MW01616730

Encouraging Words for MOTHERS

Compiled and Illustrated by Virginia H. Kreider

Poems and Thoughts from Many Sources

For permissions, please contact:
ENCOURAGING WORDS BOOKS
1231 Twin Pine Road, Metter, GA 30439

A Note About Copyrights

ISBN 978-0-9963292-0-0

Order from:
ENCOURAGING WORDS BOOKS
1231 Twin Pine Road
Metter, GA 30439

(See order form on back page.)

Foreword

In society today, motherhood is often viewed as a secondary job, one that can be managed in spare time. Many mothers hurry off to their work, leaving a hired hand to rock the cradle. Others rock the cradle out of mere duty.

Motherhood is an enduring career, a special calling worthy of complete devotion. It involves much planning and praying. The daily grind of duty may cause mothers to lose sight of their vital place and goals in life. But routine must not lead to monotony and loss of inspiration.

Mothers are co-creators with the Creator of all. They are partners with God in the formation of a new life for time and eternity. Fathers love and nurture their children too, but mothers have a special touch that cannot be duplicated.

The church of tomorrow is cradled in the arms of the mothers of today. Very early in life mothers communicate their religious values and loyalties to their children. The bedtime prayers, the Bible stories, and the answers to those sweet innocent questions are all part of the molding process.

Appreciation for a Biblical, conservative lifestyle in the rising generation is usually linked to a dedicated, self-sacrificing mother. Mothers are a potential force in shaping the destinies of children, churches, and nations.

Rise up, O godly mothers! Have done with lesser things. This is your day of opportunity. Ere long the childish chatter will cease, and the house will become strangely silent.

Mothers need sources and resources for encouragement and inspiration. The Bible is the Book of books for meeting this need. Many books have been published on this subject from a secular viewpoint. *Encouraging Words for Mothers* represents a collection of literature from a sound, Biblical viewpoint. The twenty-seven chapters cover an array of subjects that will appeal to mothers of all ages.

A mother's work is not completed until she has taught "mothering" to the rising generation. Hopefully, this book will help to fan the flame of holy ambitions in the hearts of future mothers.

The Kreiders, formerly of Lancaster County, Pennsylvania, now reside in Georgia. They are members of the Metter Mennonite congregation of the Eastern Pennsylvania Mennonite Church. The Lord has blessed them with a family of eight children and nine grandchildren.

We who have followed the development of this book rejoice with the publishers that the work is now complete. We pray that this book may serve as a bulwark of truth and a beacon of light in this dark world of deteriorating family values.

Eby W. Burkholder
Ephrata, Pennsylvania

Preface

*"For thou wilt light my candle:
the Lord my God will enlighten my darkness."*
Psalm 18:28

No matter how bright the day has been, come evening, we all
need a little light. Light to see the small things better; the fallen
button, the bedtime storybook, the fever thermometer.

And no matter how shining with blessings our day has been,
we find ourselves at evening, needing light. A keener kind of
light. Light to see the large things of life better. Light to know
how to guide the children God gave us. Light to fathom how long
and how sure the rays of our influence reach in their lives. Light
to know our priorities—whether to lean toward Martha's duties
or toward Mary's devotion. And light, as our hair grows gray, to
also grow in grace through the life-sized adjustments of helping
our children fledge and fly from our nest.

We need light to help us to see beyond our small space of here
and now. As one intense day dominoes into another, our courage
can become as thin as the worn washcloths we hang on the line.
The smudges of real life can blur our vision of raising our children
for the Lord. And even though we would not trade places with
anyone else, we can lose sight of how high and how precious our
calling really is.

We hope that these pages give just a little more light for your
mothering, some glow of encouragement to help you keep on.
You will find poems and thoughts for the spectrum of a mother's
life...first-time mothers, busy mothers, praying mothers, grieving
mothers, aging mothers, as well as mothers at heart.

These writings were gathered and assembled into a book over the course of many years. After I became a mother, the very word, *mother* leaped from the printed page in a way it never had before. I drank in those thoughts, thirsting to know how to be a good mother. Many of those choice pieces, I kept and filed.

Then, too, sterling thoughts from older mothers and from friends, truths from messages, I caught and tucked away in notebooks to use in writing. Other treasures were unearthed from fragile, old books—timeless, sparkling thoughts worthy of seeing the daylight again. Snippets and pages in a box became subjects and chapters in a file drawer and then, finally, the book I wished I had had as a young mother.

We sincerely thank our family and friends, reviewers and critiquers who took interest with wise words and helpful hints as this book developed. We would not have wanted to undertake this project alone.

Think of setting a lamp on a polished table, faintly scratched with use. Light the lamp, and see! A ring of fine lines have caught the brightness all around. So God's light shining on our little space of motherhood can illuminate a circle of encouragement in any direction we look. Dear mother friend, it is there for you. God is faithful to meet your needs when you call on Him. Find your strength and your joy in Him, in His Word, and among His people.

Kenneth & Virginia Kreider

Contents

CHAPTER 1
The New Mother

Motherhood

I cannot see how God could find me worthy
  Of giving me this little one to keep.
She is so very precious as I hold her
  Close to my heart...my baby girl, asleep!

One tiny crumpled fist lies as she dropped it,
  The other I have gathered in my hand—
So fragile, pink and white, like apple blossoms
  And yet, complete. I cannot understand
This miracle. Though old, it has such strangeness
  For a new mother who has just been born
With her first child. My heart is overflowing
  With holy gladness as I watch her form.

The fierce protective pangs that a new mother
  Wraps around her little babe, I've now possessed.
O God, that I should know this exaltation
  Has humbled me. I am so richly blessed!

Ida Mae Leatherman

The Baby Comes

"Here is your baby," Grandmother said,
"Lay in your arms his sweet little head,
  Bathe his soft cheeks with your first mother tears—
  Mothers have done this throughout the years."

"You will be happy"—Grandmother smiled—
"For paradise blooms in the eyes of your child.
  Your joys will be deeper than song or than sigh—
  Only a mother can tell you just why."

"You will be weary"—Grandmother grew sad—
"For care is companion to each little lad
  And never again will you lie down carefree—
  For this is as God has meant mothers to be."

"Weep not, little Mother," Grandmother said,
"A heavenly treasure has come to your bed.
  Drink deep those blue eyes; kiss soft his sweet hand—
  Oh, no one but mothers can quite understand!"

Author Unknown

There is perhaps no such moment
of exquisite joy,
of deep unutterable thanksgiving
taking the place of pain and sorrow,
as when a woman knows herself
to be the living mother
of a living child.

Andrew Murray, 19th Century

Firstborn

I cradle the tiny form against my heart, and delicately brush the soft wisps of hair on her head. This is my firstborn! I am amazed at the wonder of her tiny fingers, each so perfectly formed. I am awed by the helplessness of her little legs, which can only kick and squirm.

A torrent of feelings rushes over me. This is the child my husband and I have been waiting for...for so long! I cannot say that her red, wrinkled face is beautiful, but in the chambers of my heart, it can make no difference. I accept her, love her, and I am thrilled by her presence.

A joy, unlike any I have ever known, gushes from my heart and wraps both my baby and me. This child is a part of me, an extension of my own being to propagate human life.

Her dainty mouth opens, and she emits a cry—a loud, insistent cry! For a small moment, I am filled with fear at the awesome task that faces us. For, though her arms and legs flail, she can do nothing to answer her need. The sole responsibility for this helpless, demanding stranger is ours!

But my thoughts of fright cannot linger long. We have longed for this child. Now she is here, and we love her infinitely! I place her small cheek against mine, and my heart can feel nothing else. This child is a gift to our marriage, fashioned with love, from God!

Edith S. Witmer

Mother love, like an orange tree,
buds and blossoms and bears fruit all at once.
When a true woman puts her finger
for the first time into the tiny hand of her baby
and feels that helpless clutch
which tightens her very heart strings,
she is born, a mother, with her newborn child.

Kate Douglas Wiggin, 19th Century

The Newborn Babe

Into a home one blessed day
A wee sweet babe had found its way,

While through the mist of tears and pain
Sunlight fell on their hearts again!

There it lay in its tender grace—
The wee babe in its resting place.

Mother-tears fall upon the brow
Of the babe lying by her now.

She lifts her heart and simply says,
"O God! I thank Thee, give Thee praise!"

She hears a voice within her ear
That breathes this lesson, low, but clear:

*Mother! To thee this day is given
A soul to keep and fit for heaven.*

*Oh, watch and lead the little feet
Through the day's toil and pain and heat,*

*Lest from the path they go astray,
And wander from God's fold away!*

*And guide the hands that they may know
No other will than His below.*

*And train the heart so pure, so mild,
Into the likeness of the Child*

*Who came into a world of sin
And gave His life our souls to win!*

Heed well the charge! Nor hope to plead
Thou couldst not know, thou didst not heed!

The mother bowed her head in thought,
And then for guidance meekly sought.

Hence from her lips arose this prayer:
"Do Thou, O Lord, my soul prepare

"To do Thy will, and yield to Thee
This child, at last, all stainlessly!

Marian Longfellow, 1892

A Newly Made Mother Prays

Dear Lord, accept these thanks I owe,
　　That this, my child, has come to me
Unscarred and pure as driven snow,
　　Perfect in life's fair symmetry.

Thanks that Thy ever-present thought
　　Molded aright these hands and feet,
A gift that life's first workshop brought
　　To me—he came not incomplete.

And help me, Lord, that no mistake
　　Of mine may mar Thy perfect plan.
But grant me Heaven-born strength to make
　　Of this, Thy trust, a Godlike man!

Cora A. Matson Dolson, 1911

⊱ 5 ⊰

Into the Land of Motherhood

Joshua 1 for Mothers

Morning light softly fills my room, blending with the gentleness of this hour. The newness of the dawn and the newness of my motherhood seem tangibly tender.

So much love and labor is wrapped up in this little bundle in my arms. So comfortable, yet unfamiliar. So light, yet weighty. Today, everything is radiantly new...but what of the tomorrows? My feelings begin to melt around the edges as the future years crowd into view. How can I mother through the intense infant days, the toddler's training, the preschooler's preparations, the school day's disciplines, and the yearnings of youth? My arms feel weak. I am not wise enough, not strong enough, *not anything enough* to walk this path alone!

Baby is restless now and I pat small pats, hoping to encourage her to sleep. My mind searches...and recalls...long ago, a man of God also did not know the way through. But he went forward into the unknown because he knew God would be with him. And his name is nearly a synonym of what I need most—*courage*. God's words to Joshua come to comfort me...

As I was with [faithful mothers before thee], so I will be with thee:
I will not fail thee, nor forsake thee.
Be strong and of a good courage: for unto [thy little one]
shalt thou [pass on the faith of thy fathers and thy mothers].
Only be thou strong and very courageous,
that thou mayest observe to do according to all the [truth,
which faithful mothers before thee have lived and loved];
turn not from it [to harshness or to leniency],
that thou mayest prosper [in every stage of raising thy child].
[The truth] shall not depart out of thy mouth;
but thou shalt meditate therein day and night,
that thou mayest observe to do according to all [God's ways]:
for then [shalt thy child prosper], and then thou shalt have good success.
Have not I commanded thee? Be strong and of a good courage;
be not afraid, neither be thou dismayed:
for the LORD *thy God is with thee [in all the land of motherhood].*

Courage! A host of mothers before me once held their own first baby, unsure of the way to go. But God showed them one step ahead—and they took it. I may not swallow a new worry with each rock of the chair, but where I see their footprints, there I would place mine.

With this day comes light. With this path comes all I need to enter the Land of Motherhood.

V. H. K.

New Mother

"I will let nothing hurt you,"
　　She told the child asleep;
And wept because the promise
　　Was one she could not keep.

"But I will never hurt you,"
　　She said again; and wept,
Knowing it a promise
　　No mortal ever kept.

"Life has deep hurts," she whispered,
　　"Which no one can avert.
God help me teach you strength and love
　　For conquering any hurt."

Jane Merchant

Twenty Encouragements
for First-Time Mothers

1. *Sense the depth of your new trust.* A very real baby is in your arms at last, totally entrusted to you by God. The imprint of your life will be on him forever. You will sway him either to serve God or to deny Him. Such weighty work! Such inexperienced hands! But because you are weak, God gives you strength. He who gave Himself as a babe to the care of a first-time mother knows your need.

2. *Be thankful for God's mercies.* You learn the limits of language when you hold your firstborn. The relief-joy-praise that beats in your heart to God can hardly be framed with mere words. Keep your joy fresh by savoring the wonderment of each new baby stage. To roll, to sit, to crawl—all untaught—are miracles of growth.

3. *Humbly ask wisdom of God.* Looking at life in the light of motherhood raises questions you hardly imagined before. Lean on your husband as the stronger vessel and discover the answers together. Tap the resources of heaven. Ask other faithful parents. Then resolve to act on the wisdom God supplies.

4. *Devote time freely to your baby.* Feeding, burping, diapering, bathing, buttoning—over and over—may seem endless, but babies thrive on handling. You are laying a secure emotional foundation for your little one. Never feel that you have nothing to show for a day that was mostly given to baby's care.

5. *Adapt to new priorities.* Be flexible and surrender to a slower pace. Add a new reality to your goals. Baby will often be first on your list, and you may need to let the last items go undone. Those household smudges and crumbs can be forgiven until a handier time.

6. *Respect your physical limitations.* At a time when you need sleep the most, you may get it the least. Nap when baby naps. Try to get enough rest to be your best for your family. An afternoon break is not lazy luxury but a good way to relax taut nerves.

7. *Find emotional rest by trusting the Lord.* Waves of worry and unexplainable tears can sweep into your life on the tide of new motherhood. Hold on and hope on. Call on the Helper of the helpless for aid. Then try to focus outside your cycle of dark blue thoughts to see God's care for you.

8. *Seek refreshment for your spiritual life.* When you miss church services and your devotions long enough, you start to feel dehydrated. But you can be resourceful. Until you return to your routine, enough crumbs can make a meal. As you sit quietly with your baby, quiet your thoughts too. Drink from the Word, if you can, or close your eyes and pray.

9. *Accept night duty as part of motherhood.* Your mother-love is willing to rise at any hour, but sometimes your body protests. Turn away from the clock and focus on your baby, not on how much sleep you are losing. When all around you is stillness, the deeper vision for raising your child is sometimes clearer than it is in the busy day.

10. *Continue to build your marriage relationship.* Baby bands will naturally draw you closer to each other. Share Baby's big and little milestones that your husband may miss during the course of a day. Remember to thank him for his special care for you.

11. *Ask advice of others.* New motherhood is not a neat and easy pursuit, and sometimes you will be unsure of yourself. Experience has large lessons, but by asking older students in the school of motherhood, you can find good advice. Such a quest does not admit failure, but searches out pearls of wisdom to place in your own treasury.

12. *Graciously accept offers of help.* From your grandmother's warm words to your little sister's helping hands, each can be a channel of God's care for you. Do not try to do it all yourself, for times will come when a mother herself needs to be mothered.

13. *Avoid comparing your baby too closely with others.* He is a miracle—unique and unrepeatable. If your baby is healthy and normal, or if he is not, accept all his personal features. You need not hasten each milestone to keep up with others. God gave your baby his own timetable.

14. *Be aware that your baby will attract attention in public.* Do not hesitate to point to God as the Giver of your wonderful gift. Your little conversation-starter may open the door to sharing with others and discovering their spiritual interests or needs.

15. *Sing to your little one.* Baby cannot understand your words yet, but the reverent tones of the songs of the church help to mold his spirit. And who can tell when he changes from a passive to an active listener, taking the words and harmonies into his memory for life?

16. *Anticipate visitors coming.* Though they may arrive before you are feeling back to normal in every respect, receive them graciously. Do not wear yourself down by trying to achieve a spotless look. Your friends are coming to share in fellowship, not to inspect. The more relaxed you are, the more relaxed your baby and your visitors will be.

17. *Demonstrate simplicity in your baby's clothing and gear.* A pure and innocent new baby is too precious to mar with things of vanity. *Just* a baby? Think rather that you have *just* a short time to lay patterns for your little one's future path.

18. *Count it a great privilege to carry your jewel into the house of God.* At times you may feel distracted and self-conscious when caring for your baby's needs, but concentrate on the service and determine to carry some definite truths home with you.

19. *Take a moment to record memories and milestones.* Place your baby book or calendar at an available spot. You will never regret recording the little happenings too special to let slip through the cracks of time.

20. *Do not shy away from those with empty arms.* It is not easy to have, while others have not. You may wonder how you can encourage your childless friends now. But think of this: new cords of love and unselfishness have been touched in your heart. Lift your gaze from Baby's care and ask the Lord to show you how to let those virtues also flow to others around you.

V. H. K.

WORDS OF A NEW MOTHER:

"*For he that is mighty*
hath done to me great things;
and holy is his name."

Luke 1:49

If I had an eagle's wings,
    How grandly I'd sail the sky.
But I should drop to the earth
    If I heard my baby cry.
        My baby—my darling,
        The wings may go for me!

If I were a splendid queen
    With a crown to keep in place,
Would I trade for two sweet cheeks
    To cuddle to my face?
        My baby—my darling,
        The crown may go for me!

Eliza Sproat Turner

Mother, crooning soft and low,
Let not all thy fond thoughts go

Like swift birds, to the blue skies
Of your darling's happy eyes.

But on some fair curl of gold,
Let a tender prayer be told.

Mary Frances Butts, 1901

Where Can a Fussy Baby Take Me?

❖ *On an unplanned trip whose length and course I can only guess,*
  ...but also to fertile plains of patience as I learn one of motherhood's high callings: to calmly wait for better days.

❖ *Miles beyond what I would calculate to be my measure of daily strength, as my own tears mingle with my baby's,*
  ...but also to new heights of discovering God's nearness and grace for my weakness.

❖ *Into valleys of discouragement as I view unkempt scenes from my rocking chair, unable to will them to be clean,*
  ...but also to enjoy the small beauties of my landscape, realizing that though I cannot change my circumstances, I can shape my attitudes.

❖ *Through swamps of humiliation, as I fear that others will think I am a poor mother,*
  ...but also to firmer footing with the humble knowledge that I am doing all I can for my restless baby dear and that God sees my efforts.

And when my baby finally crosses over the silent border from fretfulness to fragile slumber, I know that the Lord is near. Shall I thank Him only for the quietness? No, I offer my thanks, too, for this intense journey of giving myself for my little child.

V. H. K.

Why Baby Cries

When baby cries and Mother sighs,
  She scarce knows what to do.
She hums a song, "What could be wrong,
  Oh, baby dear, with you?"

Still Baby cries. Mom wonders why—
  She simply doesn't know.
She holds him near and sheds a tear—
  Perhaps it hurts to grow!

B. Zimmerman

"Yet the LORD will command
his lovingkindness in the daytime,
and in the night his song shall be with me,
and my prayer unto the God of my life."

Psalm 42:8

Words are inadequate to express the strong consolation which
the baby brings to his mother in moments of perplexity, of weariness, or of temptation. To turn from the cares which burden or
the sad thoughts which depress, to take the little one in her arms,
to feel the clinging of baby fingers around her own, is an unspeakable refreshment, a joy in which a stranger intermeddleth not.

Louise Seymour Houghton

Peace in the Storm

A cold north wind is blowing, shaking the trees until the limbs groan. Partly hidden behind the black clouds, the moon bravely tries to send a ray of light toward the snow-covered earth. Even the night creatures have sought shelter from the fierceness of the storm.

At the edge of the woods stands a humble human abode. Let us peek inside. The clock on the wall shows midnight. The fire in the hearth burns brightly, filling the room with its warmth. A young mother is tenderly cradling a small baby in her arms, oblivious to the wildness of the night or the lateness of the hour.

"Oh, you precious babe," she whispers as she covers the soft warm face with kisses. "You are as pure and fresh as heaven's dews, a priceless gift from God to us!" She begins to sing softly; a lullaby, followed by hymns of praise and thanksgiving. As we listen to the creaking of the rocker, the clock ticks on.

The songs have ceased, and it seems some of the storm has entered the room to chill the young mother. Her song has turned into a cry of alarm. "Oh, Lord, protect my babe from the cruel, sinful world!" she cries out. "I cannot, but Thou canst. I commit her life into Thy care. Keep her safe through the storms of life, and at eventide, guide her safely back into the arms of Thy love."

Once again, the room is filled with peace. It seems as if angels are present, soundlessly ministering to the weary mother. She has fallen into a deep slumber, the precious babe in her arms.

Outdoors the wind still shrieks and roars. In this humble dwelling there is warmth and rest. There is trust in the Creator of all things — the One who created these wild winds, ice, groaning trees, and darkness. For He is also the Creator of love, warmth, safety, mothers, and babes...

Naomi Yutzy

Hand in Hand

When you look closely at the hand of a baby,
you marvel at its completeness.
You see the potential of an adult's hand,
for the essentials are all there.
It may lie softly in your own hand
as if waiting only for the mastery and skill,
the mobility and grace,
which years of training and growth
will discover in it.

When you look again at the hand of a baby,
think of the great responsibility that rests in your hands.
For here, now so dependent upon you,
are possibilities that no one can accurately gauge.
Here is a life that is of greater value
than any price you can place upon it.
Here is the living clay that can be molded
through your patience and by God's grace
into a man in the image of God.
You cannot lightly hold the hand of a baby in yours,
for its innocent trust demands of you
all the wisdom and faith that God has given you.

Author Unknown

Precious in His Sight

"Oh, let me see the baby!"

I bent down so the wrinkled woman at the nursing home could peek at my son's little face.

"Oh, he's so precious...so precious! How old is he?" she questioned.

"Six weeks," I answered, smiling.

A shadow crossed her face as she fondled my little son's blanket. "My children never come to see me. I have five of them and eight grandchildren, but they're all far away, and too busy..." Her voice had taken on a resentful edge.

"But," she brightened, "I like when you people come and bring your babies. He's so precious. He's *so* precious..." and on and on she crooned.

Yes, he is very precious, I thought to myself. Who is not drawn to a baby? Their helplessness and their innocence attracts almost anyone's affection and tenderness in a magnet-like way. Many mothers love their babies...until that child is old enough to show a temper or scream for what he wants. Then suddenly Baby may become a little less precious, and a bother instead.

Nearly all mothers love their babies, but not every mother loves *motherhood*. For true motherhood is a commitment to care for each child through the washing and wiping, the frustration and fulfillment, the sunshine and shadows, day after day after day. Those who truly love their children take time to train them, for they know that disciplined children are lovable children. And those mothers are paid that quality of love in return. An investment of unconditional, non-permissive love begins a harvest that will go on through the years.

My little son is a gift of love from God to me. May I never see him as less than my Father sees him...precious in His sight.

Rachel E. Myer

CHAPTER 2

The Trust of Motherhood

A partnership with God
is motherhood;
what strength, what purity,
what self-control, what love,
what wisdom should belong to her
who helps God fashion
an immortal soul.

Author Unknown

A Young Mother's Prayer

Oh, Lord, I come to Thee today,
And at Thy pierced feet I bow to pray.
I come, not boasting title or renown,
Nor a special skill that came hand-me-down.
I claim no wealth, nor fame, nor other—
I come—just a young mother.

Into these arms of mine so weak and frail
Thou'st placed a challenge, and I may not fail!
So young and inexperienced, scarce have I outgrown
The need of mother's care. Can I alone
Guide this young life through one storm and another?
Oh, God, can I be a mother?

I ask not pleasure, fame, or gold,
Nor worldly ease or wealth untold,
I seek not admiration from a thronging crowd
Who'd sing my praises long and loud.
Grant this petition, and I'll ask none other—
Please, God, make me a good mother.

Audre Pitts

"If there be all this burden of responsibility," a mother may say,
"who then would have children?"

We reply that nothing is gained by closing our eyes to the ac-
tual facts of life. And she who says in lowly self-distrust, "Who
is sufficient for these things?" is the most likely to look up and
say, "Help me, O my Father! who hast put the parental love in my
heart, and hast given these children into my hands that I may be
to them, in love, wisdom, and guidance, in some poor remote way,
what Thou, my all-wise God, hast been to me, Thy weak and
wanting child."

John Hall, 1883

Mother's God

"Huh, Mama, huh?" Two eyes wide
Innocence personified;
      Virgin soil soaking up
      All that flows from Mother's cup.

Open, serious, trusting heart
Cynicism knows no part —
      No — not yet, but he shall find
      Life is not all good and kind.

I must shield him while I may
Patiently each gold-wrapped day;
      Keep each promise to him made,
      Rash impulses first be weighed.

May he see my aim is true
With those eyes that look me through.
      If I fail, Lord, give me grace
      To win back that trustful face.

Tender growing hand in mine,
Pulses prove the passing time...
      Soon he'll walk with manly tread,
      Soon he'll tower o'er my head...

In my weak, imperfect way
This my goal from day to day —
      To impress him through and through
      Mother's God is always true.

Carolyn Eberly

A Never-dying Soul to Raise

From your children's earliest infancy, inculcate the necessity of instant obedience. Unite firmness with gentleness. Let your children always understand that you mean what you say. Never promise them something unless you are quite sure that you can give them what you say. If you tell a little child to do something, show him how to do it, and see that it is done.

Always punish your children for willful disobedience, but never punish them in anger. Never let them perceive that they vex you or make you lose your command. If they give way to petulance or an ill temper, you need to subdue their anger and show them the wrongness of their conduct. Remember, a little present punishment when the occasion arises, is much more effectual than the threatening of a greater punishment should the fault be repeated.

Never give your children anything because they cry for it. Teach them that the only way to appear good is to be good. Accustom them to make their little recitals with perfect truth. Never allow talebearing.

Teach them that self-denial, rather than self-indulgence, will prove in the end to be the most blessed road to travel.

"The rod and reproof giveth wisdom: but a child left to himself bringeth his mother to shame." Proverbs 29:15

Herald of Truth, 1866

THE CHARGE

❖ *"Take this child...and nurse it for me." Exodus 2:9*
❖ *"Train up a child in the way he should go." Proverbs 22:6*
❖ *"Bring them up in the nurture and admonition of the Lord." Ephesians 6:4*

THE RESOURCE

❖ *"Cause me to know the way wherein I should walk;
for I lift up my soul unto thee." Psalm 143:8*
❖ *"Give therefore thy servant an understanding heart." 1 Kings 3:9*
❖ *"And God is able to make all grace abound toward you; that ye,
always having all sufficiency in all things,
may abound to every good work." 2 Corinthians 9:8*

A Most Sacred Call

We went to the ordination
 To see how the lot would fall
To fill the spot that was vacant—
 Which man the Lord would call.
The house was filled with emotion;
 Our hearts were drawn to the Lord
As we listened with rapt attention
 To the truths of God's holy Word.
Soon we'd know the will of the Father,
 Who He'd chosen to fill this place—
A calling that must be the highest
 E'er laid on the poor human race.

Then the words of the visiting preacher
 Struck my heart like a two-edged sword,
For he asked, "What's the highest calling,
 Ever given to man by the Lord?"
He went on and said, "You mothers,
 At home with your children so small—
Yours is a very great calling,
 Yours is a most sacred call.
The ministry's load would be lighter
 If parents would all strive to guide
The precious wee lambs to the Father
 And teach them in Him to confide."

I lowered my head in submission,
 For the lot has fallen on me—
To carry this most precious calling—
 For I am a mother, you see.
So mothers, at home in our corners
 Though we think our achievements are small—
Let us strive to be true in our duties,
 For we have a most sacred call.

A. S.

Things a Mother Cannot Do

"She hath done what she could"...words of commendation from Jesus for Mary of Bethany's sacrificial act of devotion. Today these words echo as a tribute to mothers who devote themselves to doing what they can do. They feed and clothe, teach and train, pray and persevere. Every mother would like to do all she can and more, but there will always be those things that she simply *cannot* do. How shall a mother deal with the things that remain beyond her reach? Be hopeless? No, a mother can do something about the things she *cannot* do.

1. *No mother can bring into the world a child that does not have a sinful nature.* No matter how godly a woman is, she cannot bear a child that is not one of *"the children of wrath, even as others."* No matter how cute and innocent looking or well-behaved her little one is, that nature within him can lead him astray.

So what can a mother do about the things she cannot do?
- ❖ She can entreat the Lord for help to bring her child up in His way.
- ❖ She can be alert to expressions of anger and selfishness, naughtiness and stubbornness in her child. She can use discipline to keep that wayward nature from growing into a harvest of thorns and thistles, shooting out in worthless directions.
- ❖ She may not always be there to help her child choose right the first time, but a wise mother can make her child wish that he had. She can help him see where he went wrong and instill in him a sense of right.
- ❖ She can guard her own life, lest she further contribute to these inborn inclinations.
- ❖ She can be concerned that she raises her child in an environment that is as free as possible from ungodliness.

2. *A godly mother cannot take care of the sinful nature of her child only by good mothering.* She cannot mother her child to such an extent that he will be ready for eternity if he grows beyond the age of accountability. If any child grows up knowing only the influence of a godly mother, but never knows the influence of the great Savior, the Lord Jesus Christ, that child is unprepared for eternity.

So what can a mother do about the things she cannot do?

❖ She cannot give the call of God to her child or be God to him, but she can prepare him to hear God and respond to His call.

❖ She can introduce him to God through Bible stories and to the truth of God's Word through songs.

❖ She can teach him to pray while still a babe, so that at the age of accountability he will know how to pray to God— to reach out his hands to Him and find his needs met.

❖ She can instill in him a love for the Christian virtues of honesty, compassion, kindness, simplicity, separation from ungodly ways, and a love for his parents' God.

3. *A mother cannot be all that God wants her to be in her strength alone.* The task is simply too large to be done without the Lord's help.

So what can a mother do about the things she cannot do?

❖ She can lean hard on the Lord, sensing that without Him, she can do nothing.

❖ She can stay in touch with God on a daily, sometimes minute-to-minute, basis.

❖ She can count her husband's wisdom and direction a great support for dealing with the pressures of the home.

4. *As hard as a mother tries, she cannot prevent every fall and accident that comes to her child.* The protective arm of a mother can reach out very swiftly to rescue her child from danger, but she cannot stop every tumble or steer every fall.

So what can a mother to do about the things she cannot do?

❖ She can trust her children to the Lord and His angels— a power beyond herself.

❖ She can do what she can to avoid danger for her little ones, but she must realize that even with her best efforts; she will never make heaven's help unnecessary.

5. *A mother can never get all the work done.* The three C's of mothering—cooking, cleaning, and clothing—are never completed as long as her children are at home. She will always have shoes to tie, hair to comb, ears to wash, noses to wipe, snacks to serve, cuts to dress and dresses to cut, wandering toddlers to check, tears to kiss away, endless questions to answer, quarrels to settle, punishments to mete out, dishes and floors to clean, a husband to keep happy, company to entertain, shopping to manage...the list is endless! And often the things she needs to leave undone are the things she finds personally pleasurable.

So what can a mother do about the things she cannot do?

❖ She can find satisfaction in what she did do.

❖ She can try to arrange her priorities with flexibility for interruptions.

❖ She can view her work as a privilege rather than drudgery.

One more thing—

6. *A godly mother cannot do her work so quietly and unassumingly that it is unnoticed by God.* Even in this life, godly mothering will have its reward when *"her children rise up, and call her blessed."* God notices every deed of a godly mother. Though much of it is hidden within the walls of her home, God sees and remembers. He will reward every mother who has done what she could.

Harry M. Erb

"Be ye strong therefore,
and let not your hands be weak:
for your work shall be rewarded."

2 Chronicles 15:7

Seedlings

These precious ones
    Thou gavest me,
    to guard and teach awhile,
    created by Thy hand,
    in mind before the world began:

I want to teach them well,
    to love them with Thy love,
    so I can give them back to Thee,
    trunks straight,
    branches strong,
    leaves full,
    fruit ready for Thy picking.

Give me dexterous hands,
    an eye for beauty,
    and a love for pruning well.

Author Unknown

Diamonds

What if God should place a diamond in your hand and tell you to inscribe upon it a sentence which should be read at the Last Day and shown there as an index of your thoughts and feelings? What care, what caution you would exercise in the selection!

This is what God has done. He has placed before us the immortal minds of our children, less perishable than the diamonds, on which we are inscribing every day and every hour by our instruction, by our spirit, by our example, something that will remain and be exhibited for or against us at the Judgment Day!

Charles Payson, 1881

This Is My Task...

❖ To talk with God each morning before I meet my family and their needs.

❖ To perform my daily work with a willingness to serve in the most ordinary ways.

❖ To be lovable and cherishable to my husband, gentle and joyful to my children, and gracious to all I meet.

❖ To be alert to the whisper of opportunity, not shrinking from the summons of sacrifice.

❖ To work and not worry; to be energetic and not exacting.

❖ To intertwine my ideals for mothering with true life thread by thread.

❖ To be simple in my tastes, quiet in my dress, pleasant in my speech, patient for the longest mile.

❖ To hold fast to the anchors I have found in God's Word as I face a sea-deep day.

❖ To draw near to the Lord in each difficult circumstance I face.

❖ To keep my ears and heart tuned to others' needs and to reach out with prayer and with tangible expressions of my care.

❖ To perceive what each of my children can become for God's glory and to invest my time for them in timeless things.

❖ To mark a clear trail of faith in God and obedience to Christ for my children and grandchildren to follow.

❖ To be content at day's end with the span my hands have covered, ready to give myself in the same way tomorrow; for when my tasks become my joy, then I know that God is indeed my Helper.

"I delight to do thy will, O my God." Psalm 40:8

V. H. K.

Worthy Motherhood

Worthy mothers are able to look disappointment and failure in the face and say, "If I have done my best, God knows it. If I have not, I will try again." If we have not done our best, no praise of man should give us peace. If we have, no blame of man should disturb us.

God gives to all mothers who love Him the possibility of living faithfully right where we are. And though we tremble often at the seeming impossibility of it, not one of our excuses seems to stand before Him who has given us the charge to keep.

He stands before us in kindness and firmness, with a deep knowledge of our comings and goings. When He speaks, He does not say what we might wish to hear Him say: *"I will excuse you because the way is hard."*

We seem to hear, instead, the same words spoken to Job long ago when his soul trembled with effort to justify himself: *"Who is this that darkeneth counsel by words without knowledge? Gird up thy loins now like a man; I will demand of thee, and answer thou me."* After we have answered all the questions He puts to our conscience, and have told Him we are without excuse, and have the will but lack the wisdom, He speaks again, *"Ask of God, that giveth to all men liberally, and upbraideth not."*

So if, while living up to our vision of worthy motherhood, we still see things in our children which baffle us and make us feel helpless to master them, let us honestly ask ourselves whether we have given God a chance. Have we prayed definitely for specific things? Have we prayed confidently? And earnestly? If so, we may yet see how marvelously a difficulty can vanish under the hand of God.

Lois Gingerich

"Her Candle Goeth Not Out by Night"

A willful son had been away from home for several years. To his caring father, they were long years indeed. At last, the son sensed his sinfulness and determined to return. He purchased a ticket for the next ship bound for the Gold Coast where his father kept a lighthouse. Rough seas made the voyage treacherous. Entering the harbor through the fog, the son searched eagerly, then desperately, for a ray of light—for the welcoming signal that meant *home*.

The hour grew late. Utterly weary, the elderly lighthouse keeper slumped in his armchair. His eyes closed, and his chest rose and fell in an exhausted slumber. The light burned lower, and still lower, until the flicker dimmed and then ceased.

Now the ship tossed deliriously on foaming waves. No gleam from the lighthouse warned of danger. Then, in a tumult of terror, the hull dashed to pieces on the rocks.

Dawn came, and the lighthouse keeper rushed out. And there, among the wreckage washed ashore beneath the lighthouse, lay the lifeless body of his own son. Gone. Forever gone. The father wept.

O Mother! The flame of your love must never grow dim! You stand as a watchman, guarding the children God has placed within your tender care. As they mature, they will face storms of their own. They will search for a gleam of understanding, for someone to show where their ship may safely sail. Will you be awake? Will you be available? Will your light be burning on that treacherous night? You may be weary, but the waves of peril will be cold and high, and there are rocks in the darkness. The guidance of your loving devotion must keep shining through. *A mother's candle dare not go out by night.*

Author Unknown, Adapted

CHAPTER 3

A Mother's Influence

The Life Book

Write, Mother, write!

A new, unspotted book of life before thee.
　Thine is the hand to trace upon its pages
The first few characters, to live in glory,
　Or live in shame, through long, unending ages!

Write, Mother, write!

Thy hand, though woman's, must not faint nor falter;
　The lot is on thee—nerve thee then with care—
A mother's tracery time may never alter;
　Be its first impress, then, the breath of prayer.

Write, Mother, write!

Author Unknown, 1863

Early Call

Mother! Mother! Watch and pray,
Fling not golden hours away!
  Now or never, plant and sow,
  Catch the morning's earliest glow.

Mother! Mother! Guard the dew,
While it sparkles clear and true.
  No delay! The scorching noon
  May thy treasures reach too soon.

Mother! Point them to the sky,
Tell them of a loving eye
  That more tender is than thine,
  And doth ever on them shine.

Mother! Lead them soon and late
To behold the golden gate;
  When they long to enter there,
  Lead them to the Lamb by prayer.

Mother! Seize the precious hours,
While the dew is on thy flowers!
  Life is such a fleeting thing,
  Mother! Mother! Sow in spring.

Author Unknown

And say to mothers
what a holy charge is theirs—
with what a queenly power
their love might rule the vastness of the
new-born mind!
Warn them to wake at early dawn,
and sow good seed
before the world has sown its tares.

Lydia H. Sigourney, 1865

Each Day

Character building is not an exact science. A mother cannot say, "Tomorrow I will lay the foundation of honesty; then I will add these stones and this plank; and the structure will be completed on such and such a day."

However, she can make each day count for something in the way of moral and religious training; and she can be sure that her child is never tucked into bed for the night until there has been a talk, a story, or some one thing of character-forming value.

Author Unknown

The Silent Education

The mother's countenance is the unconscious study of the child. And if it be what it ought to be—gentle, modest, kind; if it be the index of a heart in which habitual peace, joy, and love abide—through the channel of such a mother, soft and holy influences will flow down from heaven upon the child.

Mothers should constantly keep in view that the eyes of their children are upon them. The mother's prayers and wishes can be ever so sincere, but if she has a care-worn face and her features are darkened and half-distracted by her anxieties, she will not mold their minds in the way of peace. The child knows nothing of the mother's wishes; but he observes and understands her outward display.

Impressions deep and lasting are made by what your children sense. Take care in the presence of your child to be gentle and tranquil. Keep your sighs and frettings for your solitary hours.

A Mother's Legacy, 19th Century

The Twig Bender

She bent the twig
  Toward home,
Toward simple pleasures
  And a firelight's glow;

She bent the twig
  Toward truth
And courage for the paths
  Where truth must go;

She bent the twig
  Toward love
To lift the heart of those
  Who only plod;

And when the tempest raged
  Her tree stood firm—
For gently
  She had bent the twig
    Toward God.

H. Charles Gallap

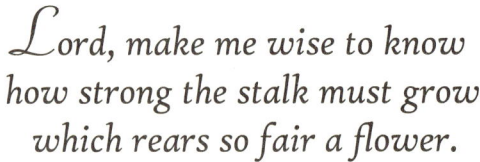

*Lord, make me wise to know
how strong the stalk must grow
which rears so fair a flower.*

Author Unknown

You Are a Mother

Temptation came the other day
Some hurtful, cutting thing to say
  About another.
The words stopped short! I seemed to hear
A warning word ring loud and clear—
  "You are a mother!"

"Two little eyes are watching you!
The unkind things you say and do
  Will be detected.
Perhaps the very words you said
You'll hear from little lips instead
  When least expected.

"Seek counsel at the Savior's feet.
When things go wrong—be kind, be sweet,
  And be forgiving.
If thus you live—how glad you'll be!
Reflected in your child you'll see
  The way you're living."

    Geneva Showerman

  Some mothers have it and some mothers do not. Children cannot explain it—but they know it—and it reaches to the deepest roots of their tender growth.

- ❖ "A double-yolk egg! Let's fry this one for Daddy."
  (*That mother had it.*)
- ❖ "I can't understand why he is late for supper—*again.*"
  (*That mother didn't.*)
- ❖ "We fold his socks this way because Daddy wants us to."
  (*That mother had it too.*)

Every child needs a mother that has it. Do *you?*

"And the wife see that she reverence her husband..." Ephesians 5:33

    A Mother

The Rose Garden

Passing by a rose garden, I looked, and looked again. How beautiful the blossoms were! I thought, "Someday, when my children are older and I am not so busy, I will lay out a wonderful rose garden. With rare and fragrant roses. Blooming beyond compare. Because of special, tender care."

I became discontented. "Lord, I am so busy taking care of necessary things for living that I have no time for rose gardens. Why, Lord?"

And the Lord said to me, *"I have given you a rose garden. A very, very special one. If you give it tender loving care, you will have rose blossoms beyond compare!"*

"But I don't have any," I said, bewildered.

"Yes, you do," He said with patience. *"Look at your daughters. They are beautiful, pastel pink buds, ready to bloom into womanhood. They can be taught to have a gentle feminine outlook that can influence each person that they meet. You were chosen to teach them how to become Christian women, willing to live for God.*

"Look at your sons. Bold, beautiful buds. With proper teaching, they can become fine leaders in homes of their own someday. You can teach them to be honest and hard working, yet gentle and loving. You were chosen to help them become Christian men willing to live for God.

"So you see, my child, I have given you roses from My own garden. Now, what will you do with your opportunity? Will you take special care of My roses while they are there? You can give them lots of love. You can surround them with prayer when they have hard times. You can train them into habits of Bible reading and church attendance. Be with them! Take care of them! If you do and they become Christians, you will have roses beyond compare. Roses, beautiful and rare. Your Christian children!"

Very humbly, I replied, "Forgive me, Lord, for my complaints. And thank you, Lord! Thank you!"

Author Unknown

Little Coats

"But Samuel ministered before the LORD, being a child, girded with a linen ephod. Moreover his mother made him a little coat, and brought it to him from year to year, when she came up with her husband to offer the yearly sacrifice." 1 Samuel 2:18, 19

What happy work it was! Those nimble fingers flew along the seams because love inspired them. All her woman's art and wit were put into the garment, her one idea and ambition to make something that should be not only useful but also becoming.

Not mothers only, but fathers, too, are always making little coats for their children, which they wear long years after a material fabric would have worn out. How many men and women are wearing today the coats that their parents cut out and made for them long years ago?

Mothers are still making garments for their children—not on the loom or with their busy needles merely, but by their holy and ennobling characters displayed from day to day before young and quickly observant eyes, by their words and conversations, and by the habits of their daily devotion.

What the children see, they imitate and unconsciously array themselves in—the gentleness or rudeness, the reverence or indifference for religion, the refinement or coarseness of manner, which are daily presented to their gaze. Children wear the robes which their mother's character and behavior, temper and tones weave for them.

By the ordering of home life, by their actions more than by their words, by the way in which they speak and spend their leisure hours, and pray—men and women are making the little coats, which for better or worse, their children wear ever after, and perhaps pass down to after generations.

Author Unknown

A Mother's Far-reaching Influence

Influence is immeasurable. Every time we try to calculate its scope, we almost always underestimate its reach and its power, especially our own influence. Everything we do—the choices we make, the things we say—make a difference. Our lives touch others with mysterious effect.

Influence carries special power when it is subtle and without conscious effort. Sometimes a mother's influence is intended, but more often it is one little thing added to another little thing. Those little things grow into something that is not small.

Influence. You cannot turn it on or off. It is a constant, perpetual force that flows from your life. Someone said, *"The work of an unknown good [woman] is like a vein of water underground, secretly making the grass green."* Influence occurs gradually; it is a lifestyle; it is *what we are.*

Think of these few areas of a mother's influence:

Children must be wanted. Mothers may find their hands full, and then God gives them more responsibility. Even so, each child should be welcomed as Hannah welcomed Samuel. It makes a definite difference. But how do mothers keep on when they wish for a reprieve? They can look ahead twenty years and try to view things from that perspective. What will the picture be then? Every true mother would want a faithful Samuel. To only wish for that is weak, but to live right today will make a mother's influence long and strong.

Cheerfulness is for everyday. Mothers need to start the day right and end the day right. A *"Good Morning!"* smile and eye contact with each of her children, whether she feels like it or not, touches the rest of their day. A little child of long ago carried memories through life of waking to hear his mother sing as she rattled the stove lids. That mother's joy in her everyday life stayed with her child.

Respect is due every person. "Guess what he did today!" say the schoolchildren as they come home with a story of their impulsive classmate. Mothers must help their children value others who may be different from them.

Each mother should take her place in the order of headship. Not much can wreck the work of God more than a woman that resists God's design for her. By a mother's response to direction, she interprets what the Bible means by *"wives, submit."* She tells her children, in essence, "This is what it says, and this is what it means." That influence becomes their frame of reference as they relate to the authorities in their lives.

Influence cannot be measured accurately. How long, how far can it go? To children? No, it will not stop there. To grandchildren? No, it will not stop there. To great-grandchildren? It probably will not stop there.

When faithful mothers envision their children thirty years from now, they should not make their focus too narrow, their box too small. They cannot tell in what way their children will serve the Lord. As they keep lending each child to the Lord, mothers see what He can do.

A mother's influence is strong, but it takes more than that to have a man or woman go right. It takes God to fill in for each mother's weakness when she gives her all to Him.

Mast P. Stoltzfus

The blossoms of flowers
cannot tell what becomes of their fragrance,
and so no mother can tell
what becomes of her influence
and example that roll away from her.

Author Unknown

The Margin of Life

Do other mothers, like me, who have little ones to care for, besides all the housework to do, ever become discouraged that they are not ministering to the spiritual development of their children as they ought?

This is the time when impressions are most lasting—when the little ones become acquainted with the things of God.

And what can we mothers do? We must feed the babies and keep them clean; we must make the home as attractive as possible. Do we have time or energy to do more? It seems as though we exert ourselves to the utmost over things that must be done, with hardly a glimpse of the things that ought to be done.

But I wonder—do we make the most of the margin of life? The margin of life! Just one instance of a "margin" and what can be done in it...

You know what happens when you wash the dishes. The children stand around and ask questions or rub their little fingers over everything they can reach. This is a golden opportunity—a "margin" to be used to its fullest.

Try repeating different psalms to the children. If you are not familiar with all the psalms you would like the children to know, copy one each week and put it above the sink. Then read it to the children as they stand beside you. In time you will know many of them by heart, and so will the children.

They are too young? Impossible! Even the tinest ones soon learn to repeat snatches of these beautiful verses. Remember, too, we are feeding the subconscious minds of these little ones. Years later, when they come to read the Book of Psalms for themselves, the passages will come back to them like strains of a familiar and well-beloved song, for having them oft repeated in childhood.

Jessie Whitney Mayshark

More Is Caught

"*Put your toys down and come to me now,*" Mother directs her toddler.

And as the child is trained to respond promptly, he learns the first steps of obedience and submission to a loving Father in Heaven.

"*There now, dear. Don't be afraid,*" Mother whispers. "*It's all right. I'm right here.*"

And as the child is comforted and calmed, he is being readied to understand that there is One in heaven who yearns to be his Divine Protector and Comforter.

"*This may hurt a little, but I will be careful. Just relax and trust me,*" Mother assures her child.

And as the child sees proof of her trustworthiness in action, he is better prepared to understand the faithfulness of his Heavenly Father.

"*I want to know what is troubling you. Just tell me all about it. I would like to help,*" Mother encourages.

And as the child finds rest in this acceptance, he tastes the unreserved love and warm security of the Good Shepherd.

"*You may not understand why right now,*" Mother firmly states, "*but our decision has been carefully weighed. It is for your best interest...for your own good.*"

And as the child slowly begins to experience the rewards of submission, he is being prepared for the discipline that is needed in his walk with the Lord.

Cynthia Ruchti, Adapted

Our Children

When our children are newborn, they are so small and helpless. I think I have never seen anything so precious before. They are like little candles glowing along the path of life. While they grow, I trim their wicks so they may shine more brightly.

❖ I care for them that they may care for others.

❖ I love them that they may love others.

❖ I respect them that they may respect others.

❖ I guide them in right paths that they may guide others aright.

❖ I try to be a godly role model to them that they may become role models for others.

❖ I point them to God that they may point others to Him.

My children are the only possessions I can take to heaven with me. I have no greater desire than to guide these precious little ones on the right path in life.

Polly Petersheim

The Way of Her Will

The child lay dying. The doctor declared he would not recover and the pastor was called. With sympathy and reverence he prayed, "Thy will be done."

"No!" the mother interrupted passionately, "not that; *my will*—the child must live!"

And the child did live, and lived to break his mother's heart and disgrace her name. He had simply breathed in her spirit of self-will and lived it out to its logical conclusion—spiritual ruin.

Children breathe in the spirit of the hearts nearest them—be it self-will or submission. Your spirit will shape the character of your child.

S. D. Gordon, 1909, Adapted

Advice to Mothers

*The first book read, and the last book laid aside by every child,
is the conduct of his mother.*

1. First give yourself, then your child, to God. It is but giving Him His own. Not to do it is robbing God.
2. Always prefer virtue to wealth. Prefer the honor that comes from God over the honor that comes from men. Do this for yourself. Do it for your child.
3. Let your whole course be to raise your child to a high standard. Do not sink into childishness yourself.
4. Give no needless commands, but when you command, require prompt obedience.
5. Never let a child indulge in cruelty, even to an insect.
6. Express sympathy with your child in all lawful joys and sorrows.
7. Be careful about correcting a child until you know he deserves correction. Hear his story first and fully.
8. Do not allow your child to whine, fret, or bear grudges.
9. Instill frankness, candor, generosity, magnanimity, and self-denial early in your child's heart.
10. Never hurt the feelings of your child by upbraiding him tediously, neither try to inspire him with self-esteem.
11. Pray for and with your child, often and heartily, in your closet.

Author Unknown, 1914

Never feel that because ideal conditions cannot be brought to influence the little one's life, there is no use to try for better things.

Conditions are never ideal.

Perhaps they appear to be in someone else's life, but if all the facts were known, difficulties exist there as elsewhere. In rising above the trying circumstances, the mother gains strength of character and infuses into her little ones the same quality.

Author Unknown

Words to a Young Mother

Go daily to an altar, there to pray
    That you be worthy of the sacred task
Of motherhood. Ask wisdom for the day,
    And heed the answer to the thing you ask.
So soon a child's grave eyes will watch to see
    Life's meaning in your voice, your smile, your face.
Each moment you will make some memory
    That all the coming years will not erase.
You will engrave upon a young child's heart
    Deep, lettered words, carved there for good or ill.
Oh, Mother, do you know how great a part
    You are to play, how much you will distill
Of truth and beauty in the empty cup
    That your child's hands will soon be holding up?

Author Unknown

Coworkers

Coworkers we with Him! Were He to ask,
"Come star with Me the spaces of My night,
Or light with Me tomorrow's sunset glow,
Or fashion forth the crystals of My snow,
Or teach My sweet June roses next to blow."
O rare beatitude! But holier task,
Of all His works of beauty fairest-high,
Is that He keeps for hands like ours to ply!
When He upgathers all His elements,
His days, His nights, whole eons of His June,
The Mighty Gardener of the earth and sky,
That to achieve towards which the ages roll,
We hear the Voice that sets the sphere attune—
"Help me, My comrades, flower this budding soul!"

Author Unknown

CHAPTER 4

A Mother's Love

Tender Loving Care

Mother, give your children Tender Loving Care...

Tenderly Touch and Talk to your baby, for this is how your baby really knows you and your presence.

Lovingly Look into the eyes of your child, and you will be rewarded. Mother's face is the most beautiful face to him.

Caringly Cuddle your children close to you. Store up these moments when you are your child's whole world, for they are fast fleeting.

It is easy to be so busy day after day, that you fail to enjoy motherhood at its fullest. Do remember to keep an unbusy portion of each day for your children. For mothering your little ones is a precious, once-and-never-again parenthesis in the span of your life.

Give your family plenty of Tender Loving Care.

Author Unknown, Adapted

Mother, Have a Heart

Everyone knows that little children love to pick flowers. But not everyone realizes that the greatest joy is not in the picking of flowers, but in the giving of them to someone. A small child very often selects his mother as the one to whom he gives his offering.

All mothers who live in the country or near a plot of ground where the tiniest weed can flower have seen the picture I am about to describe. The little child goes out to play while the mother goes about her housework. Occasionally she glances out the window to see if her child is safe. Then she sees him coming toward the house, with an absorbed, pleased expression enveloping his baby features, and in his hand is clutched a bunch of flowers. They are almost stemless, badly torn flowerlets, but held in dimpled hands!

Bless his generous little heart! He comes in and proffers his flowers to his mother. Pleased, expectant, happy, he stands there, watching his mother.

What will she do? I have watched two different mothers handle this situation.

The one mother lovingly took the battered bouquet and, with the help of her child, nicely arranged each flower in a pretty little dish or saucer, never once remarking about their battle scars, but rather how pretty they were. Then she thanked her child again while she set them conspicuously on the table. Her little child went out again to play, this time into a world dazzling with beauty, doubly enhanced by a mother's love and understanding.

There was another mother, I said. She, too, had a little child, a child with the same generous impulse as the other one. He, too, felt the need of expressing his joy in the beautiful by giving flowers to his mother.

What did she say?

"Take that trash out and stop cluttering up the house with dirt!"

Can you see the stunned look, the puzzled face, as the little one went out to throw his flowers away? All his joy was turned into bitterness because a mother could not see past the crumpled bouquet to the generous, loving soul of her little child.

Naomi Zeigler

Their Vital Need

Dear mothers, God has given you precious children to care for and love. They need more than food and clothing. They need more than to be taught what is right and wrong. They have emotional needs. Do not belittle them or impatiently send them on their way when they have something to tell you. Take time to sit down and really listen to them.

Do not make the mistake of rushing around under the pressure of your work, giving your child a half-hearted answer, pretending to be listening. Your child will soon sense that you are not really interested. Ask yourself whether you are tuned in to their heartaches and joys as you should be.

The child that is loved, and *knows that he is loved*, has a most important asset to help him through the hard places of life. And those hard times are sure to come to every child. With a feeling of being loved and needed, of self-worth, and of emotional well-being, your child will be able to say in his heart, *"Let the whole world go by, let people be cruel—I am loved!"*

The next time your child comes to you and begs for your attention, Mother, be sure, be very sure, that you are listening. It is not how big your child's problem looks to you, but how big it seems to him that is important.

Ruth Ann Stelfox

Remembering Little Things

Very little children are real people and contrary to many opinions, do remember some things. Never be tempted to think, "Oh, he'll forget it." He might not. This truth is very weighty.

It is easy to shrug off the little ones until they force our notice. But the love that we withhold would enrich their little lives if we were to give it, instead. Every Bible command that applies to love applies to our relationship with our children. We should comfort, defend, serve, pray for, and be truthful to our children. We should encourage, exhort, protect, and provide for our children. We need to discern and correct their seemingly little wrongs. We need to hold them, to look into their eyes, and to smile into their souls. These things they will remember.

It is you, Mother, it is you. You are the program, the method, the medicine, the answer. Turn the troubles in your child's life into priceless memories by the simple act of being there and caring. Turn the wood, hay, and stubble in your child's life into gold, silver, and jewels by praying for them. Give them remembrances from which they can draw truths by daily, hourly being for them the presence of God in their lives.

Help them to learn to give and receive kindness by being kind and gentle with them. Help them to learn to give and receive trust by being there when they really need you...which is always. Cause them to become whole, real, usable people when they are big, by treating them like whole, real, usable people when they are little.

They will remember.

Victoria Porter

The more a child becomes aware
of a mother's willingness to listen,
the more a mother will begin to hear.

Author Unknown

A Three-year-old's Plea

Mother, oh, Mother, I need some attention;
   You've been neglecting me all the day long.
I feel like a lowly, unwanted extension—
   I never am noticed until I do wrong.

Mother, I long for a hug and some kisses.
   Why is it that Baby gets all of the love?
She's caressed and petted. My hungry heart misses
   The last year's attention when I was "your dove."
My lonely heart's bleeding, "Please Mother," I'm pleading,
   "I only want some of your love!"

M. E. M.

 # Middle Child

Take thought for the middle child, Mother.

It was not his soft littleness that crowned you "Mother," nor his wedding day that will empty your nest. Seldom will he claim the title "First" or "Last" even though he does his renownless best in the shade of his more notable siblings. And you wonder—could there be some wordless whisper of heart-want within him?

Take thought for the middle child, Mother.

"Favorite" is a foreign word in the vocabulary of your mothering, but could it be that you are blind to some small partialities? Ask God for wisdom to love all your children as He loves all of His—equally, individually, unconditionally.

Take thought for the middle children, Mother.

As you do each of your children, enjoy them, value them, steer them, and discipline them consistently. Listen to them with your eyes, love them with your voice, pilot them with the strength of your hand.
   Keep them in the middle of your heart,
   and God will help you to not lose theirs.

V. H. K.

The Children's Friend

The clock seemed to exclaim, *"Hurry! Suppertime fast approaching!"* as I glanced at its demanding face. I had tried all day long to please this insistent master. But instead of a checked-off list of duties in my hand, it seemed I fluttered in many directions — and flew in none. What did I get done today?

Perhaps I could rest my weary feet while peeling the family-sized pile of potatoes. Seated on a kitchen chair with a dishpan of water and potatoes on my lap, I began to peel with purpose.

Mother sitting down! A virtual invitation to my four preschoolers to come cluster round, wanting attention, entertainment, even mischief. A dolly needed its bonnet tied. Books appeared with *"Mama, will you read to me?"* And a little hand dipped into the water to pull out a handful of dripping peelings.

With wet hands, the bonnet was quickly tied, the little hand got a hasty smack, and the book reading was promised for later. *"Mama must work quickly to be in time for supper,"* I said. Did my words have that impatient clip?

Softly she spoke, my thoughtful four-year-old; *"Mama, instead of you being Jesus, you're being Mama."*

The peeler stopped and I looked into her eyes. My mind searched hers...she must be thinking of the Bible story picture we had often pored over. Jesus sat with children of all sizes trustingly near to Him. No doubt His day had been an intense one. The disciples were protective of His reserve of strength. But His desire to bless the little ones was greater than His own need, and He welcomed them. He was the children's Friend! When He was pressed in, love came out. Their nearness was His joy.

The vision settled on me. And the questions came straight to my mother-heart. Had my hands taken up the clock's refrain, telling the children by my motions that *"I'm in such a hurry"*? Did they feel a perennial shortage of patient and loving mothering? Could I not give my children the gift of a non-stressed mother even though my time swirls like the potato water down the drain?

Surely those Bible story mothers, tired and worn also, were touched by Jesus' care. He had time enough to be at ease with their children.

On the way to my important goals, I need His gentle reminder.
My children are supposed to come to me. I have time enough to
be as the children's Friend in each moment of mothering.

V. H. K.

*Smile on your child.
It says to him,
"All is well between us."*

*"As one whom his mother comforteth,
so will I comfort you."*

Isaiah 66:13

*W*hen we mother our children by
tenderly easing their distresses...
by gently and persistently guiding them to maturity...
by showing a soul-by-soul care for each one...
then we should catch a vision of our Lord
stretching out His arm to us, saying,
*"That is a little the way I love thee,
but only a little, only a little."*

Author Unknown

The Fruitful Vine of Motherhood

"Thy wife shall be as a fruitful vine by the sides of thine house:
thy children like olive plants round about thy table."
Psalm 128:3

The fruitfulness of a wife and mother is not based only on the number, but also on the quality of the children she raises. Though her work may be quite obscure, seemingly endless, and sometimes monotonous, she can be a very useful tool in the hand of God.

How can a mother fulfill her role so that when her work is finished, she can look on it *"with joy, and not with grief"*? What are some things a mother should do now so that she can reap the blessing of her fruitful vine?

Mothers must see their role as a calling from the Lord. Being a good mother is not "just another job." Jesus explained the difference between the Good Shepherd and the hireling (one who simply works for pay). A mother, like the Good Shepherd, has a heart of love for her little ones. At times, a mother could feel like doing as the hireling, who *"leaveth the sheep, and fleeth."* But her accountability to God will cause her to continue to *"be instant in season, [and] out of season."*

Mothers must firmly require the submission of each child. We often think of Father as the firm one, but mothers also must require full obedience. They must stress the virtues of right and good, and be ready to punish for wrongdoing.

Too often school-age children do not really understand what a firm "No" means. Some cannot obey a simple command from Mother such as "Put your toys away now" or "You may not go outside without your coat." When mothers (and fathers) just turn the other way and let the child decide whether or not he wants to obey, they are allowing seeds to grow which will someday yield the wrong kind of fruit. By contrast, the right fruit will be developed when mothers remember that in these few short years the child's concepts of obedience to man and God are being firmly fixed.

Mothers must be a friend to each child. Every parent of more than one child is aware that their temperaments can vary greatly. Some are more likable and easier to befriend. Others are quieter and may be withdrawn. Some get into trouble easily and others keep us guessing about what is really going on inside their busy little minds.

But each child needs a very special friend. Busy mothers do many things for the entire family and may hardly find time to relate to each child as an individual. But remember, each child has special needs. Each one craves fellowship and friendship. If a personal touch can be developed early, the child will find security in coming back to his parents when questions arise and life is difficult.

Mothers must develop in their children an appreciation for the things of the Lord. True, we live in a temporal world. And most of a mother's time is spent with a constant routine of feeding, clothing, and cleaning. But mothers must somehow look beyond the daily routine.

Mothers, find time to talk to your child about God and His creation. Pray while you are working, but do not allow this to supplant your personal devotions. Read worthwhile stories to your children. Sing about the Lord as you go about your duties.

When we step back and look at life as a whole, we see that motherhood is actually an opportunity for a limited time only. But, oh, the blessing of seeing Mother's character and convictions reach out like a fruitful vine and influence the rising generations!

James W. Burkholder

Give time, give diligence, give love, mothers,
but do not give in.
For she who gives in to her child's cry,
plants a seed that sprouts a thousand cries.

George R. Brunk, Sr., Adapted

Mother

Shadows are dancing about on the wall,
Never a sound as they rise and then fall;
Softly the clock ticks the twilight away —
Children and Mother talk over the day.

Twilight with Mother! Their life she now shares;
Hears all their joys and their hopes and their prayers;
Faith that is perfect, no peace such as this —
Twilight with Mother, her guidance — and kiss!

Nellie B. Hurst

The Good Night Kiss

Always send your little children to bed happy. Whatever cares may trouble your mind, do give the dear children a warm good night kiss as you tuck them in.

The memory of this, in the stormy years that may be in store for them, will be like Bethlehem's star to the bewildered wise men. Welling up in the heart will rise the thought: "My father, my mother — loved me!"

Kiss your children before they go to sleep. In the morning, let them wake to see a smile upon your face, that they may lift their little hearts in cheerful praise to God.

Author Unknown, 1882

Bedtime Blessings

A mother is tempted at times to count it a self-denial to leave her work and tuck her children into bed. But it is a unique privilege to be shared with her husband, their father.

It is the time of all times when a child is inclined to show confidence and affection. Little secrets come out with more freedom and less restraints. Naughtiness through the day can be reproved and talked over with less excitement and with the tenderness and calmness that make a permanent impression. If the little one has shown a desire to do well and be obedient, that effort and success can be commended in a way that need not make the child vain or self-satisfied.

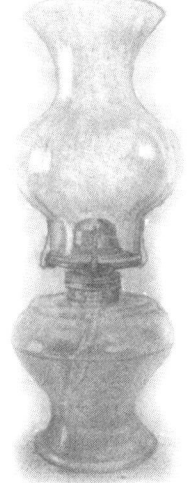

Parents must understand the character of these little beings committed to their care. They must make it a habit to talk to their children to draw out their feelings. Then they are better able to train each child wisely as their different natures demand.

Do not neglect to teach them how to pray, and pray for them in simple and earnest language that can be understood.

Mothers, your time and strength is not wasted by reviewing the day with your little boy or girl. The last words at night are of great importance, even to the babies of the flock. The very tone of voice they hear makes an impression upon them. Soothe and quiet each little heart after the experiences of the day. The little one has had disappointments and trials, as well as play and pleasures, and is ready to find rest in your care.

Author Unknown, 1882

The Mother

The while she fits her brood for bed,
    And scrubs away the dirt,
And gently brushes tangles out,
    And heals the scrapes that hurt,
She searches in their hearts as well
    Each tiny bruised spot,
Where childish woes have pressed too hard
    And left a bitter thought.

Says, "Teacher wasn't *cross* — just tired,
    She did not mean to scold."
And "Grandpa did not understand,
    For Grandpa's getting old."
"I think John said that just in fun,
    Of course you must not mind."
"*If* she was mean, just pay her back
    By being *extra kind*."

Thus, through her eyes, they view their world
    In love's most favoring light.
Then, when the whispered prayers are said,
    And all are kissed good night,
From the love-cleansed, God-guarded heart
    All bitterness is pruned,
Since patient mother-lips have drawn
    The poison from each wound.

Edna A. Collamore, 1915

CHAPTER 5

The School of Motherhood

Some wonder that children
should be given
to young mothers.
But what instructions
does the babe
bring to the mother!
She learns patience,
self-control, endurance;
her very arm grows strong.

Thomas W. S. Higginson, 1911

Lessons From Baby Mine

Baby Mine! Really here at last! Really truly here, dressed in the garments which loving hands have made. Lying in the dainty cradle which kind fingers have made cozy. Oh, precious Baby Mine!

Soon one tries to put to practice the long-thought-out plans as to feeding times, sleeping times, and going-out times. Speaking for myself, my carefully devised timetable went sadly awry. I strove so hard to train Baby, that it took me some time to realize how positions were reversed. That little bit of humanity was training me!

She trained my ears. Often, in the old days, I had been inattentive. People spoke to me, but I was daydreaming and did not hear. Now Baby Mine did something to my auditory nerve. For wherever I was, whatever I was doing or thinking, I always knew when she wanted me.

And during that period of anxiety and inexperience, how precious and real was the thought that God's ear was open to my cry. He was never too remote; never too deeply engrossed by something else to hear my continual "cries."

Baby also trained my eyes. She was not just "a baby"; she was Baby Mine. And so I became very skillful in interpreting the language written on the dear little face. I knew the symptoms that meant "a tooth coming." I learned to differentiate between the "hungry" cry and the wail that meant, "had too much." I almost knew her thoughts afar off!

And how she trained my heart! Love and ease of comfort went to the winds. It was such a joy to serve this exacting Princess. To fill up her life, I would gladly have starved out my own. Sleep, herself, seemed to know that she must draw her curtains very, very lightly across my brain; that she must be ready at any moment to wrench them back, and let me have all five senses again—sharp, bright, and alert to use them in the little Princess's service. Without force or coercion of any kind, Self just took a back seat; and Love stepped to the front row.

And further, Baby Mine opened a great big Door and showed me the vision of the Other Mothers, and of the Other Children. I would not have missed such training!

Fay Inchfawn

Progress and Perfection

"I am so discouraged," despaired the young mother to a friend. "Before Baby came, I thought that I could nearly be a perfect mother. I had never had a bit of trouble in managing the house. I had studied all the books about the care of babies that I could find. But I've made so many mistakes. I let baby cry with colic, thinking that it was just temper. He won't sleep according to schedule. I can't get through my work in the time it is supposed to take, and *everything* goes wrong."

"Can you tell a hunger cry from a temper cry, now? Did you do today's washing in less time than you did his first load of clothing? Are you a bit more deft about his bath?" asked the good friend.

Wonderingly, the mother answered all three questions in the affirmative.

"Then you can gather up your courage and go on," was the comforting assurance. "But change your watchword. Substitute *progress* for perfection. There's no such thing as a perfect mother. You wouldn't reach that goal if you lived to be the mother of ten children and then brought up forty of your grandchildren...but you can achieve progress."

Martina G. Owen

Perfection is not so much reaching, as "reaching forth."
It is an attitude more than an attainment.
Its hope is attainment, but its heart is intention.
Attempt today and accomplish; but, succeed or fail,
today or tomorrow, still attempt.
You may not accomplish your purpose,
but you are a more accomplished [mother] for the attempt,
and that was God's purpose.
To do your best every day betters your best.
That is the perfection God seeks.

Malthie D. Babcock, 1901

Wait and See

When my boy, with eager questions,
   Asking how, and where, and when,
Takes all my store of wisdom,
   Asking o'er and o'er again
Questions oft to which the answers
   Are like finding a lost key,
I have said to teach him patience—
   "Wait, my little boy, and see."

And the words I taught my young son
   Taught to me a lesson sweet;
Once when all the world seemed darkened
   And the storm about me beat,
In the children's room I heard him,
   With a child's sweet mimicry,
To the baby brother's questions
   Saying wisely, "Wait and see."

Like an angel's tender chiding
   Came his trusting words to me,
Though my Father's ways were hidden,
   Bidding me still wait and see.
What are we but restless children,
   Ever asking what shall be?
And the Father in His wisdom,
   Gently bids us, "Wait and see."

Author Unknown, 1910

*E*very inward aspiration
   Lends her beauty, undefiled.
And for every, "Oh, my Father!"
   Answers deep, a "Here, my child."

Dscheladeddin, 1892

A Prayer for Mothers

As a little child forgives,
  Forgetting the wrong that is done,
Holding no malice or spite,
  After the trial is gone,
  Would I forgive.

As a little child believes,
  With confidence tender and strong,
That Father knows all things,
  In all things never is wrong,
  Would I believe.

As a little child submits
  To him who beareth the rod,
Chastened, but lifted and loved;
  To Thee, my all-wise God,
  Would I submit.

Mabel Hale

Except your Father lead you,
You cannot find the way
Among the snares and pitfalls,
The lures that lead astray;
Except you be like children,
And hold the skirts of love,
You'll miss the narrow pathway
That leads from earth above.

Mary Frances Butts, 19th Century

The Lesson of the Tipped Table

It wouldn't have happened if we had built-in cupboards with convenient work space. But since those were still only a house-wife's dream in our case, it *did* happen. And what a lesson it taught me.

It was a busy Saturday morning and I was mixing buns on the drop-leaf kitchen table. They were almost ready to set aside to rise—just the spices to add, and the lemon rind, the raisins, and

a bit more flour. At either side of the table sat a little boy. Two blue eyes and two brown eyes sparkled as they watched this wonderful creative process. But when is it enough for a child just to watch? Ah, no! He must touch; he must smell; he must taste; he must help. He must do these things—not because he takes a delight in imped-ing Mother's progress, but because God says to him, *"Smell, touch, taste, see, learn all you can about your environment."* And motivated by this God-given eagerness of mind, he experiments with the various components of his world.

And so, as I stepped over to get the lemon, the blue-eyed one leaned far over onto the table, to learn something that he had not known before. It all happened so quickly—and there it was—an upset table; two wide-eyed boys staring at the messy debris on the floor; Mother's mixing bowls—all she had—broken; the jars of lard and sugar and flour smashed, with all their fresh supplies now useless; and through it all, the sticky mass of dough that was to have been the tasty buns.

Now I would like to say that after looking at the forlorn heap on the floor, I smiled at the boys and said, *"Well, now accidents will happen, even when we are very careful."* And perhaps, while cleaning it up, we would have sung, *"When we all work together, how happy we'll be..."* But I cannot say that. None of us care to have people know what things we do and say in the unguarded moments; what sharp words are released when no one "important" is around to overhear. And yet I must tell it.

"*Who did that?*" I asked severely. The blue eyes fell, and he said, "*I did, Mother.*" I remember the harsh words that overflowed. And then the "offender" was ordered to sit on a chair in another room.

As I determinedly cleaned up the mess, I heard his sobbing. "*Why did you do that?*" I asked myself. "*You know it was an accident. You could have done it; a guest in your home could have done it, and you would have taken it in stride. You should apologize to your son!*"

With God's help, I did. I called him to me, and as he sat on my lap, I confessed to him that I had not done what God would have been pleased to have me do. I told him that I knew he didn't mean to upset the table. (*"An' I din't, Mother, really, I din't mean to!"*) And that I had been wrong to say the unkind words to him. I asked him to forgive me, and as the dear arms went about my neck, and the wet face pressed against mine in an all-forgiving kiss, I knew I had done right to humble myself before my child.

Since, I have pondered this question: "*What would I want my sons to write as a tribute to me someday?*" I would not want them to say in a gush of emotion, "*Mother always did what was best.*" For there were times when I did not do what was best; times when I had to ask their forgiveness, and God's, for my wrong actions. Let them say, rather, that when I was wrong I had the grace to admit it; that I kept my account with my children open and clear.

May God help us as students in the school of motherhood to be true Christians, the totality of whose influence will be for the good of our children. Then our children may truly rise up and call us blessed.

Miriam Sieber Lind

*Make that possible to me,
O Lord, by grace,
which appears impossible to me
by nature.*

Thomas á Kempis

Clearing the Ground

Sweaters, gloves, rakes, Edwin's express wagon—all were ready for clearing up the garden and lawn. Leaves lay thick and crisp in the yard. The garden was filled with the dry stalks of summer flowers—a rough, unkempt garden now, it looked to be.

Mother and Edwin and Katherine worked busily, happily. Even wee Toddler helped, carrying small stalks and twigs to toss on the growing brush pile. As the children shouted and laughed and made play of their work, Mother's thoughts dwelt on her little children.

She mused, "If only I could make a fresh start as we can in the garden—forget all the mistakes; clear up and burn all the rubbish; do better next year because of my small successes and even because of the failures of the summer just gone!

"Well, why not? God must have intended we should. Every day and week and month and year He gives us a chance to begin over. I've been depressed by my failures. Edwin is willful and selfish; Katherine is growing more self-satisfied and forward—like my dahlias, too rank and tall for best flowering. I'll do better with dahlias next year, because I've learned how."

Mothers, do not drag around with you the thought of past mistakes. It is as difficult to do good work under such a handicap as it would be to plant a garden with all last year's rubbish left on the ground. Use past failures as warnings, as lessons; get from them all the help they have for you. Then turn your thoughts resolutely toward the future—the fresh, new start. Clear your mental and spiritual garden plot. God will bless all mothers' gardens as they sow and tend and water the good seed!

Agnes Noyes Wiltberger

Development

Forbid me an easy place,
O God, in some sequestered nook
    Apart to lie
With folded hands, in quiet rest,
To doze and dream, and weaker grow
    Until I die.

Give me, O Lord, a task so hard
That all my powers shall taxed be
    To do my best,
That I may stronger grow in toil
And fitted be for service harder still
    Until I rest.

This my reward—*development*
From what I am to what Thou art;
    For this I plead;
Wrought out by being wrought upon,
By deeds reflective, done in love
    For those in need.

Charles C. Earle, 1908

A Prayer for the Journey

O, Lord, do not give me tasks equal to my powers,
    But give powers equal to my tasks,
For I want to be stretched by things too great for me.
I want to grow through the greatness of my tasks,
    But I shall need Thy help for the growing.

E. Stanley Jones

Big Mud Puddles and Sunny Yellow Dandelions

When I look at a patch of dandelions, I see a bunch of weeds that are going to take over my yard. My children see flowers for Mother and fluffy white stuff to blow away.

When a stray puppy by the roadside lifts its pleading eyes as we pass, I see a dirty, scrawny animal that will dig up my flowerbeds if given a chance. My children see a lovable pet to run and jump with and to fetch a stick.

When I feel the wind on my face, I brace myself against it. I feel it messing up my hair and pulling me back when I walk. My children close their eyes, spread their arms, and fly with it, laughing.

When I see a mud puddle, I step around it. I see muddy shoes and dirty carpets. My children jump in it. They see dams to build, rivers to cross, and worms to play with.

It seems we are given children both to teach and to learn from. The time is short to stop and see things through their eyes. Enjoy the little things in their lives; for one day you may look back and realize they were the big things.

Author Unknown

If a mother is not a learner, she will become a lesson.

Author Unknown

CHAPTER 6

The Dailyness of Motherhood

O trifling tasks so often done,
  Yet ever to be done anew!
O cares that come with every sun,
  Morn after morn the long years through!
We shrink beneath their paltry sway—
The irksome calls of every day.

The restless sense of wasted power,
  The tiresome round of little things,
Are hard to bear, as hour by hour
  Its tedious iteration brings;
Who shall evade or who delay
The small demands of every day?

Dear Lord! Amid the press,
  The whirl and hum and pressure of my day,
I hear Thy garments sweep, Thy seamless dress,
  And close beside my work and weariness
Discern Thy gracious form, not far away
But very near, O Lord, to help and bless.

Author Unknown, 1892

No Wings for the Morning?

No wings for the morning? When high, singing mountains
Fling down from their summits the crystal-cold fountains?
When darkness is gone with its secret and shadow,
And warm lies the light on the green-golden meadow—
Oh, sweet lies the light on the green-golden meadow!

No wings for the morning? When joy like a river
Is poured from the hand of the Infinite Giver?
The noontide has wings of loving and giving,
Of working and striving, and fullness of living—
Oh, strong, gentle wings of loving and giving!

No wings for the morning? When children are waking
Star-eyed to the promise the new day is making?
The evening has wings of the weary birds' homing,
Of lamps all alight for the loved ones' home-coming—
Oh, sudden, soft wings that stir at their coming!

But no wings for the morning? Then how can you bear it,
This bright, brittle challenge? Oh, how can you dare it?
My heart rises early, it soars and it sings,
   "The morning hath wings!
      Yea, morning hath wings!"

Lorie C. Gooding

*Let your face be like the morning,
While the days are going by.*

George Cooper, 1905

The Morning Glory's Message

"Open yourself to the light from above." Bend your heart toward the Maker of your new day. Unfurl your soul before the warmth of the Word. You may be heavy-eyed, but shake off the dew of night and raise your eyes to Him.

"Look what mercies crowd around your door." Don't miss the profusion of blessings that quietly return each morning to grace your home. Be buoyant before your children because you see God's goodness afresh.

"Color your corner with beauty." Be as the five-pointed flower; simple in character, but strong in hue, making a small space rich and beautiful. Smile on your family when it would be easier to sigh. Adorn your children's hearts with your song.

"Remember, splendor can be a daily event." Each perfect bloom is fleeting. But God sends another one just as lovely in its place tomorrow. The Artist of your daily canvas faithfully places scenes of beauty in your mothering, if you but look for them.

"Stretch upward steadily, grasping new things." The vining habit calls for something higher and stronger than the vine, lest the tendrils wrap around each other and become a stunted, tangled mass. Aspire, by God's strength, to be just what you want your children to become.

"When the heat fades your glory, keep making shade." When a stressful day threatens to wilt your spirit, draw nourishment from your roots to keep a comforting shield of calmness over your family. God can uphold you for your loved ones when the temperature rises.

"Drop your seeds on fertile ground." Your courage is contagious. Your tone sets the tune. Give them bright words to ripple on to others. Not only is it the morning of your children's day, it is the morning of their life. And you have the first chance to sow.

"It is of the LORD'S mercies that we are not consumed,
because his compassions fail not. They are new every morning:
great is thy faithfulness." Lamentations 3:22, 23

V. H. K.

Beautiful Motherhood

Tread the home grounds softly, Mother,
    Tenderly your duties do,
Gentle as the soft spring raindrops,
    Refreshing as the morning dew.
Mother's love can melt the heartaches
    And can soothe the baby's cry
As tenderly she treads the home grounds,
    With prayers ascending to the sky.

Mother often holds the keynote
    As life's melody is played,
Reflecting on the family circle
    As a Christ-life is displayed.
Together with a loving husband,
    Bound in fervent, mutual love,
Being knit in love and action
    As the wings upon a dove.

The place you're called to serve, dear Mother,
    Is a gift from God above.
So in tenderest love be patient,
    Serving God throughout the home;
Yielding to your dear, dear husband,
    Serving in submission sweet,
Tread the home grounds softly, Mother,
    Angel guards thy vigil keep.

Ruth R. Groff

Light From Heaven

Let us bow our souls and say,
"Behold the handmaid of the Lord!"
Let us lift up our hearts and ask,
"Lord, what wouldst Thou have me to do?"
Then light from the opened heaven
shall stream on our daily task,
revealing the grains of gold
where yesterday all seemed dust;
a hand shall sustain us and our daily burden
so that, smiling at yesterday's fears,
we shall say, *"This is easy, this is light"*;
every lion in the way, as we come up to it,
shall be seen chained
and leave open the gates of the Palace Beautiful;
and to us, even to us,
feeble and fluctuating as we are,
ministries shall be assigned,
and through our hands blessings
shall be conveyed in which "the spirits
of just men made perfect" might delight.

Elizabeth Charles, 1896

*G*rant me, dear Lord, for my life's term to pray,
A threefold grace to sanctify each day—
Grace so to guide and to control my tongue
That none by me may be misled or stung;
Grace to detach my mind from worldly snares,
From trivial talk, or worrying Martha-cares;
Grace in adoring love to take my seat
Like Mary in peace and silence at Thy feet.

Author Unknown, 1894

The Everyday Mother

True beauty lies with the commonplace mother—the mother who not once in ten thousand instances fails in the fulfillment of all that routine, so seldom estimated at its worth when performed, so sorely bringing condemnation if it is in any iota neglected.

True beauty, we repeat, is with the mother who rises in the middle of the night to see if her children are covered; who springs from warm and comfortable and needed rest at the hoarse breath or the restless toss; who lies awake plotting and planning, in the early years, how to get two articles of dress out of the cloth meant for one—in the later years, how to foretell the bent of this child's intellect, of that child's inclination; who perhaps kindles the fires, perhaps prepares the breakfast, certainly sees the children contentedly off to school; who toils and moils all day long, endeavoring to keep the home desirable for her husband and children; measuring this way and that to make both ends meet; not glancing aside at the enticing storybook; forbidding her feet to follow the pleasant path to some neighbor's gossipy fireside; denying herself sometimes necessaries in order that her children may have luxuries; foregoing outside social pleasure that the evening lamp may always be trimmed and burning, and the best-loved spirit of the bright fireside never wanting; bearing her pains and her sorrows with silent composure, that no thought of them may darken the young lives about her, and when all is done, and while all is doing, finding perfect recompense in the happiness afforded by the opportunity of the sacrifice and devotion.

Author Unknown, 1897

*It does not need to be an easy day
or a perfect day to be a good day.
Any day lived in the will
of our heavenly Father
is a good day.*

Author Unknown

A Woman's Prayer

O Lord, who knowest every need of mine,
Help me to bear each cross, and not repine:
Grant me fresh courage every day;
Help me to do my work alway
    Without complaint.

O Lord, Thou knowest well how dark the way,
Guide Thou my footsteps, lest they stray.
Give me fresh faith for every hour,
Lest I should ever doubt Thy power,
    And make complaint.

Give me a heart, O Lord, strong to endure;
Help me to keep it simple, pure;
Make me unselfish, helpful, true
In every act, whate'er I do,
    And keep content.

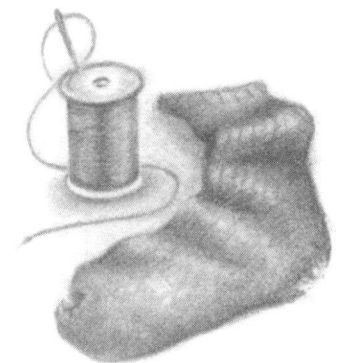

Help me to do my woman's share;
Make me courageous, strong to bear
Sunshine or shadow in my life;
Sustain me in the daily strife
    To keep content.

Anna B. Baldwin

Blessed are the mothers of the earth,
for they have combined the practical and spiritual
into one workable way of life.
They have darned little stockings,
mended little dresses, washed little faces,
and pointed little eyes to the stars,
and little souls to eternal things.

William L. Stidger

A Mother's Daily Dozens

Devotions   Darlings   Diapers   Dishes   Daddy   Directions

Dusting   Decisions   Darning   Dinnertimes   Drawing

Decorating   Dictation   Discipline   Displays   Dainties   Diets

Distractions   Dispositions   Dedication   Ditties   Disarray

Daydreaming   Diligence   Designs   Desk-work

Dressmaking   Debates   Dirty wash   Disturbances   Drinks

Dimensions   Details   Discussions   Discomforts

Diagnosing   Dough-making   Doorbells   Drudgery   Drills

Donations   Defeats   Dabbles   Disasters   Deference

Discounts   Decipher   Dawdles   Diversion   Disappointment

Dollar-marks   Daisy-chains   Deficiencies   Dashing

Dexterity   Discretion   Dallying   Dirty Floors   Drizzles

Dollies   Disagreements   Diseases   Deadlines

Developments   Dependency   Dispatches   Determination

Dates   Disinterest   Decorous   Debris   Diary   Departures

R. D.

Only a Mother

One evening a mother of several children complained, "It seems as if I didn't get a thing done today." Her small daughter looked up at her and said, "Well, you were the mother."

Just stop some evening and take inventory of your day. Did you hustle your little one out of the way while you said, "I'll read to you when I have more time?" Did you scold him for spilling his milk on the newly waxed floor, even though you knew baby hands could not hold a glass very steadily? Did you fail to listen to the school-children tell about the happenings of the day? Oh, what instruction you give by your attitude toward the events of a school day!

When your older children say, "I didn't think you'd be interested," let it be a warning to you. It means that sometimes you have failed to listen and be interested in what they were telling you. It is very easy to think that childish chatter is rather unimportant, but that is wrong. It is by listening to such chatter that you build confidence and open the way for them to bring their problems to your attention. You will be able to avoid many unpleasant situations if you listen in time.

Don't forget, you are mother for today even though nothing else is done. If that one task is well done, what joy can be yours! Do not be just a housekeeper or cook. You are called to a higher work. Remember, today you are "Mother."

Mildred Graber

Isn't There a Noble Task?

There seems to be so little that I can do for Thee;
Isn't there a noble task that You would have for me?
   Something that the world may know I'm busy for my King
   Besides the dull and daily tasks that every new day brings?

For how can stacks of dishes and piles of dirty clothes,
Tackled and completed, ever tell Christ rose?
   Or stories, mud, and Band-Aids—read, cleaned up, applied,
   Tell the world of Jesus, my Savior, crucified?"

"Oh, busy, busy mother, your task is very great.
I've given you eternal souls to teach and educate.
   Not in worldly wisdom, in fame or honor grand,
   But how to love and serve My cause, and seek that better land.

For as you tackle homey tasks with children by your side,
You have the greatest privilege, within their hearts to hide
   Bits of goodly treasures from My Holy Word,
   Which many mighty men of faith first from their mothers heard,

Oh, busy, busy mother, I need you where you are.
Your task at hand is very great, you need not travel far.
   Oh, love and teach these little souls, and help them grow to be
   Steadfast within the simple faith, to be of use to Me."

Author Unknown

A Mother's Meditation

*"Commit thy works unto the LORD,
and thy thoughts shall be established."*
Proverbs 16:3

The house is still, the children in their beds —
The dawn has not yet ushered in the day.
But Baby's hunger cry drove sleep away
And called me from my dreamland fantasies.
So while my darling nestles in my arms —
Picture of sweet content and utter trust —
I lift my soul to Thee, and through Thy Word
I hear Thee speaking softly, heart to heart.

My works, dear Lord — what very trivial things —
No sermon great to stir a waiting crowd,
Or song, or music played by master hand!
These hands of mine will deal with dust and dirt.
(Thine dealt with dust and made a blind man see!)
This voice be used to counsel and command.
My works, dear Lord, from morn till late at night —
A ceaseless round of very little things.

Commit these works to Thee? Yea, Lord, just now,
And from Thy hand of love receive them back
Moment by moment, till the evening falls.
Thy promise is my thoughts shall settled be —
Thoughts that are often filled with doubt and fear,
With discontent and dismal dark foreboding.
My work, dear Lord, I now commit to Thee —
With Thine own peace, establish Thou my thoughts.

M. L. M.

Nighttime Meditations

Dear God, loving Father,
Thou who hast silently watched me today,
  Through my rush and hurry,
  All my impatience and worry,
Thou hast seen it all in Thine own loving way.

Dear God, all-knowing Father,
I remember how I forsook little two-year-old.
  He came, "Mommy, me hold you."
  He heard, "Go, find something to do."
I was so busy; my love for him must have felt cold.

Dear God, forgiving Father,
I thank Thee for end of day, the nighttime.
  We can bring our mistakes,
  All our sins and forsakes,
To Thee: for there's no heart so knowing as Thine.

Dear God, all-powerful Father,
Grant me strength and love to begin another day.
  Thy forgiveness brings release,
  Now there's quiet sleep and peace.
O Lord, give me wisdom and teach me Thy way.

Grace Yoder Gehman

CHAPTER 7

The Pressures of Motherhood

How She Rose Above

"You are never out of temper,"
was once said to a woman
well known to be much tried at home.
"Is it that you do not feel the injustice,
the annoyances?"
"I feel them as much as you do,"
she replied,
"but they do not hurt me."
"You have, then, some special balm?"
"Yes; for the vexations caused by people,
I have *Affection*;
for those of circumstances,
I have *Prayer*;
and over every wound that bleeds,
I murmur the words,
'Thy will be done.'"

Charlotte Younge, 1880

A Picture of a Good Mother

How much is involved in that word *good!* Good inside, outside, all over, all through, all the time. Good to live with, to live beside; good to everybody in and outside of the home. Good to pattern after, good to look at. How shall one fit herself to fill such a place? Here is one picture of a good mother:

> *She lived with her children. There was never enough*
> *time to do all she felt she ought, but without complaining*
> *she did the best she could and was comforted in knowing*
> *"angels can do no more." So she kept cheerful, played, and*
> *laughed, and understood. There were burdens that took*
> *her to the very earth sometimes, but as soon as she rose*
> *above these, there were hearts of rejoicing because Mother*
> *was happy again.*

Mrs. Evaline Green

Busy!

Who of us is not busy? Busyness walks hand in hand with motherhood. But what does our busyness achieve if it excludes our children? What good do we accomplish by hustling and bustling to keep the house absolutely spotless and the washing done with laundry-like perfection if we must neglect our children to do it?

Children have been known to grow up happy and well-adjusted in homes that were not models of cleanliness, but not in homes where Father and Mother showed little interest in their activities.

Children are our business. Let us be busy with them!

Lois Duffield

Before and After School

"Quarter to eight! Boys and girls, do you hear?"
"One more pancake, then—be quick, children dear!"
"Oh, where is my lunch box?" "Under the shelf,
 Just in the place where you left it yourself!"
"I can't say my times table!" "Oh, find me my cap!"
"One kiss for Mamma and lil' Ruth on her lap."
"Be good, dear!" "I'll try!" "9 times 9's 81."
"Take your mittens!" "All right." "Hurry up, John—let's run!"
 With a slam of the door, they are off, girls and boys,
 And the mother draws breath in the lull of their noise.

"Don't wake up the baby! Come gently, my dear!"
"Oh, Mother! I've torn my new dress, just look here!
 I'm sorry; I only was climbing the wall."
"Oh, Mother, my map was the neatest of all!"
"And Sarah, in reading, got all her words said!"
"Oh, say! can I go on the hill with my sled?"
"I've got such a toothache!" "There's glue in my hair!"
"Is supper 'most ready? I'm hungry as a bear!"

Be patient, worn mother, they're growing up fast,
These nursery whirlwinds, not long do they last.
A still, lonely house would be far worse than noise;
Rejoice and be glad in your brave girls and boys!

R. I. Schoolmaster, 19th Century

Doing the Most Important Thing

I have learned a wonderful secret which is an untold blessing to me in the busy days that make up my life, and I would pass it on to my equally busy sisters. A woman's life cannot be blocked off into days and hours, this time for this, and another time for that, with full success; for the many ends of her responsibilities overlap each other in a way that is confusing, four or five things coming up and demanding attention at the same time. No wonder a woman's nerves give way and her strength fails with the many demands put upon them.

But this secret is greatly helping me to solve my problems, and I believe it will help others. It has to do with values and consists in this—*doing the most important thing first.*

There can be but one most important thing at any one time, no matter how many other things may clamor. It may be the hushing and quieting of a child, the preparing of a meal, or the tidying of the house. At one certain hour of every day the bedtime story is the most important thing, and unfortunate is the child that is habitually sent off to bed without it.

There are times when the most important thing is writing a letter or calling on a friend. There are half hours that can be most profitably spent in courting the husband and father of the children, keeping alive the coals of married love and happiness. Reading of God's Word and secret prayer are most important things each day.

When the matter is faced squarely, the most important thing can be chosen instantly, and that thing can be done with no worry about the rest. If they are really necessary, they will come to be the most important thing each in its turn.

When a nap and relaxation are the most important thing, I go and take my rest, no matter what is waiting for me. And when I rise from my rest, the work seems to melt away when it had been hard to keep it going before.

Those who have learned this secret find that doing the most important thing, with the assurance of heart that it is the thing that should be done, relieves the mind of much anxiety and worry. There come days when much work must be left unfinished. It is so in every busy life. Yet the most important thing can be done each day. I hear some worried mother exclaim, "If you had a home full of little children to care for, you could not cast things off so lightly."

I am not casting things off lightly. I am in earnest in my work and know well that there is more to do than I can ever get done. Yet I know that at any given moment, there is but one most important thing to be done, and I want to recognize that thing and do it. The other fifty things can wait till their turns come. If they are really important, the moment will come when they are the most important.

I cannot do all my work by schedule, although schedules help; nor can I get my work into such a system that I can know ahead just what I shall do, yet system helps. There are always things coming up that demand immediate attention. This upsetting of schedule and system was at first a great cause of confusion and worry. Now I have capped my system with the happy rule of doing the most important thing first, and it takes much of the friction out of life.

If you have never worked by this rule, try it and see its wonderful results.

Mabel Hale

"*S*he hath done what she could."
Not what she could not do—
not what she thought might be done—
not what she would like to do—
not what she would do if she had more time—
not what somebody else thought she ought to do—
but "she hath done what she could."

W. A. Shipman, 1893

A Mother's Resources

for the Pressures of the Home

It takes strength to be a mother. It always has—especially to be a faithful mother. Think of Hannah of old. She faced many pressures, but she knew where to turn for answers. She found a way through unfulfilled hopes, and later, the urgency of child training, along with the unending schedules and routines.

Three of her resources are right at hand. They are nothing new. You have heard them before. Just remember, they are within your reach too.

Resource 1: Your God

Listen to Hannah's prayer...

"My heart rejoiceth in the LORD." The Lord may not remove your demands and difficulties, but He can give you a song in the midst of them.

"Neither is there any rock like our God." He has not abandoned His post. God has not allowed anything in our lives, but that He first considered whether we are able to handle it. We tend to evaluate our situation by how it affects us; whether we are happy or whether we are sad. God evaluates the same circumstance on the basis of His glory and His will. And He says, "Be faithful in it."

"The LORD is a God of knowledge." If you are taking your parental role seriously at all, you live with a sense of inadequacy. How often life's demands rob you of your sense of accomplishment! But God fills in the gaps for the honest, willing heart. He gives a sense of blessing in the menial tasks of life. He sees and honors your inner desires.

"The bows of the mighty men are broken." What serious mother has not looked into her child's innocent face and wondered if there is a way for this one to be faithful in an increasingly sinful world? But the Lord has a grip on the evil about us and will protect His own.

"The LORD...maketh alive...and lifteth up." God touches faithful stay-at-home mothers with His richness and fullness. Nothing transcends the feeling of being in God's will.

"He raiseth up the poor." Do you struggle to see God's purposes in the midst of the trivial and routine? Right amidst the commonplaceness of your life, He wants to prepare His pillars for the church.

"*The LORD shall judge the ends of the earth.*" The Lord will triumph, and faithful mothers will share in the victory. Don't grow weary!

Resource 2: Your Husband

As a worship partner. Praying together and sharing spiritual concerns is so vital. See him as a spiritual shepherd and protection for you.

As a leader in the home. Let him face the rigors of decision making and earning a living. God did not equip you to do so. Leave it in his hands.

As a mature, affectionate friend. Give up your idea of a perfect marriage. You can have a good marriage by showing true patience with failures and by avoiding criticism. Love him, instead of what would come naturally. As you do these things, you will find an inspiration and energy that this world knows so little of to face the pressures of life.

As a communicator. Express your ideas, feelings, goals, opinions, and convictions to each other, even when the truth hurts.

As an ever-present companion. Find partnership in the project of raising children together, not in leaving them behind with others.

Resource 3: Your Church

As a worship center. Like Hannah, keep a true perspective of life by being with godly people. How often have you gone to church feeling loaded...life is all work and nearly all drudgery...only to leave with a clearer focus and a lighter step to face your duties again?

As a place to share and bear burdens. Don't be so aloof that you would be embarrassed to unveil a hidden load to your sisters. Confess your faults, even your struggles, that you may be healed. You can find security in knowing others will tap you on the shoulder if you need it.

As a safe haven. Like Hannah, have confidence in the temple and take your child there. In a faithful church, your children can mingle with others and find inspiration for living right.

As an opportunity for contribution. Oh, the enrichment Hannah must have felt as she saw the product of her faith standing in the temple! When life's pressures fray the fabric of your day and you begin to wonder what it's all about, remember every small thing done faithfully contributes to your child's life and to the Lord's church.

 H. Lynn Martin

A Woman's Work Is Never Done

You tell me your work is never done. I am in the same case. I know the sort of snowed-up days you can get. It is the rush that is so wearing; the sight of Duty, treading upon the heels of Duty. And the long line of Duties, still waiting, one behind the other; each one pushing and hustling for its turn.

And so, your hands work feverishly, your tired feet hurry to and fro, and up and down stairs, while your brain schemes and plans, and remodels schemes and plans, until you grow weary of it all.

"This is not life!" you say, "This is drudgery! It seems I have no time now for higher things. They are crowded out. It takes all the faculties I possess just to keep the home going. How is it possible to keep in touch with God when one is beset behind and before, and inside and out?"

But friend, there is a way of knowing God, of seeing Him and serving Him, right in the midst of "pot and pan life." He can pilot your spirit through the most tiresome day, and bring you out tired, very likely, but unruffled and conscious of victory.

The very first step toward living the victorious life is to hand one's self up to God. To say to Him something like this: "Here I am, Lord. Do what You wish with me today."

And, after that take every little trifling circumstance as coming from His hand. Do not be upset about the hindrances. He could have prevented them, but He saw blessing in them for you.

Oh, the difference that such an attitude makes! The very duties that were so wearisome before take on a kind of spiritual beauty.

And what about the children committed to our care? Perhaps some tender touch of mine, as I perform the little everyday tasks, may linger on, when the soapsuds and sponge are put away. May some "virtue" go out of my mother-heart and help those tiny hands to move "at the impulse of His love"; and may the restless feet feel the power of it and walk in right paths.

Look around your table this very evening. Smile at the children's faces and into your tired husband's eyes, remembering this:

"You are the Bible they will read the most.
They shall see the Father, Son, and Holy Ghost
Within its pages; reading, they shall claim
Their great possessions in the fragrant Name."

And so, in a very real and blessed way,
your work will never be "done,"
because it will outlast the ages.

Fay Inchfawn

My Day

It was Monday. Mommie and the Day looked at one another, and the Day was bigger than Mommie.

There was twice the usual amount of daily washing (and seven children keep us well supplied!). There was a messy house to straighten up, and there were six babies to care for on a rainy day.

After Daddy left with Jane for school, Mommie just sat and thought while the Day just sat and waited, and the children swirled and swarmed throughout the house.

When the Lord said, *"My grace is sufficient for thee: for my strength is made perfect in weakness,"* did He really mean it? And is it not true that, if we do not come to know the Lord in the circumstances of everyday life, we'll not come to know Him well?

Mommie thought...and the word came, *"Come unto me, all ye that labour and are heavy laden, and I will give you rest."* Matthew 11:28

The Day grew smaller when Mommie remembered, *"I can do all things through Christ which strengtheneth me."* All things—even a houseful of children, a rainy day, and a Monday.

Doris Coffin Aldrich

A Walk Through the Psalms
For Weary Mothers

When we feel empty and needy, a page-by-page journey through the Book of Psalms can pour God's refreshment back into our hearts. Mark a trail of stepping-stones by underlining these verses and others in your Bible.

Thou O LORD, art...the lifter up of mine head. 3:3

The LORD sustained me. 3:5

He forgetteth not the cry of the humble. 9:12

It is God that girdeth me with strength. 18:32

Thy gentleness hath made me great. 18:35

The LORD is the strength of my life. 27:1

My times are in thy hand. 31:15

Make thy face to shine upon thy servant. 31:16

Be of good courage, and he shall strengthen your heart. 31:24

Rest in the LORD. 37:7

Lord, all my desire is before thee. 38:9

Withhold not thou thy tender mercies from me, O LORD. 40:11

But I am poor and needy; yet the Lord thinketh upon me. 40:17

Thou...settest me before thy face for ever. 41:12

My soul thirsteth for God. 42:2

His song shall be with me. 42:8

God is our refuge and strength, a very present help in trouble. 46:1

The goodness of God endureth continually. 52:1

Cast thy burden upon the LORD, and he shall sustain thee. 55:22

Wilt not thou deliver my feet from falling? 56:13

I will cry unto God...that performeth all things for me. 57:2

From the end of the earth will I cry unto thee, when my heart is overwhelmed: lead me to the rock that is higher than I. 61:2

Trust in him at all times. 62:8

Thou shalt...comfort me on every side. 71:21

They go from strength to strength. 84:7

Rejoice the soul of thy servant: for unto thee, O Lord, do I lift up my soul. 86:4

O turn unto me, and have mercy upon me; give thy strength unto thy servant. 86:16

Shew me a token for good. 86:17

And let the beauty of the LORD our God be upon us. 90:17

He shall cover thee with his feathers, and under his wings shalt thou trust. 91:4

Light is sown for the righteous, and gladness for the upright in heart. 97:11

Serve the LORD with gladness. 100:2

Mine eyes shall be upon the faithful of the land. 101:6

Like as a father pitieth his children, so the LORD pitieth them that fear him. 103:13

Seek the LORD and his strength. 105:4

Through God we shall do valiantly. 108:13

Unto the upright there ariseth light in the darkness: he is gracious, and full of compassion. 112:4

He maketh the barren woman to keep house, and to be a joyful mother of children. 113:9

The LORD hath been mindful of us. 115:12

The LORD shall increase you more and more, you and your children. 115:14

Stablish thy word unto thy servant, who is devoted to thy fear. 119:38

Let, I pray thee, thy merciful kindness be for my comfort. 119:76

Thou art near, O LORD. 119:151

Great are thy tender mercies. 119:156

Let thine hand help me. 119:173

I will lift up mine eyes unto the hills, from whence cometh my help. My help cometh from the LORD, which made heaven and earth. 121:1, 2

In the day when I cried thou answeredst me, and strengthenedst me with strength in my soul. 138:3

The upright shall dwell in thy presence. 140:13

Cause me to know the way wherein I should walk; for I lift up my soul unto thee. 143:8

The LORD preserveth all them that love him. 145:20

Great is our Lord, and of great power: his understanding is infinite. 147:5

V. H. K.

Why Did You Fail?

A mother is sometimes called to great trials of patience. Her home cares lay upon her trembling nerves a sore strain. There are a thousand things to try her. It is hard for her to always keep sweet and patient.

Sometimes, in a moment of weakness and weariness, she loses her self-control and speaks unadvisedly. It seems a little thing to fail in temper. Is nothing more common? It is easy to soothe one's conscience and allay the momentary feeling of shame, by thinking excusingly of one's tired nerves and of how hard it is to be always calm and self-poised.

But meanwhile what has been the effect of the mother's unseemly conduct on the tender lives of the children? Bad temper is usually unjust. Its hot, hasty words are unkind and hurtful, words that burn and pierce, words that should never have been spoken. Besides, the mother was standing for Christ before her children, and she has failed to show them the strength, peace, and beauty of Christ.

We need God's help in the common days just as much as in what seem to us great days. We all need to pray very often a prayer like this:

"God help us through the common days,
 The level stretches, white with dust,
When thought is tired, and hands upraise
 Their burden feebly, since they must.
In days of slowly fretting care
 Then most we need the strength of prayer."

Our Lord is very patient with our weakness when He knows that we do what we can do; yet we should strive not to fail Him in temper, even if the strain is sore. It is in these pages of everyday life that we must write our word or two, and we ought to write only what will truly interpret the spirit and life of our Master.

J. R. Miller, 1896

CHAPTER 8

The Sacrifices and Rewards of Motherhood

The New Baby

Here is a sweet, fragrant mouth to kiss;
here are two more feet to make music
with their pattering about my nursery.
Here is a soul to train for God,
and the body in which it dwells
is worth all it will cost,
since it is the abode of a kingly tenant.
I may see less of friends,
but I have gained one dearer than them all,
to whom, while I minister in Christ's Name,
I make a willing sacrifice of what little leisure
for my own recreation,
my other darlings had left me.
Yes, my precious baby,
you are welcome to your mother's heart,
welcome to her time, her strength,
her health, her life-long prayers.

Elizabeth Prentiss, 1869

I Surrender

A white flag means surrender,
   Or so I've heard them say.
I think of that as I hang out
   My white flags every day.

What is it I surrender?...
   Hours uninterrupted
To use for work or play;
   Rooms clean and uncluttered
(How I wish they'd stay that way);
   Time for rest or reading
Or just good fellowship;
   Plans for active service
Or making that long trip.

These I do surrender
   And many, many more,
But there are also things I gain
   To even up the score.

What do I gain?...
Little hands that cling to mine
   While walking down the street;
The innocent smile of a half-year-old
   (There's nothing quite so sweet);
Little eyes that look for me;
   Little feet that run
To bring me "ouchies" to be kissed,
   Or maybe share some fun.

These are but a sample
   Of what I gain. Their worth?
I could not buy them anywhere
   For all the wealth on earth.

So my surrender's not defeat,
   For motherhood is mine.
Those white flags I hang out each day
   Are diapers on the line.

Clara E. Headrick

Tied Down

I am tied down...

By clotheslines
   On which I hang
   Baby clothes and dishtowels.

By strings...
   Just commonplace white threads
   With which I sew on buttons,
   Patch faded, threadbare, little suits,
   And hand-sew uncounted yards of dress hems.

Ropes tie me down...
   Jumping ropes made of twine,
   And those that pull small wooden toys about.

By bandaging...
   Young, bleeding, grimy thumbs there are
   To kiss and bind with lengths
   Of clean, white gauze.

And baby arms about my neck,
   Oh, yes...I am tied down...*I thank Thee, God!*

Author Unknown

The Cost

A lady called on a friend whose two well-mannered children came in during the visit. As they talked together, the visitor said eagerly and yet with little thought to the meaning of her words, *"Oh, I'd give my life to have two such children."*

The mother spoke with subdued earnestness from the depth of her experience: *"That is exactly what it costs!"*

Yet the gleam in her eye and the intensity of her manner spoke more plainly than words, that though she had given much, she had gotten more. She had gained the possession of her children and the enrichment of her spirit.

S. D. Gordon, 1909

Just to Be Needed!

"She always seems so tied,"
    Is what folks sniff and say.
"She hasn't e'en the slightest
    Chance at all to go away."
        Home, husband, children small,
        Keep her at their beck and call.

But she confides with loving smile,
    And laughter in her eyes,
She never has felt fretted,
    Or worried by those ties.

Says she:
"Just to be needed is more sweet
    And makes me more than free,
Than any freedom in the world
    Or anywhere could be!"

Mary Eversley

When the Song Begins

*"And when the burnt offering began,
the song of the LORD began also." 2 Chronicles 29:27*

The house of the Lord had been utterly forsaken and desecrated.
But now King Hezekiah had opened its doors, cleansed its rooms,
and restored its worship. Now the sacrifices were ready to be offered. The great temple choir waited in silence, ready to break
forth into song. But *not a note* was to be heard until the moment
the sacrifices began to burn on the altar. As the holy fire started to
consume the offering, only then did the great choir begin to sing.

These ancient burnt offerings expressed the people's devotion
and consecration to God. We do not deal with animals and altars,
but we have our own sacrifice to make. As we surrender our lives
to God, then and only then does the song begin in our hearts.

The sacrifice of motherhood calls for the denial of many former
pleasures—an uninterrupted night of sleep, time alone with one's
husband, the usually tidy house, the freedom to come and go at will.

But when mothers devote themselves to the care of their children and sacrifice ease and strength with complete self-abandon-
ment, then the song begins. Then there will be a song of joy in
the midst of drudgery, peace in the midst of trial, and strength in
the midst of burden. And as the load grows heavier and the need
for self-denial grows greater, the song becomes stronger and richer
in its melody.

Human love is a marvelous transformer of dull duties and tedious tasks. It wakes up the best in life and calls out its sweetest
songs. But there is another love which has far more wondrous
power—love for Christ. *"Whom having not seen, ye love."* This
mighty motive in our hearts, can change our whole life. It sur-
passes all earthly love in its power to inspire service, sacrifice,
and song.

If we have not learned to find joy in self-sacrifice, we need but
to look at the face of Christ, remembering His love and His infinite sacrifice—for us. Then think that these things which seem so
dreary, so hard, so costly, are simply His biddings, *bits of His will
for us.* Then love will spring up in our heart for our Master and all
will be transformed.

J. R. Miller, 1905

Motherhood

The joy of motherhood — ah, who can tell
　Of richness in the heart, who hath a child:
A little hand to snuggle in your own,
　Two eyes upturned, with look so sweet and mild;
A happy shout, "Come, Mother, play with us!"
　A kiss and hug, as day draws to a close;
So many things to teach, to learn, to share —
　There is no measure for such joys as those!

The pain of motherhood — ah, who can tell
　The bitter ache, the sting within the heart
Of those who try to guide a dear child's steps,
　But see at last their wandering feet depart?
So many sleepless nights and weary days,
　As sickness comes, and crosses hard to bear;
The tasks attempted with a strength too slight —
　How great the pain, which hearts of mothers share!

And yet, if you were asked to take your choice
　Between the burdens every mother knows:
The mental stress, the physical as well —
　If it were yours to say, that all these woes
Would never, never be your lot to bear,
　Yet choosing this, you'd also forfeit, too,
The joys and blessings, deep, of motherhood —
　I wonder what you'd say. What would you do?

Oh, it is well that mortals cannot choose —
　That God alone bestows, in His design,
On whom He wills, the gift of motherhood,
　According to His sovereign plan divine!
Our God is good, to mingle joy and pain.
　Too much of either one, we could not bear!
We thank Him that, although the pain is great,
　The joys outweigh, and keep us from despair!

L. B.

Which Mother Are You?

A mother sat by a hearthside place,
Reading a book, with a pleasant face,
　Till a child came up, with a childish frown
　And pushed the book, saying, "Put it down."
Then the mother, slapping his curly head,
Said, "Troublesome child, go off to bed;
　A great deal of Christ's life I must know
　To train you up as a child should go."
　　　And the child went off to bed to cry
　　　And renounce religion — by and by.

Another mother bent o'er a book
With a smile of joy and an intent look,
　Till a child came up and jogged her knee,
　And said of the book, "Put it down — take me."
Then the mother smiled as she stroked his head,
Saying softly, "I never shall get it read;
　But I'll try, by loving, to learn His will,
　And His love into my child instill."
　　　That child went to bed without a sigh
　　　And will love religion — by and by.

Author Unknown

*L*et the alabaster box
　Of my will be broken
That my very self may freely pour,
Spreading fragrance
　O'er my loved ones.
　　Costly to me,
　　Needful to them,
　　Pleasing to my Lord.

Thus may I anoint the feet of Jesus.

A Mother

Who Notices?

Who notices if Mother's night
    was shortened by a child who needed tender love and care?
Who notices if Mother's back
    is weary, tired, and sore after a long day's labor?
Who notices little patches
    added to small garments and large,
    because of frugality and necessity?
Who notices the stacks of pans and dishes
    that pass through hot and soapy water so they are clean for
    "next time," which may come three times a day?
Who notices the host of soiled towels,
    socks, dresses, trousers, and shirts
    that pass through the water twice a week?
Who notices the effort to clean the floors,
    windows, and beds or the labor in the hot kitchen to prepare
    a year's supply of fruits and vegetables?
Who notices the salves, bandages, and love
    applied to elbows, knees, and chins, or all the soap and water
    used to wash dirty hands and feet?
Who knows about all the Bible stories read,
    toys picked up and repaired, or the songs sung at request
    when it seems the body is too tired and busy?

Who notices? God does!
    He notices if one sparrow falls to the ground.
    Fear not, you are of more value than many sparrows.
Even though your efforts seem unnoticed
    or unrewarded publicly,
    in heaven you shall receive a reward
    for what you have faithfully done.

Let us therefore labor that we may receive
    the rest and reward.

Author Unknown

The Blessings of Motherhood

A true mother does more than give birth to a child. She is a child of God; a new creature in Christ Jesus. She is willing to lay down her own wishes and give herself to carry out God's will for her life, whether she has many children or few. To her, motherhood is not a restriction or something that robs her of her full potential. It is a blessing. And she knows that her attitude toward her calling reaches into the lives of her little ones and into eternity.

She desires the very touch of God's love on her fingers. Her eyes carry both command and compassion. Command to enhance her realm of responsibility, and compassion to guide her children to God. Her lips correct misdemeanors with a soft rebuke that at times the correcting rod of a father is unable to reach. Her heart is so full of desire for the spiritual success of her children that no price of self-sacrifice is too great to pay. She would rather burn out her very life than see her children suffer or stray.

Mothers, the load may be heavy and you may wonder where to find enough strength. Trust God, and bear children in joy as a service to Him. He will never forget you, leave you, or forsake you. Take courage. It is a blessing to be chosen of God to be a mother.

Marion P. Hoover

Mothers, be careful to not sacrifice too much for your children. If you do, you can train them to be selfish and to treat you with neglect. Doing a great deal for them does not guarantee that they will be grateful and do a great deal for you.

The mother who does not hold herself too cheap before her children, who pleasantly requires them to hand her a chair, get her a drink, and take her wraps when she comes home from church— in short, makes them wait upon her, instead of her always waiting upon them, is the mother who is treated with loving respect.

The loyalty that is in every child's heart will lead him to pay devotion somewhere. She can be the rightful place for their homage if she has shown them how.

Celesta, 1890

An Offering

"Whosoever is of a willing heart, let him bring it,
an offering of the LORD." Exodus 35:5

Dear Lord, my heart is willing.
   An offering I would bring,
Not to build a tabernacle
   But the kingdom of Christ my King.

No jewels have I, nor gold,
   But, Lord, here are some irises
      Of perfect golden hue
   I cut for our home this morning
      Still sparkling fresh with dew.

No priestly garments can I weave,
   But unto Thee I dedicate
      Those little dresses there.
   As I ironed them this morning,
      I thought of Thy loving care.

No brazen laver can I shape for
   ceremonial washing,
   But, Lord, here is our two-year-old
      All scrubbed and ready for a nap.
   (An encounter with a muddy ditch
      Called for an unscheduled bath.)

No sacred ark nor mercy seat can I make,
   But, Lord, this afternoon I kneel
      In quiet, private prayer,
   And as I intercede and praise
      I find Thy mercy there.

No shewbread can I fashion,
   But here's a fragrant pie crust;
      It gave me great delight
   To mix and shape it quickly
      For my family's meal tonight.

No sacrificial altar can I form,
But, Lord, tonight I read my girls
    Precious stories about Thee
And Thy great sacrifice of love
    Upon Mount Calvary.

Indeed, my heart is willing;
    This offering is mine:
My home, my time, my everything,
    Dear Lord, I would make Thine.

Clara E. Headrick

'Tis not thy work alone the Master needs,
but thee, thee, Mother;
the obedient spirit,
the believing heart,
the willing life.

Author Unknown, 1893

Surprise, Mother!

The sooner you accept this fact, the better! Life as a mother is going to hold some unpleasant surprises.

You may as well count them into your day's work—the spills, messes to clean up, ouches to soothe, a change of plans, mishaps, articles to search for, and many more. Plan time for them. Expect these surprises.

These are very important little jobs in your web of life. So do them quickly and pleasantly, and someday they may come back to bless you.

Author Unknown

To Mothers of Missionaries

So send I you—to give your own with gladness,
  To let them go unhindered to the lost;
To hide the tears and every trace of sadness;
  So send I you—to taste with Me the cost.

So send I you—to anxious days of waiting
  For word that often leaves so much untold;
To nights of burdened vigil unabating;
  So send I you—to watch the gap you hold.

So send I you—to walk alone when aged,
  To need the strength of one you cannot call;
To lean on Me and on the ones I bring you,
  So send I you—to find in Me your all.

So send I you—to know the joy of serving,
  To share the triumphs of the one you send;
To reap the fruit of sacrifice unswerving,
  So send I you—to joy without an end.

As the Father hath sent Me—so send I you.

Mrs. Winona Carroll

Love, struggle, sacrifice, victory—
great peace.
These are the ever recurrent
notes in the sweet hymn
of motherhood.

Author Unknown

CHAPTER 9

The Joyful Mother

Keep Sweet

Amid the duties of today
In all I think, and do, and say,
Whether I work, or rest, or play —
Lord, keep me sweet at home.

When pressing duties claim my care
And I seem needed everywhere —
Then tune my heart to praise and prayer
And keep me sweet at home.

No matter what the day may bring,
Or night — I pray, in everything,
My life may glorify my King
Especially at home!

Laura A. Barter Snow, 19th Century

My Flowers

The catalog came yesterday
And nearly took my breath away:
    Fascinating,
        Captivating—
The glossy pages were so gay
    With brilliant, dewy flowers.

The roses! Oh, those gorgeous flowers!
I sighed for scented, shaded bowers...
    Beautiful,
        Enchanting,
I'd linger there through pleasant hours
    Amidst the sweet perfumes.

I closed it with a wistful sigh
Because I heard my baby cry...
    Cherubic,
        Loving.
He cooed, content with me nearby
    And smiled a trusting smile.

I hugged him and he cuddled near
I'm blessed to have three children dear...
    Precious,
        Innocent.
My children are my joy and cheer—
    My children are my flowers!

Emily Royer

A Mother's Prayer

So many cares to burden all the day,
  So many wounds to bind, and hurts to heal,
So many steps to guide along the way,
  So much for hands to do and hearts to feel.
Thou knowest, Lord, how weary mothers grow;
  How at the close of day, we come with lagging feet
And oftimes aching head, to ask Thy help
    Just to keep sweet.

The cup of little things, things that worry so
  Comes often to a mother's lips to drink.
The griefs and joys that only mothers know
  Make up her chain of days, forged link by link.
Dear Lord, a mother draws her strength from Thee,
  Her wisdom, too, to guide the childish feet;
But always, Lord, our daily need will be
    Just to keep sweet.

Helen P. Metzger

*The path of a good woman
is indeed strewn with flowers;
but they rise behind her steps,
not before them.*

John Ruskin, 19th Century

The Mother of Joy

❖ Violets dot her windowsills like flowering ellipsis points; each a cluster of beauty, each blooming approvingly in its pot-bound life. She can imagine folks nearly tisking as they pass by those windows, pronouncing her *housebound*, confined to a narrow existence. But they are mistaken. She loves her small queendom of home! And it shows. Her family circle thrives as she gives them her best energies. She shines, she sings, she steadies, amid the clatter and chatter within those four walls. No escape needed. *She is the mother of joy I long to be.*

❖ Her son's health had faded week by week, but his trousers kept their color. Much too clean for a six-year-old boy. She stuffs them down, down into the washer. Questions and fears tangle in her mind like the pile of hangers beside her. With a sigh of release, she places all her cares in her Father's hands to make better or not to make better—and a mellow, trustful joy now sustains her. *She is the mother of joy I long to be.*

❖ The girlish notes were nearly flat enough to level the mother's enthusiasm. But Mother sang on with pleasure, the hymnal a bridge between her and her young daughter struggling to learn the alto part. Even though yesterday's bit-off pencil eraser, today's trailing shoe strings, and tomorrow's tipped trashcans are scattered across her life, she sees each day, no matter what it holds, as marked by God's hand to *"be glad in it."* *She is the mother of joy I long to be.*

❖ A little hand led her away from her tasks to the garden corner—all his own—to see the few valiant sunflowers that had emerged that dry spring. "Keep watering," she told him, "and see how tall they will grow." She had laid down her efficiency to show affection. She joyed in his joy and it tied him to her. He would not wonder if she liked being his mother or what kind of a Master she served. *She is the mother of joy I long to be.*

❖ The pain of parting…It was just a small grave, but it cradled a brief, beloved life. It was just a short letter, but it cut off her son's budding courtship. "Little," but a great loss. In the depth of her sadness, she finds that the joy of the Lord is underneath each disappointment. She does not fall through. *She is the mother of joy I long to be.*

❖ The children were to work diligently. They were to play quietly. It was a day of precarious peace as she kept all six occupied while her husband prepared for the Sunday morning service. That evening her children caught their father's words of thanks for her help. They saw again how a happy marriage works. *She is the mother of joy I long to be.*

The mother of joy... Does God mean for her to be a distant, elusive ideal as I place her perfect ways next to my imperfect ways? No! He has words for me to grow by...

"With joy shall ye draw water out of the wells of salvation." That means I should quench my deepest yearnings *in the Lord*, not in pleasures or in people or in some happy harmony of circumstances. Joy comes from my link with God.

"Rejoice in the Lord alway: and again I say, Rejoice." That means I should choose joy this minute. And choose joy the next. Resolute step by resolute step. It means I should make my will a compass needle pointing toward joy in whatever God sends.

"Light is sown for the righteous, and gladness for the upright in heart." That means I should plow daily furrows of self-denial in the field of my life. Then seeds of joy will find a home there.

"Weeping may endure for a night, but joy cometh in the morning." That means my trials are temporary, though they may not seem so. That means I only need to mourn till morn. Light *will* come.

"That my joy might remain in you, and that your joy might be full." That means I should put my countenance in God's hands even though it is easier to let my family know how tired and discouraged I am.

"Giving thanks always for all things unto God." I cannot count *all* my blessings, but God wants me to try, for I will gain perspective and grow stronger in joy. And if the joy of the Lord is *my* strength, then *my* joy will be my children's strength.

As I turn my whispered longings into real living, as I focus not on what I am *going through* as a mother, but on what I am *growing to*...then I will be that mother of joy.

V. H. K.

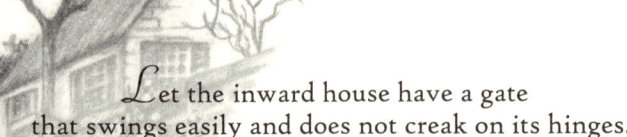

*L*et the inward house have a gate
that swings easily and does not creak on its hinges.

Let truthful transparencies stand for the panes of plate-glass,
and patiently listening ears be doors
which no just petition seeks in vain.

Let a watchful conscience
dust and sweep and wash every nook and corner.
Ventilate with every honest opinion that blows.
Then, under this little but wondrous arch and dome
guarding the mind, this instrument of the soul—will be *joy*.

Bartol, 1909

A Mother's Smile

How easily our smile shines forth to welcome guests into our home! Let us not shut these sunbeams from our own children. They are the tender plants we are training for immortality.

A mother's smile! I doubt whether we realize how precious it is to the unfolding heart, how widely it casts its radiance into its future life, or how it is remembered amid heavy hours.

Oh, feed your little one with your smile and the sweet tones of that love which is so deep in your own heart. And if you die, may he remember together the mother who nurtured him and her loving smile.

From an Old Book

The Fountain

Into the sunshine,
  Full of the light,
Leaping and flashing,
  From morn till night!

Into the moonlight,
  Whiter than snow,
Waving so flowerlike
  When the winds blow!

Into the starlight,
  Rushing in spray,
Happy at midnight,
  Happy by day!

Ever in motion,
  Blithesome and cheery,
Still climbing heavenward,
  Never aweary.

Glad of all weathers,
  Still seeming best,
Upward or downward,
  Motion, thy rest;

Full of a nature
  Nothing can tame;
Changed every moment
  Ever the same;

Ceaseless aspiring,
  Ceaseless content,
Darkness or sunshine
  Thy element;

Glorious fountain:
  Let my heart be
Fresh, changeful, constant,
  Upward like thee!

James Russel Lowell, 19th Century

*You have not
fulfilled every duty,
unless you have fulfilled
that of being pleasant.*

Charles Buxton, 1884

Joy Lessons

Life is made up of habits. We ask God to help us to keep sweet and to live joyfully. He is ready to do it, but the way He would help us is in little lessons which we must learn for ourselves. He will never take out of our life all our miserable ways at one time and put in place of them a full set of lovely ways, as one might change the works of a watch. That is not God's way of remaking us.

We are scholars in Christ's school and are to learn of Him. No pupil can master an art or a science in a day: it takes months and years. We cannot learn in a day to live joyfully and victoriously; but we can get a lesson today and another tomorrow, letting no day pass without its line.

Meanwhile, God will help us continually, encouraging every effort. If only we are diligent and persistent, the most cheerless of us can at last learn the habit of joy that we may lift our day with song.

J. R. Miller, 1898

How does the soul grow? Not all in a minute,
Now it may lose ground, and now it may win it.
  Now it resolves, and again the will faileth;
  Now it rejoiceth and now it bewaileth;
Now its hopes fructify, then they are blighted;
Now it walks sunnily, now gropes benighted,
  Fed by discouragements, taught by disaster.
  So it goes forward—now slower, now faster,
Till, all the pain past, and failures made whole,
It is full-grown, and the Lord rules the soul.

Susan Coolidge, 19th Century

The Balancing of the Clouds

"Dost thou know the balancings of the clouds,
the wondrous works of him which is perfect in knowledge?"
Job 37:16

But have you watched it, child of God?
And have your eyes been wide-awake
To see His thought for you?

A cloud is overshadowing,
The light grows dim and you depressed.
But watch! He balances the clouds!
That extra bit of joy has come from Him
Today—just when you needed it.
That word of cheer, that evidence
Of seed that rooted and bore fruit,
That flash of insight to His truth,
That radiant glimpse of loveliness;
Are they not all His sunshine rays
To balance clouds and give His light?

O thank Him for His lovingkindness now—
How sweet to think He cares,
And plans the happy things
To counterbalance those with stings!

Dorothy J. Langford

*L*earn the sweet strength
of a cheerful face;
not always smiling,
but at least serene.

Author Unknown

The Last Day

Were this the last of earth —
  This very day —
My life's work finished quite
  And put away;
And I from fam'ly dear
  About to part,
How gentle were my thoughts!
  How kind my heart!

And yet this fleeting life
  Is one last day;
How long soe'er its hours,
  They will not stay.
O heart, be soft and true
  While thou dost beat!
O hands, be swift to do;
  O lips, be sweet!

Mary Francis Butts, 1898

*I want a heart
so full of joy,
life's withering storms
cannot destroy!*

Author Unknown

CHAPTER 10

The Patient Mother

Prayer of a Tired Mother

Hear my whispered prayer to Thee,
O Father; may I patient be.
  Keep my voice soft, gentle, low;
  Help me serene and calm to grow.
The little hands that clutch and cling,
The wilted flowers they often bring,
  The restless feet that track in dirt,
  The many little cuts and hurts—
    They fill my days.

So often I am tired and hurried
When I have need to be unflurried.
  Help me to know which things are real;
  Their true importance help me feel.
And may I kiss the clinging hands,
With eagerness, receive the flowers.
  Help me to guide aright those feet—
  Each hurt to bind and then repeat
    Soft, soothing words.

Amy Elizabeth Taylor

Prayer for Patient Hands

Lord, give me patient hands—
Not hurrying through their ministry
Toward tasks more pleasing unto me,
But less to Thee.

Lord, give me quiet hands
That work in calm and harmony—
A mirror of the peace that we
Receive from Thee.

Lord, give me tender hands—
A gentle touch of sympathy
In answer to each frightened plea
Upon life's sea.

Lord, give me patient hands,
However small their task may be.
For patient Thou hast been with me
Unfailingly.

Author Unknown

Have a heart that never hardens,
a temper that never tires,
a touch that never hurts.

Charles J. Dickens

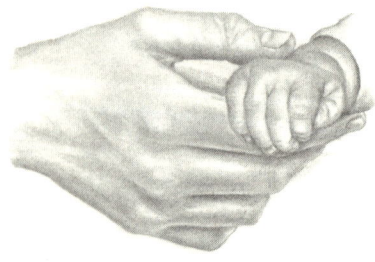

The Violet

Lord, make my life a flower in the garden of Thy kingdom.
Let me grow close to Thee so that I may be filled
    with Thy beauty and fragrance.
Let me, as a sweet-smelling flower,
    shed the perfume of Thy love upon those who are close to me.

Lord, I would be the violet.
A violet is near to the heart of the child.
        I would not be the gorgeous rose.
            Children admire its beauty and delight in its fragrance,
            but they are hurt by its thorns.
I would be the violet which little hands may find
    and pin near to their hearts without being wounded.
        I would not be the brilliant zinnia
            nor the gaudy dahlia nor the towering sunflower.
            Children stand off in awe and gaze upon them.
But they leave them for the little violet which they can reach
    and which yields its life to their little hands.
        I would not be the orchid, rare and costly.
            Only a few can share its beauty.
I would be the violet,
    hidden from the eyes of the rushing throng
    but found where the feet of children tread.

Lord, then, let me be a violet growing close to Thee.
When the eager eyes of little ones search for a flower,
    let them find me.
Let them feel delight in the fragrance and beauty
    which is from Thee.
Let them feel that they are close to Thee. And when they take me
    and wear me near their hearts, let them see Thy face and feel
    Thy love, and breathe of Thy Spirit.
Let them, with the eyes of faith, look up and say,
    "It is from God; I would be a violet, too."

M. Irene Stauffer

Patience

I prayed for patience:
  "Lord," I cried, "I know I sin when in frustration.
  I give way to angry words and reckless deeds.
  I cannot conquer this—I've tried.
  I trust You for the victory."
  I prayed sincerely, and in faith.

Time passed:
  Again I kneeled before the Lord.
  This time in weariness I wept;
  "O God, I've failed again, again!
  I spoke harsh, angry words to them.
  And spanked them, too, beyond all need.
  Will they remember me, O Lord,
  Impatient, scolding, and unnerved?"

Then, to excuse myself, I said:
  "Lord, I love order in my work—a time for this, a time for
  that—and now's the time for cleaning house. (There's no
  doubt that's what it needs!) But three-year-old begs for a pail
  of water! She will scrub the porch. The water spills. She's
  sopping wet and cries until her clothes are changed. Now
  two-year-old is at the cats. (She carries them so close, they
  squeal.) I've told her twenty times to stop. Poor kitties, just
  ten hours old. And Baby's crying when I thought she'd sleep at
  least another hour. But I've the bathroom floor to scrub! And
  when will I stir up those rolls? Heavenly Father, Lord of all,
  hear me in my weakness now. How can I face my day with
  calm? Where's the patience for which I prayed?"

I paused:
  Deep within my consciousness, a voice spoke clearly to my soul.

  *"Daughter, do not despair, but learn the lesson which is yours. In wis-
  dom, I have given you the multitude of homey cares. I could have sent
  you sickness, want, or great disaster, as the tool for learning patience.
  But in love I sent instead, these little ones. Strength in every task
  is yours. Arise and face each day with joy; and patience, too, will
  surely come."*

  "O Lord, I hear. Amen. Amen."

  Clara E. Headrick

Gentle and Wise

Far down through the shadowy tunnels of time,
  The mothers of Israel came,
All servants of God in an unbroken line.
  The prophets recorded their fame.

And, oh, they were faithful! Beloved of Him!
  Now here I am left in their place.
I cling to a lamp that is feeble and dim,
  Not daring to look in His face.

For I am a child, though in years not a youth,
  Yet still I am young in His eyes.
So often I stumble in seeking the truth,
  And how can I judge or advise?

In Gibeon, Solomon prayed in the night.
  "My God, I cannot do it all.
I ask for a heart to discern what is right,
  For I am unworthy and small."

King Solomon thought of his calling to lead,
  Much more than it seemed he could do,
And though my position is humble indeed,
  Yet I am responsible too.

So now I will go to the Ancient of Days,
  Who never reproaches the weak.
The hands that are hanging, He gently will raise;
  He gives them the good that they seek.

I have no temptation to ask Him for gold;
  My needs, He already supplies.
I only request, like the ruler of old,
  A heart that is gentle and wise.

Janice Etter

*N*o position is subject
to more petty annoyances
than that of the mother of a family.
It often happens that she is interrupted
ten times while trying to complete a task.
To discontinue one's work
without any apparent trouble,
to reply smilingly,
to wait patiently until the end of a long conversation,
to resume calmly the interrupted work—
this is the mark of a soul which possesses itself
and which God possesses.

Author Unknown

*T*he many troubles in your household will tend to your edification if you strive to bear them all in gentleness, patience, and kindness.

Keep this ever before you, and remember constantly that God's loving eyes are upon you amid all these little worries and vexations, watching whether you take them as He would desire.

Offer up all such occasions to Him, and if sometimes you are put out and give way to impatience, do not be discouraged, but make haste to regain your lost composure.

Francis de Sales, 17th Century

A MOTHER'S SUPPLY FOR UNLIMITED PATIENCE:

"That ye might walk worthy of the Lord
unto all pleasing,...
strengthened with all might,
according to his glorious power,
unto all patience and longsuffering
with joyfulness."

Colossians 1:10, 11

A Quiet Spirit

In my attempts to promote the comfort of my family, the quiet of my spirit has been disturbed. Some of this is doubtless owing to physical weakness; but, with every temptation, there is a way of escape; there is never any need to sin.

Another thing I have suffered loss from is entering into the business of the day without seeking to have my spirit quieted and directed. So many things press upon me, that this is sometimes neglected; shame to me that it should be so.

This is of great importance; to watch carefully not to over-fatigue myself, because then I cannot contribute to the plea-sure of others. A placid face and a gentle tone will make my fam-ily happier than anything else I can do for them. Sometimes our own will leaks sadly into the performance of our duties.

Elizabeth T. King, 19th Century

"Thy Gentleness Hath Made Me Great"
Psalm 18:35

David attributed his greatness to God's gentleness. Our sons and daughters can also become great in the work of the kingdom as they feel the touch of God's gentleness and observe it in their parents' lives.

Gentleness is the expression of kindness and meekness. It is soft in manner and amiable in disposition. Gentleness will be heard in the tone of our voice, felt in the loving touch of our hand, and seen in the expression on our face.

A gentle soul is like a great rock in a weary land. Troubled hearts grow calm and peaceful under the touch of gentleness. How do we respond when our teenager comes, wanting to share a troubling situation? Do we tap our fingers on the desk, anxious to move on to the demanding pressures of the day? Or are we ready to give our full and patient attention?

Children observe gentleness as we are patient with them, ready to offer a helping hand. The two-year-old notices the very gentle touch given to the newborn and with patient guidance will also learn to give loving touches. The sick child feels our love as we are gentle and considerate in meeting his needs.

Parents should remember the value of love and gentleness when correcting children, especially when they have performed to the best of their knowledge. When discipline is needed, firmness should be tempered by gentleness.

We do not know what the future holds for the children growing up by our side. Will our son be a master with servants? a leader of God's people? When our daughter grows into womanhood, will she be a mother of children? a nurse to the elderly? or a teacher in the school? Regardless what station in life our children grow up to fill, they will need to use gentleness. The gentle, careful hands of parents are far-reaching as our children pass to horizons beyond us.

Donald L. Kauffman, Adapted

Be Still...

"Be still, and know that I am God: I will be exalted among the heathen, I will be exalted in the earth. The LORD of hosts is with us." Psalm 46:10, 11

This Bible command extends to mothers in some of the most frustrating scenes of life.

Be still...
when the living room has a fresh bestrewment of dolly clothes and toy tractors, and unexpected company has arrived.

Be still...
when a child's scream of pain strikes lightning through your frame.

Be still...
when you find crayons in the cookie jar, Legos in the lid drawer, and a bottle in the boot box.

Be still...
when your baby wants to stick to you like Velcro and the days go faster than you do.

Be still...
when the overlapping noises of kettles clanging, chairs scraping, and voices calling, drown out key words in your conversation.

Be still...
when you catch your big-little boy stomping the laundry he took off the line into the wash basket to make room for more.

Be still...
when the flu bug strikes and the children go down like dominoes and you fear you are next.

Be still...
when there are big tears for little reasons.

Be still...
when your master plan for your day does not match your Master's plan.

Be still!

Being still does not mean you do not take appropriate action when that action is necessary. You can be still while your hands or feet move rapidly. Being still, for a busy mother, is usually more of an inner posture than an outer one. It is a quiet trust in a personal God and a confidence that He will be exalted. For He is with you.

Adapted from Mary Foxwell Loeks by V. H. K.

Depth

Out on the ocean, where waves tumble about in riotous tumult, one gets the impression that the waters are being churned to their uttermost depths. But this is no more than a surface confusion. For if the waves are fifty feet high, then seventy feet below them is abiding calm. The higher the waves, the deeper the calm!

Even so is it on the ocean of life. Life's unresting surface forever bears storm and disaster, and those who live a surface life are no more than driftwood on an angry sea.

But those who descend beneath the surface find a twilight world of eternal calm. The greater the waves, the deeper must one go to find tranquility.

To live on the surface of daily events is to see nothing as being related; each event and experience becomes no more than a broken, meaningless segment. But to find "the depth that's deeper still," one must submerge himself in the ocean of life, and discover that "there abides a peace which man did not make, and cannot mar."

Author Unknown

That woman who is calm and collected,
who is master of her countenance, her voice,
her actions, and her gestures,
will be the mother who is in control of her children
and who is greatly beloved by them.

Author Unknown

Equilibrium

Just when we think we've fixed the golden mean—
  The diamond point, on which to balance fair,
  Life, and Life's lofty issues—weighing there,
With fractional precision, close and keen,
Thought, motive, word, and deed—there comes between
  Some wayward circumstance, some jostling care,
  Some temper's fret, some mood's unwise despair,
To mar the equilibrium, unforeseen,
  And spoil our nice adjustment! Happy she
    Whose soul's calm equipoise can know no jar,
      Because the unwavering Hand that holds the scales
    Is the same Hand that weighed each steadfast star—
  Is the same Hand that on the sacred tree
  Bore for her sake the anguish of the nails.

Margaret J. Preston, 19th Century

A Mother's Prayer

Lord, at the dawn of this morning,
  Busy with care though it be,
I would kneel down and look upward,
  Yielding myself unto Thee.

    Open my heart to Thy blessings;
      Close it to worry and greed.
    Work in my life true contentment,
      Trusting my God with my need.

Fill me, oh, fill with Thy Spirit!
  Pour of Thy sweetness and grace
Into my soul as I labor.
  Give me a calm, smiling face.

    Make me more patient in spirit,
      Gentle in manner and word;
    Let only answers of softness
      From my lips ever be heard.

Banish from me irritation
  Both in my manner and tone;
Oh, let Thy presence be with me!
  Let me not labor alone!

    I would not live by my feelings,
      Simply by faith I would pray,
    Yielding myself to Thy promise,
      Grace to supply for my day.

      Mrs. Curtis Yoder

CHAPTER 11

The Trustful Mother

Mother's Prayer

Dear Father, Thou knowest how deeply I love
Those whom Thou hast given me.
Next to Thy love for them, is mine.
Thy love surveys all with perfect wisdom,
While mine is partly blind because of human frailty;
Therefore I commit them into Thy care,
Confident that Thy love will do the right thing
For them at all times.
Spare them, oh, save them, at all cost!
Overshadow them with Thy mighty power
And keep them in temptation's hour.
Oh, let none of them be lost!

Author Unknown

Keep This for Me

"Keep this for me."
What child has not said this
And placed a treasure in his mother's hand
With this injunction, she should keep it safe
Till he return?
He knows with her it will be safe;
No troubled thought or anxious fear besets his mind.
And off he runs lighthearted, to his play.

If children can so trust, why cannot we
And place our treasures, too, in God's safe hand?
Our hopes, ambitions, needs, and those we love,
Just see them, in His all-embracing care,
And say with joyous heart,
"Keep these for me."

Author Unknown

Our Keep

In olden times, there was a strong place in every castle called "The Keep." All the weak and helpless and precious things were hidden there in times of danger. Today, God is our Keep, and we must hide our precious children in His safe care and keeping. If we are hidden in this divine Keep ourselves, surely we will not leave our children outside.

And we must let our children know that we trust God about them. We must tell them we do, and then we must act as if we did. What sort of pictures are we hanging up in the gallery of our children's memory? See to it when your boys and girls are grown, that they do not remember you as an anxious, worried, irritable mother. But live such a trustful life before them that they will have a picture of peace and trust when they think of you.

Hannah Whitall Smith, 19th Century

"Why Art Thou Disquieted?"

Some, like Martha of old, spend an infinity of trouble on the smallest things; worry themselves and the household about the arrangement of a room, the preparation of a meal, the loss of a shilling. They dream of misfortunes if their children are an hour behind time. They give to their fears the careful thought which might win them the knowledge of a science... Why, what sort of life is that? It is made up of *peacelessness*.

Leave the future in the hands of Eternal Love. Understand what it is to trust God. Be not over-careful for what is to come. He who has watched over you will watch over those you love. A wiser love than yours directs your little world!

Stopford A. Brooke, 1898

Finding the Bright Side

It may not be very bright, and the side may be small, yet it is certainly there. Our duty is to find it. Perhaps it is bright only in contrast with the darker portions around it. Be thankful that it is not quite as black as it might be.

We mothers can become old before our time by not resting in the thought that God does know and care for us in our daily life. We can lose sight of the protecting oversight of our Heavenly Father. We look at the dark shadows of the picture, not taking time to see the beauteous highlights. We add tomorrow's burdens to those of today. How can we see anything bright if we are continually overcoming the difficulties of next week and fearing tomorrow's hardships?

Mothers, look Godward! He will disclose to our view the "silver lining," the bright—or, at least, less dark—side. He will open our eyes, that we may see His hand in it all.

Author Unknown

Mothers Exuding a Spirit of Trust

Mothers need to trust their children. No child functions well in a climate of distrust. Expecting a child to misbehave, to forget something, or to perform below par is quite likely to produce just that. Letting your child know that you trust him to do his best will likely motivate him to do better.

Mothers also need to distrust their children—well, let us say that mothers need to avoid an absolute trust in their children. Why? Because their children are just as much the sons of Adam as anyone! The carnal nature loves to slant a story in its own favor. It also will do things secretly to avoid exposure. And the heart is still as deceitful as ever. So the children are blest whose parents check up on them at times. It may mean a private conversation with the teacher or another child's parents. It may mean trusting another's judgment above your own. It may even mean punishing the child for something he will not admit to, if there is sufficient evidence against him. Children appreciate it when they must earn their parents' trust.

Mothers need to put their trust securely in their Heavenly Father. The doubts and the "what ifs" will come. But happy is the child whose mother quenches her fear in a loving Father's care. He has given promises and is worthy of our trust. Even faithful friends can fail us, but God never has and never will. Such a trust will seep out and bless others.

Mothers need to teach their children to trust others. That is done mostly by example. Whether it is trusting her husband, or a teacher, or another child's parent, a mother who trusts, inspires trust.

Mothers need to be trustworthy. Can your child depend on you to love constantly, to discipline consistently, and to criticize carefully? In this fashion, mothers teach their children to be trustworthy. Do your children know from your example the importance of being dependable? Have they learned to shun wild mood swings? Are they tidy and punctual by force of habit? Learning the value of being trustworthy brings present and future rewards. Children who have learned to trust and are worthy of being trusted, will rise up and call you blessed. God has entrusted you with them for that purpose.

Leon Leinbach

"Be It ... According to Thy Word"

Mary, may I know the secret
　　Of thy humble trust in God?
How you must have sat and marveled
　　That you'd bear the Son of God!
To human mind, impossible,
　　Yet 'twas what the angel said:
"Your Son will be the King of kings;
　　His reign will have no end!"

Your answer to this startling news
　　Still a shining model stands
To womankind all these long years
　　Who before their Maker stand.
"Behold the handmaid of the Lord;
　　Be it...according to Thy word."
Such simple words, so full of faith
　　From a pure heart so deeply stirred.

May we follow in thy footsteps,
　　Calmly trusting without sight,
Knowing not what lies before us,
　　Trusting God to lead us right,
For miracles cannot be wrought
　　In faithless hearts and cold.
"O Father, lead Thy handmaids
　　As in the days of old."

Rosanna

Abraham and Isaac

My heart said:
　　I'm glad God did not ask me
　　　My son to offer up.
　　Such test of love for me would seem
　　　Much too severe a cup.
　　Moriah miracles may come
　　　To one of Abram's strength;
　　I could not exercise my faith
　　　To such a bitter length.

God's voice said:
　　I ask of all My followers
　　　What they have power to do.
　　When you have need of Abram's strength
　　　I'll give that strength to you.
　　My miracles are worked in hearts
　　　As feeble as your own;
　　In humblest human instruments
　　　My mighty grace is shown.

Author Unknown

Mother Questions

When the difficulties of life curl
into big question marks before you—
turn to the Lord and say,

*"Neither know we what to do:
but our eyes are upon thee."*

2 Chronicles 20:12

Our Dearest Treasures

*Written at the hospital bedside of a seven-year-old son
who had undergone an operation.*

His hand outstretched with love, the Lord entreats us
    To yield our dearest treasures to His care;
Then while we struggle with, "Thy will be done," still
    He waits in tenderness to hear that prayer.

Not for Himself, but for our good He asks it,
    That treasures of our heart might be above.
Can we commit our life and that of loved ones
    To God's perfecting and refining love?

Though outcome yet unknown, God wants submission;
    (Yield, heart of mine, and cease to struggle more.)
Then in surrender we oft find our loved ones
    A little dearer than they were before.

While here on earth in human flesh we tarry,
    This conflict to God's children is not odd.
His love calls often, through life's situations
    To trust our dearest treasures in the hand of God.

Mrs. Andrew N. Miller

A Mother in the Hospital

I know it all...I know.
For I am God. I am Jehovah. He
Who made you what you are; and I can see
The tears that wet your pillow night by night,
When nurse has lowered that too-brilliant light;
When the talk ceases, and the ward grows still,
And you have doffed your will;
I know the anguish and the helplessness.
I know the fears that toss you to and fro.
And how you wrestle, weariful,
With hosts of little strings that pull
About your heart, and tear it so.
I know.

Lord, do You know
I had no time to put clean curtains up;
No time to finish darning all the socks;
Nor sew new hemming in the children's frocks?
And do You know about my Baby's cold?
And how things are with my sweet three-year-old?
Will Jane remember right
Their cough mixture at night?
And will she ever think
To brush the kitchen flues, or scrub the sink?
And then, there's John! Poor tired, lonely John!
No one will run to put his slippers on.
And not a soul but me knows just exactly how he likes his tea.
It rends my heart to think I cannot go and minister to him...

I know. I know.

Then, there are other things,
Dear Lord...more little strings
That pull my heart. Now Baby feels her feet
She loves to run outside into the street.
And Jane's hands are so full, she'll never see...
And I'm quite sure the clean clothes won't be aired—

At least, not properly.
And, oh, I can't, I really can't be spared—
My little house calls so!

I know.
And I am waiting here to help and bless.
Lay down your head. Lay down your hopelessness
And let Me speak.
You are so weary, child, you are so weak.
But let us reason out
The darkness and the doubt;
This torturing fear that tosses you about.

I hold the universe. I count the stars.
And out of shortened lives I build the ages...

But, Lord, while such high things Thy thought engages,
I fear—forgive me—lest
Amid those limitless eternal spaces
Thou shouldest, in the high and heavenly places,
Pass over my affairs as things of nought.
There are so many houses just like mine.
And I, so earthbound, and Thyself, Divine.
It seems impossible that Thou shouldest care
Just what my babies wear;
And what John gets to eat...and can it be
A circumstance of great concern to Thee
Whether I live or die?

Have you forgotten then, My child, that
I, the Infinite, the Limitless, laid down
The method of existence that I knew,
And took on Me a nature just like you?
I labored day by day
In the same dogged way
That you have tackled household tasks. And then,
Remember, child, remember once again,
Your own beloveds...did you really think —
(Those days you toiled to get their meat and drink,
And made their clothes, and tried to understand
Their little ailments)—did you think your hand,
Your feeble hand, was keeping them from ill?

I gave them life, and life is more than meat;
Those little limbs, so comely and so sweet.
You can make raiment for them, and are glad,
But can you add
One cubit to their stature? Yet they grow!
Oh, child, hands off! Hands off! And leave them so.
I guarded hitherto, I guard them still.

I have let go at last. I have let go.
And, oh, the rest it is, dear God, to know
My dear ones are so safe, for Thou wilt keep.
Hands off, at last! Now, I can go to sleep.

Fay Inchfawn

*B*e not miserable about what
may happen tomorrow.
The same everlasting Father,
who cares for you today
will care for you
tomorrow and every day.
Either He will shield you
from suffering,
or He will give you
unfailing strength to bear it.

Francis de Sales, 17th Century

In Convalescence

Not long ago, I prayed for dying grace,
For then I thought to see Thee face to face.

And now I ask (Lord, 'tis but a weakling's cry)
That Thou wilt give me grace to live, not die.

Such little prayers! I know. Yet pray I must,
Lord help me—help me not to see the dust!

And not to nag, nor fret because the blind
Hangs crooked, and the curtain sags behind.

But, oh! The kitchen cupboards! What a sight!
'Twill take at least a month to get them right.

And that last cocoa had a smoky taste,
And all the milk has boiled away to waste!

And—no, I resolutely will not think
About the saucepans, nor about the sink.

These light afflictions are but temporal things—
To rise above them, wilt Thou lend me wings?

Fay Inchfawn

Sufficient Unto the Day

The Present is all we have to manage:
  the Past is irrevocable, the future is uncertain;
  nor is it fair to burden one moment
  with the weight of the next.
Sufficient unto the moment is the trouble thereof.
In looking forward to future life,
Let us realize that we do not have to sustain all its toil,
  to endure all its sufferings,
  or to encounter all its crosses at once.
One moment comes laden with its own little burden,
  then flies,
  and is succeeded by another, not heavier than the last.
If one could be sustained,
  so can another and another.

Jane Taylor, 19th Century

Because in a day of my days to come
There waiteth a grief to be,
Shall my heart grow faint and my lips be dumb
In this day that is bright for me?

Margaret E. Sangster, 19th Century

CHAPTER 12

The Thankful Mother

Thanksgiving Day

It is so small, one little day, to hold
    My thanks, with all the rest! To rise, slow-stealing
Beside a crib, to watch wee eyes unfold
    In pink round cheeks — what mother but, there kneeling,
Must every day feel thankfulness untold?

Love binds itself to serve, with many a smile,
    And seldom finds regret. The hours, returning,
Bear me new tasks in seeming endless file;
    And I, from each some new love-lesson learning,
Know life is good, and offer thanks the while.

One day? Ah, no; how may a mother say
    The half her gratitude in one day's waning,
When every hour gives some new prayer to pray,
    Some fresh-born happiness? With love remaining
Each day is my most blest Thanksgiving Day.

H. Bedford Jones, 1910

At Eventide

This very day, while I with sweet content
Fulfill the common daily round, on homely duties bent,
  From many a happy home, with careless unconcern
  And gay good-bye, have fared forth feet that never will return.
And what hath she who sits with all the world beside,
If nevermore, her loved ones come home at eventide?

And what indeed am I, that God should give to me
So glad and blest a life, a home from grief so free?
  That this sweet common day, for me without a tear,
  Should bring for some the crushing loss of all life holds most
  dear?
That kept secure from whatsoever danger may betide,
My own come safely back to me today at eventide.

Help me, O Lord, I pray, my gratitude to show
In tender, loving ministry where falls the sudden blow;
  In daily walking softly, lest the terror nigh
  Descend in darkness swift and deep, o'erspreading all my sky,
And there should come to sit my own hearthstone beside,
The grief of one who waits alone, alone at eventide.

O Father loving all, I gladly trust to Thee
The days to come, that good or ill, I still may see
  Thy tenderness in each; and whether stress or peace
  They bring, I still can praise with praise that shall not cease,
That for so many years love hath not been denied,
And I have welcomed home so long, my own at eventide.

Lillian Manker Allen, 1918

Gold Mining

There! Did you see it? A yellow glint! It was the smallest flash of light, a trace of a shine, but it means…that you stand upon a whole mine of gold! Some is ready and waiting, some you must dig for. It looks like this:

- ❖ A stack of breeze-scented, freshly-folded diapers.
- ❖ Your little boy's laugh in his sleep.
- ❖ Your daughter, volunteering the truth, instead of using a convenient lie.
- ❖ Little hands that reach for you over the top of the crib.
- ❖ The full circle of love when your children mother you on one of your rare sick days.
- ❖ Hymn medleys by a stool-perched, apron-clad dishwasher.
- ❖ A little bookworm enjoying each page, even though her book is upside down.
- ❖ A dirt-splattered wash-up sink as evidence of a hard-working husband and boys.
- ❖ Stress-melting baby smiles.
- ❖ Your young man's open Bible and notebook on his desk.
- ❖ Each uneventful day.

A lode of gold lies right where you live and serve; imperishable blessings known only to a mother. Each fleck, particle, and nugget reflects the light of His love for you. Keep finding yours.

"In the house of the righteous is much treasure." Proverbs 15:6

V. H. K.

Treasuring Sunbeams

A little child sat on his playroom floor, playing with a sunbeam that lay across the carpet. He tried to catch it with his tiny fingers and giggled at each failure. Again, he would bathe his little hands in its warmth and brightness, and then clasp them for joy. Grown-up children, too, are found treasuring sunbeams. They are happy in the enjoyment of the intangible when the tangible is wanting.

Mary Miller was such a young woman. She had grown up in an unusually happy home and had passed into one of her own, which promised her all the comforts she had been accustomed to. But her husband met with heavy losses just as he had won his bride, and she was obliged to live in a lowly style she had not known before. Her husband thought he knew what a sweet spirit she possessed when the day of prosperity shone for her without a cloud. But he was astonished and cheered when adversity revealed her true character.

"It is going to be very hard for you, my dear wife," he said to her, "to descend with me into all sorts of scarcities and sacrifices which you have never been used to."

"We shall see," she returned with smile.

"It is easy to smile in advance," he said in reply, "but you do not know how hard it will be for you."

It is true she did not know. She now had to do with her own hands what she had other hands do for her; she had to make a very little money go a long way; and in short, she must have that grim and unpleasing master, Economy, sit with her at the table, reign in her kitchen and preside over her wardrobe. But her friends found her unchanged by circumstances and when they consoled her, she replied, "But think what a kind husband I have!" And she treasured this sunbeam and made herself glad with it. Yes, she was so genuinely happy, it was refreshing to meet her.

"But it will not last," said the ravens. "By and by, when she has children, and must clothe and feed them, we shall have a different tune."

Well, the children came and she scarcely had a moment of leisure. She was industrious and arranged her time wisely, but she could not work miracles. She felt a great deal of the time like a straw blown hither and thither by the wind, trying to complete her unending tasks.

"Now, then," quoth the ravens, "we shall hear you complain. You have to work like a slave, and see what miserable wages you get!"

"Miserable wages!" she cried. "Why, I don't know anybody so rich as I am! With such a husband and such children and such friends, I am happy as the day is long."

"You have a great deal of leisure for your friends, to be sure."

"Well, I should like to see more of them, it is true. And some day when the children are older, I shall."

"By that time you will be so old yourself, that your heart will have grown cold."

"Oh, no; it is too busy to grow cold."

So she made sunbeams out of her daily homespun tasks, and went on her way rejoicing.

The ravens were puzzled. "It must be her perfect health," they whispered to each other.

Time passed; the children grew up, and just as the long-needed prosperity began to flow into the house, the young people began to pass out of it into homes of their own, until father and mother sat at their table alone.

"Now you have spent nearly a lifetime in toiling for your children, and what is the good of it all? As soon as they get old enough to be a comfort to you, every one of them goes off and leaves you."

So said the ravens.

"Just what I did at their age!" she replied cheerily. "Why shouldn't they get married as well as I? And instead of losing, I have gained children. I had only six, and now I have twelve. And I have time now to see my friends, to read, to take journeys, and to enjoy my husband."

But now long, long days of ill health came and laid leaden hands upon her. Her children were scattered far and wide and could only come occasionally to make brief visits.

"Very hard!" said the ravens.

"Oh, no! It is such a relief to me that they all moved away before this illness overtook me. It would have cast such a gloom upon them to be at home and miss Mother from the table."

"But the time is so long! What a sad pity that you are not allowed to use your eyes!"

"Oh, do you think so? I was just thanking God that in my days of youth and health, I learned so many passages in the Bible, and so many hymns. I lie here repeating them over, and they are like honey to my taste."

"It would surely be a good thing if you could see your friends more."

"I do see them, in imagination. I call on this one, and now that one; and make him or her repeat the pleasant words they used to speak. I am never lonely. And I have other encouraging things to think of: books I have read, sermons I have heard, little kindnesses shown me by some who are in heaven now."

"Have you forgotten that you have wept over little graves?"

"No, I have not forgotten. I lie and think of all the sweet ways my little ones had, and how tenderly the Good Shepherd took them away in His arms. They might have lived to suffer or what is far, far worse, to sin. I can't help rejoice that three of my children are safe and happy in heaven."

"Is it no trial to lie there, bound, as it were, hand and foot, and often racked with pain?"

"It would be a great trial if I had not such a devoted husband, who does all he can for my comfort. And what a delightful room this is! In the summertime, when the windows are open, I can hear the birds sing and the voices of children at play. In the winter, the sun shines in and cheers me."

"The sun doesn't shine every day."

"No, and that is a mercy because it is so welcome after its absence. On cloudy days, I think over the sunny ones and remind myself that clouds never last forever. 'The saddest birds find time to sing,' they say, and it is true. Nobody is sad all the time or suffering all the time."

"You are in the prime of life; others your age are at work in the Master's vineyard. Doesn't it pain you that you are doing nothing for Him?"

"It did at one time. I said all I'm good for is to make trouble for other people and use up my husband's money. But it was made plain to me that 'they also serve who only stand and wait.' I might be nothing but a cold, flat stone to be trodden on and fit for nothing else. But if the Master's hand put me here, I ought not to complain that He did not let me build part of a palace instead. Some of us need to give others the blessing of serving by being served. You see, everything has its good side."

By this time the ravens were exhausted and flew away.

And now, let us see whether this faithful sufferer was doing no work in the great vineyard...Here are six homes where she is quoted regularly. Her children have all learned the songs she used to sing to them in her nest, and they are teaching them to their children. And the influences going forth from these lives are beyond computation.

Her friends often heard her wonder what made God so good to her, though they knew her life seemed so full of trials. They had gone away with lessons impressed on their memories to bear fruit she never knew of. Those who were with her when death stole away three little ones knew it was not stoicism that kept her from complaining. She thanked God that she could enjoy them for a season, knowing they were now safer, happier with Him. Yes, when she wept over the little graves, she caught sunbeams even then, and said, "'Though he slay me, yet will I trust in him.'"

The truth is, our own hands have more to do with shaping our lives than we realize. We cannot and would not control God's providence. But we can be willing to see the silver lining in the cloud, to "nurse the caged sorrow till the captive sings," to count up our mercies through those dark days, knowing that it never rains always.

And now, let us go back to the sick room and its patient occupant. She has grown old and her strength has greatly declined. She cannot talk much and no longer hears earthly voices.

"Yes, I knew you would come to me as soon as you heard he died, so kind of you. We lived together fifty years. God was always so good to us. I always did say we had mercies when other people had miseries. He slipped away so gently that nobody heard him go.

"Don't grieve for me. The parting will not be long. My old feet will soon go tottering after. It has been a great shaking, but I think I could hardly have borne to go and leave him alone."

As she faltered forth these words, slowly and at intervals, her children and a few dear friends standing about her, watching the smile that mingled with tears, a sunbeam darted suddenly across her bed. She laid her cold hands upon it, in the tender way in which she would clasp that of a friend, and said, "I've had nothing but mercies all the days of my life."

And so she passed painlessly away, treasuring sunbeams to the last.

Author Unknown, 1872

Not in the
Abundance of Things

Ripe rich carpets—like plum butter spread
To the very edge of the bread;

Too fragile, 'most, to stand upon its base—
A thin blue vase,
Veined like an old woman's hand,
From some far land—
Chaste china; and crystal the thickness of a hair
Was there.

"O God, she has such lovely things! And why not I?"
I all but prayed...
Then came her cry
From the next room—pitiless; and a child's—afraid:
"One of my imported cups!
Irreplaceable since the war!
You awkward child! Oh, what are children for!"

Back in our small rooms—square
And sunny with the rag rugs on the bare floor,
More and more
I pondered what I saw and heard,
Deep joy then stirred
Within me; overwhelmed me; and in gladness
for my lot
I suddenly forgot
The battered beauty of her loveless home. I laid
My arms against my baby's crib and prayed:

"Lord, keep me from the tyranny of things—
A house—a dish—a chair—whate'er it be
That turns my heart from this, my son, and Thee.
Lord, spare me from the tyranny of things.
Oh, may I covet these: the faith that sings
And springs to meet a Hand outstretched above;
The friendship of His chosen ones; the love
Of this dear boy whose merry laughter brings
More beauty to our home than worlds of things.

"Lord, keep me from the love of Here and Now—
That I might rightly teach these small ones how
To love Thee, the eternal King of kings—
The One who bears His sons on eagle's wings
To timeless loveliness, unmarred by breath—
To beauty freed of dust, unscathed by death;
Teach me to seek the gifts His spirit brings—
Lord, save me from the tyranny of things."

Miriam Sieber Lind

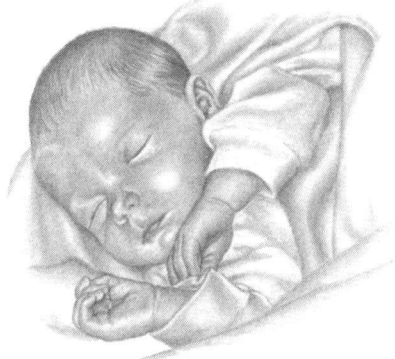

A Mother's Reflections

Sometimes she feels that this is not enough—
The dull routine—the daily chore—
And then she tucks them in their beds at night
And sighs—*"Could there be more?"*

Virginia Gibbons

*L*ive with the light of God's love
shining into your *common* day.
Take old gifts and joys
as though they were fresh gifts.
So we can sing a new song
unto the Lord every day.

Malthie D. Babcock, 1901

When Nothing Happens

In youth one sighs for happenings
    To flash across life's story,
Some startling change, or swift event,
    Or hint of coming glory.
I used to long, in those old years,
    To burst some bonds asunder,
To rush from slow monotony
    Into a world of wonder,
To find some unexpected guest
To rouse me from ignoble rest
And force me to an arduous quest—
But now I think I love the best
    Those days when nothing happens.

They mean—no death within my house;
    No fever, pain, or riot;
No loss to darken all the skies;
    No storm to break life's quiet;
No sudden sickness for myself
    Or for my best and dearest;
No startling news; no battle cries,
    But all good things the nearest,
And joys that stay with folded wings,
And love's own gentle comfortings,
And dear familiar household things—
    These days when nothing happens!

And yet I will not be afraid
    Of any new tomorrow,
For God, who orders all my ways,
    Chooses my joy or sorrow;
Nothing by chance can come to me,
    Or find me undefended,

My Father's care encircles me,
And I am well befriended;
So I will wait and trust His will,
His love with peace my heart shall fill;
I know that He is with me still
Whatever else may happen.

Marianne Farningham, 1908

Thorns and Roses

There are those who see
only roses in life,
pretending the thorns are not there;
and those who see no roses at all,
constantly scorning the thorns.
Then there is the child of God
who sees both,
knowing whom to praise for the blossoms—
and where to go
when the thorns cause pain.

Marcia K. Leaser

A Reminder to Mothers

You teach your children by your attitudes:

❖ Thankfulness is contagious—
   and so is the lack of it.
❖ Do not major in what is missing—
   and overlook what is there.
❖ Troubles and mistakes are inevitable—
   but complaining and discouragement
   are optional.

V. H. K.

Thankful

"For boyish quarrels swift and hot?
For household rules so soon forgot?
For aches and pains, for joys soon lost?
For days when we are tempest-tossed?
For disappointments, each reverse?
When all things go from bad to worse?
    Oh, no, Lord, not for these
        Thou my thanks dost ask!

"For song of bird, for blue of sky,
For twinkles in a baby's eye,
For green of grass, for clouds so high,
For rainbow wings of butterfly,
For autumn leaves a-sailing by,
For every proof that Thou art nigh.
    Oh, yes, Lord, yes, for those
        Thou my thanks dost ask!"

"My child, 'In every thing give thanks.'
Boyhood's quarrels are soon forgot
And household rules are sometime learned.
In heaven, pain you will not know,
And adverse winds don't always blow,
Each disappointment holds from Me
Numberless blessings. Wait and see!
    When nothing good at all you see,
        Child, use your 'faith-full' eyes.

"It takes the bitter and the sweet
To keep you sitting at My feet.
And too much sun or too much rain
Would be your loss and not your gain.
I know what's best for you, dear child,
Of sunny skies or tempest wild."
    "Oh, yes, Lord, all things work for good.
    To Thee I offer thanks."

Author Unknown

CHAPTER 13

The Singing Mother

Sing It, Mother

Sing it, Mother—sing it low,
　Deem it not an idle lay;
In his heart 'twill ebb and flow
　All the lifelong day.

Sing it, Mother—softly sing,
　While he slumbers on thy knee;
All that after years may bring
　Shall flow back to thee.

Sing it, Mother—love is strong:
　When the tears of manhood fall,
Echoes of thy cradlesong
　Shall its peace recall.

Sing it, Mother—when his ear
　Catcheth first the Voice divine,
Dying, he may smile to hear
　What he deemeth thine.

J. B. Tabb, 1893

Her Songs of Love and Home

The little joys of life she sings
  In measures true and strong;
But through her theme of common things
A note of love and gladness rings,
  For love inspires her song.

Ah, better might we sing if we,
  So wont for themes to roam,
Would sing as sweetly wise as she—
  A song of love and home.

Eugene C. Dolson, 1909

Mothers...

Mothers, sing with your children!

Little Freddie, aged four, pinched his finger in the car door. The finger was badly mangled, but Freddie tried not to cry. Soon he was on his way to the doctor, held securely in Mother's arms.

"Sing to me, Mama," said Freddie gravely. Together they sang one song after another of the songs that Mother had been singing to him since birth. Mother felt Freddie relaxing in her arms. The singing helped to ease her own tenseness.

The doctor went to work on Freddie's finger. He marveled at the small boy's calmness. Twice he remarked on it. "Most children would have had to be held down to do anything like this," he said.

Mothers, sing with your children!

C. C. C.

*O*h, that we might sing evening and morning,

and let song touch song all the way through!

Oh, that we could put songs under our burden!

Oh, that we could extract the sense of sorrow by song!

Then sad things would not poison so much.

Sing in the house; teach your children to sing.

When troubles come, go at them with song.

When griefs arise, sing them down.

Lift the voice of praise against cares.

Praise God by singing;

That will lift you above trials of every sort.

Attempt it.

They sing in heaven,

and among God's people on earth,

song is the appropriate language of Christian feeling.

Henry Ward Beecher, 19th Century

A Mother's Song

A story from Pennsylvania during the French and Indian War
of the mid 1700s

The young girl struggled through the brush and tangle of an almost path, the pain of her bruised and bleeding feet outweighed only by the pain of her bruised and bleeding heart. Behind lay her dear and familiar home, torn apart and smoldering. Before her, a fearful wilderness life with merciless red men who snatched children from the side of their peaceloving parents, never to see them again. Beside her, the company of other captive children, smaller ones carried by the bigger, stunned and silent in their grief. Within her, the memory of songs and prayers of home...all that she could carry with her.

After unknown miles and days of trudging and nights of over-tiredness, one by one the kidnapped children were given to Indian families, now to be slaves. The young girl found herself with an old squaw who was as harsh in manner as the work she demanded—gathering branches and bark, digging nearly immovable roots, and catching furtive mice to add to their meager diet.

With the passing of time, the red people were pleased to see the white blood wash out of their captives. Nine years, marked by the changing seasons, brought gradual changes to the girl. Her fair skin browned, her hands and feet grew rough, and her thoughts and speech became that of the Indians.

But something lay in the heart of the young girl that no Indian ways could quench. As she roamed the quiet forest, songs and prayers of her beloved German mother floated to her on the unseen swell of memory, *"Allein und doch nicht ganz allein bin ich in meiner einsamkeit..."* she sang, the very words a comfort to her.

> *"Alone, and yet not all alone,*
> *Am I, in solitude; though drear.*
> *When no one seemeth me to own*
> *My Jesus will Himself be near."*

Winter snows had come and war clouds had all but gone. Pennsylvania soldiers had captured a few hostile Indian bands. These former captors, now captives themselves, pled for freedom. Only if they would meet certain conditions, was the answer. One important one: Return all stolen children.

A ragged, shivering cluster of grown children was released by the remaining Indians to the colonel at Fort Pitt. Sympathetic soldiers supplied them with blankets and wraps from their own scant supply to make the arduous trip eastward to Carlisle.

Meanwhile, a notice—not the first of its kind—was published in all the papers. Any who had children or other kin carried away by the Indians during the war were to come to Carlisle to identify and claim their own.

It was hope that brought the German mother to the appointed meeting place, a hope as tattered as her widow's garb. Since that long-ago day when she had taken grain to the mill, since that awful day when she had returned to find her daughter missing, their house burned, and—grief of griefs—her husband's lifeless form—ever since that day, she had prayed that the Lord would keep her child and bring her back.

The mother gave the decade-old memory of her daughter to the officers…light hair, blue eyes, fair skin…but her words trailed into silence as she saw the unkempt, forlorn youth. Impossible! Yet she had prayed, and hope moved her nearer. She peered into their faces, one after another, but there was nothing in them that she could claim; nor was there anything in her to light their pitiful eyes.

"*Did your daughter have a birthmark or scar to help you identify her?*" the officers gently probed the mother with bowed head. "*A song or prayer she might recall?*"

"*There was,*" she said as she timidly lifted her face. "*There was a song we loved to sing at evening time…Allein und doch nicht ganz allein bin ich in meiner einsamkeit…*" and her words flowed into melody.

A look of wonder crossed the face of one young woman. It was her song of comfort, the song of her lost home! With a cry of joy, she rushed forward to her mother. Their reunion was complete. This is said to have happened at Carlisle, Pennsylvania on December 31, 1764.

Faces fade. Houses crumble. Pathways grow over. Names disappear. But a mother's song endures in the heart of her child.

V. H. K.

Knowing the Joyful Sound

The things we enjoy doing in everyday life tell quite a bit about ourselves and what is really important to us. This is true about our singing. The Christian's song should be heard beyond the church doors. When we love the Lord and His Word, we will not be satisfied to express it only on Sundays.

Singing a variety of songs over and over again impresses them in the minds and hearts of our children for life. Our children's memory is quite active. They can learn to sing and to love many of the songs in our hymnbooks, not only the children's choruses. Teaching them these songs in our homes will put enthusiasm into their singing in church.

Singing while we go about the routine experiences of life teaches our children a number of valuable lessons.

- ❖ It gives them a glimpse of the One who means the most to us.
- ❖ It shows them where we turn in times of disappointment and trouble.
- ❖ It convinces them that we are not ashamed to be identified as Christians or to give our testimony of His saving, keeping power.
- ❖ It is a message of trust and contentment.

"Blessed is the people that know the joyful sound:
they shall walk, O LORD, in the light of thy countenance."
Psalm 89:15

Stanley C. Wine, Adapted

*L*et us try to make our lives like songs,
brave, cheery, tender, and true,
that shall sing themselves into other lives,
and so help to lighten burdens and cares.

Author Unknown, 1893

The Remedy of Song

O mother, if your dishes have become a weary chore,
And if you sometimes wonder, "Must I do them all once more?"
Then you have need of seeking for the remedy of song,
To fill your kitchen and your heart with joy when things go wrong.
You need to feel the heartfelt cheer which praise to God will bring;
Lift up your heart, lift up your eyes, lift up your voice—and sing!

Prop up a book behind the sink, with hymns you love and know,
With songs you recently have learned or tunes of long ago.
Then start right in—it matters not who hears you, or if none;
The Father hears—and you will find the blessing is begun.
Sing cheerfully, sing thoughtfully—oh, make your kitchen ring!
Lift up your heart! Lift up your eyes! Lift up your voice—and sing!

We mothers need to look beyond the tasks of every day,
Our little cares that seem so big, sometimes along the way.
A mother singing in the kitchen fills the home with cheer;
It is a sound of happiness our families love to hear.
We need to keep a singing heart, whate'er each day may bring;
Lift up our heart, lift up our eyes, lift up our voice—and sing!

Mrs. Curtis Yoder

A Few Notes on Singing

❖ Have you noticed this cycle in your home? A singing mother makes happy, relaxed children. Happy, relaxed children make a mother sing.

❖ Sometimes we sing to small ears, "Little ones to Him be-long, they are weak, but He is strong." and it comforts us too. "[She] that watereth shall be watered also [herself]." Proverbs 11:25

❖ A question to consider: Do I sing enough for my family to know which songs are my favorites?

❖ Trade places with your children and ask them to teach you the songs they are learning at school.

❖ What can you learn by hearing your children sing for pure joy? When there is a song in your heart, sing along. When your heart is heavy, covet your children's free spirit. Through their weakness and innocence, God has "perfected praise."

❖ Sing of your love for your Savior and the fresh victory He gives you. Your children need to hear the sound of your joy.

❖ Teach your children the deeper, richer songs of the church. Even if such songs seem above their understanding, even if they *misunderstand* some words, still invest in their growing love for truth.

❖ Sing above the dirty dishes, cluttered counter, and baby blues by keeping a song at eye level. Position a hymnbook in a cookbook holder on your sink sill, ready for use.

❖ Cradlesongs should be soft and rich with meaning. Use your voice and the rhythm of the rocking chair to closely weave these songs into your child's heart.

❖ Memorize a lifting song. Think about it and follow its words in the realities of your day. Try *Above the Trembling Elements.*

❖ Encourage your children to sing while doing simple, lowly tasks. It will help them to do the unpleasant things of life willingly. You may be raising Pauls and Silases to sing in the stocks someday.

❖ The little child by your side at church will sense if your singing is passive or purposeful, personal or impersonal. So...sit up. Look up. Sing out!

❖ Sing the scale to your growing babies on the changing table. Notice how closely they watch your mouth. They may begin to imitate you and eventually sing with you.

❖ A song in the night of sorrow or trial, can give light when the darkness seems impenetrable. We can remind our loved ones that at all times God is good, and spread over them *"the garment of praise for the spirit of heaviness."* Isaiah 61:3

❖ Have a regular medley of songs to sing, a chain of your own creation to repeat with your children. It will keep you singing rather than searching your mind for another song.

❖ Gather your own mental arsenal of songs that are uplifting and re-focusing for times when "pity city" seems an inviting place to go. Two choices often beckon; we can sigh or we can sing.

❖ Your songs have wings and will traverse miles and years. Imagine your grandchildren singing the very songs you now sing to the little ones at your knees.

❖ Paint song pictures of beauty beyond this world for your children: the Happy Land with its pearly gates and golden streets, the jasper walls and the crystal sea, the angel forms and the ransomed throng on the evergreen shore in an everlasting spring. You can give a glimpse beyond heaven's door to joys unspeakable.

V. H. K.

When It Is Hard to Sing

...apply this five-fold treatment

1. Sing daily. Vocal cords grown rusty need the oil of gladness.

2. Sing daily. Dislodge the lump of pride and self-consciousness that hinders your airflow.

3. Sing daily. Expel the inner claim that your thoughts are already too full with important matters as you bustle about your home.

4. Sing daily. Repel the clouds of negativity standing between you and the sun.

5. Sing daily. Beware of excuses. The two times a mother should sing are when she feels like it—and when she does not.

Recover your voice. You can sing!

V. H. K.

Birds do not sing because they
have an answer.
They sing because they
have a song.

*W*alk with the woodland creatures; note the hush
And whisperings among them. Not a sprig
Or leaf but hath this morning hymn. Each bush
And oak doth sing, *"I am!"* Canst *thou* not sing?

H. Vaughan, 1892

CHAPTER 14

The Mother Who Reads

Wise is the mother,
the bridge-building mother,
who spans the way
from her heart
to her children's hearts,
placing little planks together
with care and purpose—
a book read here,
a letter written there,
a verse shared today,
a poem penned tomorrow—
imparting her loves, her loyalties,
her faith, her foundation,
to form a bridge of trust
in God and one another.

"For precept must be upon precept, precept upon precept;
line upon line, line upon line; here a little, and there a little."

Isaiah 28:10

Read, Mother, Read

Evening. The supper dishes all washed and put away. Mother seated in her soft, roomy chair with a very small boy on each knee. A book in her hand, her voice rising and falling. Our attentive faces fixed on the scene being made so real to our little boy imaginations. Our eyes flashing with indignation, softening with pity, or sparkling with the sheer thrill of the story. And then, a pause, as Mother stopped to rest her voice. A momentary silence, then two small voices in unison, "Read, Mother, read. Please read, Mother!" And Mother would take up the book again, the story would hold us captive once more, and the evening hours would slip all too quickly by.

Those are almost the earliest memories of my childhood and among the most significant. Because in them, my mother laid foundations, and laid them deep, that her children should instinctively love the noble things of life.

They are among the most precious memories because now I can see, as I was too small to understand then, the tender love and patience that held her to her task, that glorified it, that took it out of the realm of "doing something to keep the children quiet," and made it a labor of love. For the winter nights were long, and incessant reading is not always easy after the work of the day. It would have been easy, and natural, to have left us to ourselves. We were wiggling and squirming with life; there would have been no fear of our not being able to pass the time.

But Mother would not have been satisfied with that. She wanted her children to grow in mind as well as body. As bit by bit her two boys grew bigger there was a change in posture of our little group. First one, then the other, moved to the arm of the chair. Then my brother, older than I, drew up a chair for himself beside Mother's, and after a while, I did the same. But though the posture changed, the plan never did. And on through the years we boys would still look at her whenever she paused, and plead, "Read, Mother, read."

The reading of those years had a profound and good effect on our young minds. For one, it taught us the habit of reading something long, and actually reading it through, not merely skipping here and there.

Mother taught perseverance in reading by making it so attractive that we wanted to read things through.

We also learned to listen to rapid reading, and to understand it easily. Rapid does not mean hurried. It is the sort of reading that keeps the listener on edge to be sure he misses nothing. This makes one "sit forward" mentally. When reading is too slow, one "slumps backward" in his listening and the mind dozes.

Mother was a wise selector. She took as much or more care as to what entered our minds as she did to what entered our stomachs—and she was by no means negligent of the latter!

She wanted books that would be interesting to her boys. But not only interesting, they must be wholesome. There must be no questionable ideals or bad men held up in admiration because of one "redeeming trait."

Mother evidently knew that small children absorb and hear a great deal more than they are given credit for. She knew that in order to entertain us, she must not read something silly to be "on our level." She would rather read things that took a little effort to understand instead of things that were easy. At the same time, she did not read things that would have been foreign to our boyish enthusiasm and interest.

Slowly, but surely, our reading was made up of books just a little deeper and harder to understand than before. But never once did she let down the bars for books that were not worthwhile.

Above all, I am grateful that early on Mother read us stories from the Bible. And I am grateful that later on she, under a compelling constraint of the wonder of the Book, led me to love it as I never had before. She led me to know its central figure, the Son of God, who loved me and gave Himself for me.

Through the passing years, we boys have thanked God from our hearts that He gave us a mother who would read to us. And often the echo of those words comes back to me, whispered as if they were a mandate and invitation to all mothers who have in their care the destiny of their children: If you want your children to be all that they ought to be, *"Read, Mother, read!"*

 *Author Unknown*

To a Good Mother

Mother, the songs you are singing
 Though simple they seem today,
They are deathless things with tireless wings
 That travel a long, long way;
Sometimes, though you may not know it,
 When you are a world apart,
They'll come to a man as such things can,
 And nestle and sing in his heart.

Mother, the things you are telling
 Seem simple stories, in truth,
But these wondrous deeds are life-filled seeds
 That fall on the heart of youth;
Sometime, though the days be many,
 Your spoken word shall outring;
Then here where you sow, will green things blow,
 All sweet with the fragrance of spring.

Mother, the tasks you are doing
 May seem commonplace, 'tis true;
But your happy ways and words of praise
 Are building high in the blue;
Sometime, when the world grows dreary,
 As it does for all who roam,
Lo, for such an hour in love's tall tower,
 Will be shining the joys of home!

Author Unknown

Please, Mother, Read to Us

Of all the childhood memories
  That linger 'round my heart,
There's one that's very precious now
  And makes the teardrops start.
Somehow amid her busy days
  Of keeping house and all,
Our mother found the time to read
  To us, her children small.

She didn't get the things all done
  She would have liked to do;
She didn't go away so much,
  But, when her work was through,
She'd read to us; and I believe
  More than by what she said,
She taught us of eternal things
  Just by the books she read.

Our house may not have been as clean
  As Jones's o'er the way,
Our meals may not have been so fine
  As if she'd spent all day
Preparing rich desserts and things
  That take a lot of fuss;
But those things do not matter now—
  And Mother read to us.

Dear mothers, when your little ones
  Come begging you today,
"Please, Mother, read to us again,"
  Oh, do not say them nay.
But read some worthwhile books to them;
  It is not wasted breath—
You're molding soft and tender hearts
  That do not die in death.

Author Unknown

On Reading Bible Stories

❖ Effective training to respect and love God's Word begins in infancy. If a mother does not possess love for the Bible, she cannot instill love for it in her child. If you object to the word infancy, you do not understand how early a child is affected by the mother's attitudes. — *Lloy A. Kniss*

❖ What book takes the highest place in the training and development of the mind? The Bible. But during some of the most important years of life, the child cannot read and understand the Bible. Here is the parent's opportunity to tell Bible stories. Why tell the story rather than read? Because telling makes it more direct and forceful; the child's attention is caught and fixed. — *The Book of Life*

❖ Ye, who train the young, beware of the first gallery in which you put your child! One picture that the child's heart can safely hold is the form of Jesus. Put it there early, before all things. Let it be the first painting in the soul—the child's first ideal of greatness! Let the morning message of heroism be a message of unselfishness. Let it see the strength of gentleness, the courage of meekness, the might of restraint, the victory of forgiveness, the majesty of patience, the triumph of peacemaking, the manliness of compassion. — *George Matheson, 19th Century*

❖ Suit the story to the child's mind, but not by the use of baby talk. The child must be treated as a rational being. Much has God hidden from the wise and prudent and revealed unto babes. Some of these Bible words, beautiful and significant, rich with the usage of the centuries, will be treasured in the child's mind. It is well that he hears a few words which are full of music: solemn, stately, and glorious. — *The Book of Life*

❖ "Tell me a story" is a plea heard in many a home. The Bible is a mine of stories; its pages contain an abundant store. The ideas are wholesome and exalted. Evil is recognized and punished. Goodness stands approved. — *The Book of Life*

❖ Mothers, read Bible stories to your young children often. They will pick these up and "read" them back to you by the time they are four-years-old. Establish these good, solid Bible stories at a young age, and your children will never forget them. — *Jesse Neuenschwander*

❖ Children will ask questions. They may cause the parent frustration in knowing the wisest way to answer. Storytelling is a good way to engage the child's mind and to take some control over what questions they might ask. This idea can be found in the Bible. Several times when God instructed Israel to tell their children a story, He also taught them how to get their children to ask questions that would make opportunity for them to tell a story. — *The Book of Life*

❖ The Good Shepherd's final words to the disciples were this command: *"Feed my lambs"* (*John 21:15*). The lambs are tender, needing a carefully chosen, wholesome diet. They are vulnerable, receiving so readily the impressions that will help to mold their spiritual characters. Only by God's grace and wisdom can any parent fulfill that solemn charge. — *Bruce A. Good, Adapted*

❖ Consider that when we read Bible stories to children there is absolutely no enmity between them and God. They find the stories fascinating, and they say, *"Read some more, please."* Even if a story would convict an older person, children make no connection like that. Young children are innocent before God. — *Peter Baer*

❖ Let all parents who truly love their children take heed that they rightly and clearly instruct them from the Word of God as soon as they may be able to receive and understand it; that they may guide them in the way of truth and zealously watch over all their life; that they may from their youth learn to know the Lord their God, to fear, love, honor, thank, and serve Him.
— *Menno Simons*

❖ If we tell the great stories of the Bible and tell them reverently and earnestly, we may trust them for the most part to make their own impression. We shall find them again in the hearts and minds of our children. — *The Book of Life*

10 Ways to Look at a Reading Mother

1. *As a Garden Planter.* The God of springtime stirs her. The seeds of reading must enter the soft, warming soil of her children's hearts—early—and at just the right depth. Then spring bows to summer's heat. Her garden needs her touch. And so she cultivates often, combining the tools of her voice, her lap, and a book. Her children learn to listen, they are trained to trust, and the mother thinks of the harvest to come.

2. *As a Gentle Shepherdess.* With her lambs around her, she creates a tiny green pasture for their regular story time. They are drawn to her warm attention, her familiar tones, the pretty pictures...and the love between the lines. It is her time to move beyond the details of their care into the realm of relationship—that she may truly *know* each one of her flock. Thus, each little question and comment is welcomed and guided.

3. *As a Wool Spinner.* She deftly twists short strands to form long lengths of yarn. Strands of spontaneous storytelling; of her memories of God's care for her and for others. Strands of a favorite book; read and reread and re-reread to please its little owner. Strands of newsy letters that knit her home with other faithful homes. And so she draws her children in, twining them together with qualities that will live on and on.

4. *As a Gatekeeper.* She guards the entryway, with black marker and scissors on hand. Her husband entrusts her as a sentry over the constant passage of script into their home. From the cereal box to the encyclopedia, she censors or bars all unworthy material. Clean books, realistic books, books deep with character and high with lofty thoughts, books that take no pleasure in wrongdoing—these gain entrance.

5. *As a Trailblazer.* She wants to take her children to never-been-there places. She wants the joy of telling them never-heard-before things. Not in a spirit of high adventure, but in a pursuit of the hows, the whens, the wheres, the whos, and the whys in the spheres that books explore. Someone will feed her children's natural inquisitiveness. And so *she* deliberately opens the way by reading stories of God's world and works, marking a trail for them to follow.

6. *As a Gift Giver.* She would rather *"wear the old coat and buy the new book."* She would rather spend more on a new book that shows her children the beautiful and true, than spend less on a used but questionable book. She would rather write her child's name and a sentiment inside the front cover of a book than buy an expensive greeting card that is soon laid away. And so she gives books that will become tattered with use, yet live beyond her short days.

7. As *a Skilled Painter.* The brushes of her enthusiasm paint scenes and characters in living color before her children. She reads fast or slow according to the sense of the story. She softens her voice at tender places and strengthens it at forceful ones. She pauses at a moment of suspense. Sometimes a gentle tear cannot be withheld. She shuns the monotony of a typewriter voice; a black-and-white picture. And so her interest begets their interest, and meaningful images are painted on the canvas of her children's hearts.

8. *As a Practiced Dietician.* Books lay invitingly on the end table, the stair steps, the nightstand awaiting the return of her book-hungry children. Her part? To see that they keep a balanced diet. She serves them books with life-sized lessons in an easy-to-swallow form. She monitors highly seasoned and light reading so they do not lose their taste for the wholesome. And she stretches their appetites by pointing out the hidden treasures behind the dull cover.

9. *As a Torchbearer.* When she was a youth, she clasped and held the torch of truth. Now her children are the same age she was. Now she watches for the same fire to spread to their hearts. At times she kindles this quiet transfer by applying a small flame of Scripture to a matter. Other times she encourages her youth to read doctrinal writings, knowing that the torchbearers of tomorrow are reading the church's literature of today.

10. As a Wise Investor. She asks: "Whose time is more precious? Mine or my children's?" She answers: "I will forgo my book for theirs. I will make one more deposit in their treasury. I cannot wait till the slower pace of grandmothering to read to the little ones. The time is now!" The turning pages may become a blur in her children's memories, but her imprint on their lives will remain.

V. H. K.

A Reader's Prayer
for Mothers

Lord, let me never minimize
the meaning or the moral of any truth I read.
Show me my sway upon my children
that I shun what has no meaning or moral.
Help me to choose with equal care my words and my books,
because they both shape my life.
Show me that as in a river, so in reading:
the depths hold more of strength and beauty than the shallows.
Teach me to value variety, but not be blind to vanity.
Keep me from caring more for much reading than for careful reading
and from caring more for books than the Book.
Give me an ideal that loves the pure and true,
and counts these treasures of paper and ink invaluable for my home.
Repay me with wisdom to teach my children,
and then help me to say from a disciplined heart,
a grateful Amen.

H. H. Barstow, 1905, Adapted

Reading, however slow and plodding, has God's blessing on it,
and none of us is too good for it. Studying books and periodicals
and Sunday school lessons, is one way to begin a humble learning process that the Lord finally rewards with direct inspiration
through His Holy Spirit.

We should be teaching our children what a privilege and pleasure it is to dig buried treasure out of books for themselves. And,
finally, we should be leaving a good example. Let us be careful,
not only what we read but also what our children see us reading.
Where our reading interests lie today, our children's interests will
lie tomorrow.

David L. Martin

CHAPTER 15

The Mother's Devotional Life

She who sits and waits
on the Lord's guidance
shall soon rise up
and soar above her duties
with wings of eagles.
She can run with her children
and not be weary.
She can keep up with
her daily homemaking tasks
and not faint,
for God gives her new strength.

Ella Mae Miller

A Mother's Thoughts

I'd like to be a Mary—just
　　To sit at Jesus' feet
And spend my time, enjoying there,
　　Communion blest and sweet.

Oh, how refreshed my soul would be
　　To have a quiet hour;
To read God's Word and meditate,
　　Receiving His great power.

But "Martha" duties claim my time;
　　The children call for me.
The baby cries; "It's time to eat"
　　My quiet time now flees.

How can I fill another's need,
　　When my own need's not met?
How can I find my strength in God
　　To escape the tempter's net?

God's servant spoke to me these words,
　　"To spend more time with Him
Think of His Word while at your work,
　　Not of the shadows dim.

"Write down a gem of truth you learned
　　In your devotion time.
Review it often through the day—
　　From it new strength you'll find.

"Pray often as you do your work;
　　Ask God for grace today
To help your husband, teach each child
　　About the heavenly way."

Although life's full of "Martha things,"
　　In spirit I can be
A Mary, and commune with God,
　　His strength sustaining me.

Marla Horst

Finding Time With God

Someone once said, "Motherhood is a time of leanness of soul." If a mother were to measure solely the undisturbed quiet time she has to spend with God, this statement would sometimes be all too true.

It is good to be scheduled, but a mother must be willing to shift with the changing stages of her children. Early morning can be a prime time to meet with God if she has not been up several times during the night. Shifting to the children's afternoon nap time can also work for a time. Then there are days when she must seek for several rich nuggets rather than one long period of time with God.

Some days when it has been totally impossible to have her quiet time, a mother should not allow herself to feel guilty before God. Rather, she should try again tomorrow and never give up striving to reach her goal. Remember, God has placed each mother where she is. He knows her desires and what she needs to face each day. Finding time with God will be a lifelong pursuit for the busy mother.

Ruby L. Mack, Adapted

The Quiet Hour

Long ago, in the early 1800s a mother lived with her family in a crowded, cramped, little house. She worked so hard from morning until night that she sometimes found herself growing irritable, though she longed to be always serene.

The little house was full of children who could be active and annoying, as the dearest of children are once in a while. There were in-laws too, who sometimes failed to understand and who criticized the tired mother just at the hardest times, as people are apt to do in a crowded little house.

There was very seldom a sixty-minute quiet hour for this mother, and never a spot in all the house where she could be alone, free from interruption. But there were a few moments at twilight when she might slip away by herself without sending the domestic machinery clashing into discord.

Then she would steal away into the calming peace of God's blessed out-of-doors. She hadn't time or strength for a long walk; she had no beautiful garden in which to stroll and commune with God; but just a little beyond lay the spacious grounds of a rich neighbor. There she knelt in one corner among the shrubbery while she poured out her heart in confusion, entreaty, praise, and fellowship to Him whose ear is attentive to the least whisper of a loving tongue.

In a little while, she would return, refreshed and stronger, to the hum-drum round of toil in the crowded little house. And out of those precious moments of high communion, Phoebe H. Brown's familiar hymn was born:

> *I love to steal awhile away*
> *From ev'ry cumb'ring care,*
> *And spend the hours of setting day*
> *In humble, grateful prayer.*

Perhaps no beautiful hymn will come out of our quiet hour, since He does not call all of us to the composer's seats of this earth. Yet we cannot doubt that somehow the influence of our time spent with God will make sweeter the world for others as well as for ourselves. There is a fragrance of life that reaches many whose ears are deaf to the harmonies of music. And that fragrance shall dwell long in the memories of all children whose mothers forget not the quiet hour.

Mary S. Stover

Mother's Morning Prayer Time

Unsounding morning
Is filled with God.
And silent with footpaths
Where comfort has trod.

I seek His soft strength
Before waking the boys;
It unlocks my heart
To let in the day's noise.

Romayne Allen

"Seven [seven!] times a day do I praise thee....
Great peace have they which love thy law:
and nothing [nothing!] shall offend them."

Psalm 119:164, 165

On the Wing

Life, dear Lord, makes so many demands
On a woman's heart, of a woman's hands!
Oh, I seldom have time for slipping away
From my duties in some quiet corner to pray;
But like meadowlarks that soaring, sing,
I must talk to Thee, Lord, as it were on the wing.
Do acknowledgments hold less of gratitude
If sent in the midst of preparing food?
Are petitions less fervent if one only asks,
As one works, for strength for finishing tasks?

Author Unknown

What Is a Mother's Prayer?

A mother's prayer is sometimes clothed in beautiful words stitched together with the needle of love in the quiet chambers of the heart. Sometimes it is arrayed only in the halting, deep soil of human emotion. It is a frequent watcher of the night. It has often seen the dawn break over the hills and flood the valleys with light as it waited and cried at the gates of God.

A mother's prayer has no language it cannot speak, no barrier of race or color that causes its feet to stumble. It is born before the child is born. It has often stood at the altars of the Lord blending its joyful and tearful voice with the prayers of the father. It has sat dumb and mute in delight over a tiny bit of humanity, so overwhelmed it has been able only to sound the notes of gratitude: *"Oh, thank the Lord!"*

A mother's prayer has watched over the cradle of her tender, feverish little one. It has sighed with relief over the sweat on the little one's curls because the crisis was past. It has sustained her when she must lay her little lamb in the arms of God. It sets its hope in the promises of God and waits until it feels the everlasting arms underneath.

A mother's prayer has walked and knelt in almost every room of the house. It has followed each of her growing children and circled their ever-widening friendships and fields of interest. It has filled pantries with provisions when the earthly provider was gone. It has sung songs in the night when there seemed nothing to sing about but the faithfulness of God.

A mother's prayer has lingered on the lips of the dying mother, but has not died with her. It is deathless, because it lives before God, who continues the work it has set in motion.

Praying mothers, take courage! Your pleas have entered into the ears of the Lord. They have ascended to the heavenly throne. Your earthly eyes may never see the fullness of their harvest hour, but your prayers will live on!

Author Unknown

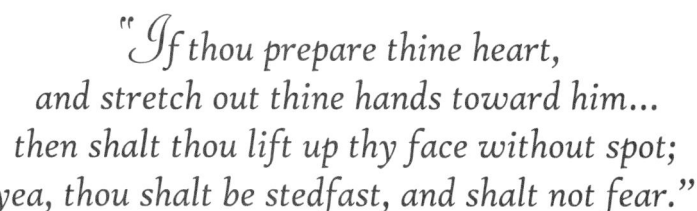

*"If thou prepare thine heart,
and stretch out thine hands toward him...
then shalt thou lift up thy face without spot;
yea, thou shalt be stedfast, and shalt not fear."*

Job 11:13, 15

"He will be very gracious unto thee at the voice of thy cry." Isaiah 30:19

That has comforted me often, more than any promise of answer; it includes answers, and a great deal more besides. It tells us what He is toward us, and that is more than what He will do. And the "cry" is not long, connected, thoughtful prayers. A cry is just an unworded dart upward of the heart, and at that "voice," He will be very gracious. What a smile there is in these words!

Frances Ridley Havergal, 19th Century

*L*earn to entwine with your prayers the small cares, the trifling sorrows, the little wants of daily life. Whatever affects you—be it a changed look, an altered tone, an unkind word, a wrong, a wound, a demand you cannot meet, a change you cannot notice, a sorrow you cannot disclose—turn it into prayer and send it up to God.

Disclosures you may not make to man, you can make to the Lord. Man may be too little for your great matters; God is not too great for your small ones. Only give yourself to prayer, whatever be the occasion that calls for it.

Octavius Winslow, 19th Century

*G*od is at the helm of the ship, and is working in the hearts of your children in answer to your prayers. Go on in confidence and trust Him because He hears your prayer and is working in many, many places you cannot see.

A Mother

The Daily Interview

Today a small Voice whispered:

> *"For My sake, keep tryst with Me!*
> *There are so many minutes in a day,*
> *So spare Me ten.*
> *It shall be proven then,*
> *Ten minutes set apart can well repay.*
> *You shall accomplish more*
> *If you will shut your door*
> *For ten short minutes just to watch and pray."*

"Lord, if I do
Set ten apart for You—
The baker's sure to come, or John will call
To say some visitor is in the hall;
Or I shall smell the porridge burning, yes,
And run to stop it in my hastiness.
There's not ten minutes, Lord, in all the day
I can be sure of peace in which to watch and pray."

But all that night,
With calm insistent might,
That gentle Voice spake softly, lovingly—

> *"Keep tryst with Me!*
> *You have devised a dozen different ways*
> *Of getting easy meals on washing days;*
> *You spend much time on hopeless socks,*
> *On scrubbing stains from tiny frocks;*
> *'Twas you who found*
> *A way to make the sugar lumps go 'round;*
> *You, who invented ways and means of making*
> *Nice spicy buns for tea, hot from the baking,*
> *When margarine was short...and cannot you*
> *Who made the time to join the butter queue*
> *Make time again for Me?*
> *Yes, will you not, with all your daily striving,*
> *Use woman's wit in scheming and contriving*
> *To keep that tryst with Me?"*

Like ice long bound
On powdered frosty ground,
My erring will all suddenly gave way.
The kind soft wind of His sweet pleading blew,
And swiftly, silently, before I knew,
The warm love loosed and ran.
Life-giving floods began,
And so, most lovingly I answered Him:

"Lord, yes, I will, and can.
I will keep tryst with Thee,
Lord, come what may!"

Envoy

It is a wondrous and surprising thing
How that ten minutes takes the piercing sting
From vexing circumstance and poisonous dart
Hurled by the enemy straight at my heart.
So, to the woman tempest-tossed and tried
By household cares, and hosts of things beside,
With all my strength God bids me say to you;
"Dear soul, do try The Daily Interview!"

Fay Inchfawn

If we are going to keep a strong inner life, it means
that we will set apart, almost stubbornly, regular periods
of time for private devotions.

— It may mean getting up earlier or staying up later
than usual.

— It may mean a change in our work schedule.

— But whatever it means, it will be worth more than it
costs.

Our days will be brighter, home life happier, and
family relationships sweeter, because our hearts are in
tune with God.

Ruth B. Stoltzfus

How She Found Time

"This book of the law...thou shalt meditate therein day and night, ...and then thou shalt have good success." Joshua 1:8

The promise sounded good to the busy young mother.

The first week she managed to find at least ten minutes each day to read God's Word and to pray.

The next week company came and the work piled up. *"The Lord will surely understand if I miss a day,"* she mused.

The following weeks, there were more excuses. *"There's so much canning to do. God surely expects me to provide nourishing food for my family."*

Early in the morning had been the best time to be alone with God. *"But,"* she argued, *"this is the best time of the day to get things done that I can't do while the baby is awake."*

A new idea transpired. She called it "meditating on the run." *"I'll keep my little Testament in my apron pocket where I can quickly get it and be memorizing Scripture while I'm peeling potatoes, rocking the baby, and such."* She even tacked Bible verses above the kitchen sink so she could meditate while washing dishes.

It worked for a while. But gradually the Testament stayed in the apron pocket more than in her hands. The birds outside the window caught her attention more than the Bible verses at her eye level.

Another frustration was getting her down; every morning for a week now the baby insisted on waking and crying at an early hour—just when she was going to get all that work done. The thought was sobering. *"Do you suppose God is allowing the baby's early risings because I was too selfish to give Him the best part of my day?"*

She came to grips with herself. There was nothing very prosperous in the way she had cheated God out of His share of her day. He faithfully gave her twenty-four hours to use every day, but she couldn't even give Him ten minutes of it!

Spending time alone with Him during the best part of the day was really not for His sake. If she did it willingly, *she* would definitely receive the benefits!

"For then thou shalt make thy way prosperous." Joshua 1:8

Lavina Gingerich

Your Prayer Closet

One of the best places to learn to pray is in our own prayer closet. It will not be all mountaintop experiences, but we need to continue faithfully. If we meet difficulty, we should not give up in despair. Difficulty is normal. Satan recognizes the power of our devotional life, and he will attempt to make it as difficult for us as he can. It will become one of his main targets of attack.

We should not use our prayer closets as an escape from work, but rather as a place where victories are won. A good plan is to turn every care into prayer.

We must always pray with submission. Hannah wanted a son and prayed for a son. But God wanted a leader. As God delayed His answer, Hannah finally came to the place of submission where her prayer included a vow. It was no longer Samuel for Hannah, but Samuel for Israel. Her prayer was finally answered when her will conformed to God's noble plan.

Harry M. Erb

God is waiting to answer.
Why are you waiting to ask?

Harold M. Weaver

Beware of the barrenness of busyness. You can survive on snatches of prayer and Bible reading throughout your hectic, demanding days for a time. But if you stay there, you will not really grow. You will never go deeper with God until you are willing to pay a greater price.

A Mother

A Mother's Quiet Time with God

What to Do When Special Quiet Time Is Elusive

1. When going about your work, singing can cheer your spirit and give you encouragement.

2. Breathing a word of prayer when washing the dishes or hanging the wash is time with God.

3. Keeping your eyes open for lessons to teach the little ones in everyday happenings helps to draw their minds—and yours—to God.

4. When you send a card or letter, taking time to add a Bible verse gives encouragement and food for meditation.

5. At the preschooler's nap time, reading a story that teaches a lesson can also be blessing to you. The story of the lad who shared his lunch with Jesus teaches children about sharing. It also is a precious thought that God blessed and used what the boy's mother took time to do for her son. The simple deed of packing a lunch for him was done for the Lord! It inspires you to meet the needs of your children for the Lord's sake.

6. At times your husband might help by taking the toddlers along for a while, giving you an opportunity for devotions or to make use of your prayer list.

7. When you are awake at night with an infant or sick child, use that time for prayer and meditation. *"When I remember thee upon my bed, and meditate on thee in the night watches."* Psalm 63:6

 Iva Lynn Kreider, Adapted

The child's first idea of prayer comes to him when an infant, by the mother kneeling beside the crib in silent prayer. Her bowed head and kneeling body tell of submission to and reverence for a power greater than herself. Her tone of voice when she speaks of sacred things is far more effectual with the little listener than the words she says.

Frederich Froebel

CHAPTER 16

A Mother's Link in Passing on the Faith

Mothers, we should

so live and labor

in our time

that what came to us as seeds,

may go to our children as blossoms,

and what came to us as blossoms,

may go to them as fruit.

Author Unknown

Faith of Our Fathers

What guided our fathers across the sea?
What stirred their hearts so forcefully?
    Why risk the perils that hence may come
    By leaving their homeland to sail the unknown?

'Twas a faith, strong faith, that beat in their breast.
So they sought God's will till they found rest.
    With faith that God was leading the way,
    They embarked for a land where freedom lay.

How stark were the partings, one may ne'er again see.
But they had a faith in eternity.
    Press onward they must — there were children to lead
    To a land where their God they could fervently heed.

Their trials and toils did not melt away
When they climbed the new shore that wonderful day.
    There was more to be faced. Would their faith in God stand?
    Could they stay nonresistant, calmly meet hostile band?

The faith's been passed on. It's come down to me.
Is this faith living still? Is it living in me?
    Can my children see that God is my stay
    When the billows would sweep o'er my stony pathway?

Oh, my heart's desire would ever be
That this living faith would not cease with me.
    Lord, help me to live in obedience to Thee,
    Be a link of the faithful through eternity.

Sherene Weaver

Written with a deep burden from seeing this precious faith being lost by
some and with fear that it could happen to me and my family.

The Need of the Hour

The church needs mothers, strong of soul, yet lowly
    With that rare meekness, born of gentleness;
Mothers whose lives are pure and clean and holy,
    Those mothers whom all little children bless;
Brave, earnest mothers, helpful to each other,
    With finest scorn for all things low and mean;
Mothers who hold the names of Wife and Mother
    Far nobler than the title of a queen.

Oh! These are they who mold the men of story,
    These mothers, oftime shorn of grace and youth,
Who, worn and weary, ask no greater glory
    Than making some young soul the home of truth;
Who sow in hearts all fallow for the sowing
    The seeds of virtue and of scorn for sin,
And, patient, watch the beauteous harvest growing
    And weed out tares which crafty hands cast in.

Mothers who do not hold the gift of beauty
    As some rare treasure to be bought and sold,
But guard it as a precious aid to duty —
    The outer framing of the inner gold.
Women who low above their cradles bending,
    Let flattery's voice go by, and give no heed,
While their pure prayers like incense are ascending;
    These are our church's strength, our church's need.

Ella Wheeler Wilcox, 19th Century, Adapted

Mother, Stand by My Cross

Follow the pressing crowd north out of Jerusalem. Before us march a group of Roman soldiers. In their midst, Jesus and two thieves tread heavily under their crosses. Worn out from His arrest and trial, Jesus stumbles and sinks to the ground. Throwing His cross on a passerby and pulling Him to His feet, the soldiers continue the relentless pace to Golgotha.

Holding our breath at the terrible scene, we watch the piercing nails, the yelling thieves, and the calloused soldiers. Yet our Lord is silent. As the crosses are lifted and dropped into the ground, the Jewish leaders break out in taunts, above the distressed cries of Jesus' followers.

Under the central cross, an older woman stands with her head bowed, weeping. *"Now there stood by the cross of Jesus his mother."* John 19:25

Forward to January 5, 1527. Step close by the edge of the Limmat River on Zurich's cold cobblestone street. Shivering in the January wind, look at the silent stone jail tower in the middle of the river. The constables' boat is nearing the tower. When it docks, an Anabaptist, Felix Manz, is brought out. He steps into the boat. The constables take him to a fishing hut in the middle of the river, just beyond the bridge near the Council Hall. A Reformed minister urges Felix to recant as the constables tie him up.

At the edge of the river, a motherly woman leans fearlessly into the chilly wind. Over the sound of the slapping waves, she shouts encouragement to her son to be faithful to the bitter end.

Unrelenting in his commitment, Felix is pushed into the dark water to drink his death.

Today. The church needs fathers and mothers who stand by their children's crosses. We need to stand like Mary, who encouraged her Son, but did not attempt to reduce His load. We need to lean forward in the face of adversity, as Felix's mother did, calling encouragement to our children as they face the challenge of living for Christ in a sinful world.

The crosses we saw were crosses of seriousness. Our children need to begin bearing crosses of their own when they are converted. Naturally, the lighter responsibilities of youth will produce a more carefree view of life than older Christians have. That is a gift of God for their stage of life.

But parents need to let that carefree view die a natural death as the teenager grows older. Marriage, voluntary service, an occupation, and church and financial responsibilities are serious matters.

Lead your children to and through the heart-searching questions of music, games, and personal friendships. Help them to understand the impact their influence and counsel has on the church. Lead them by example and teaching into full-hearted service and giving.

Discuss with them the hard questions of church divisions, wayward relatives, and fellowship boundaries. Help them to contribute to a sound atmosphere among their friends. Be able to open your Bible and show them the danger of casual trends.

If our children will carry on the faith, they will need to *have* the faith. They will need parents who lean into the wind, not with the wind. We will need to call fearlessly above the slapping waves. We must teach and live the great commitment of the Christian life.

By example, we need to rally all who will follow the Lord Jesus. By loving admonition and prayer, we need to revive the faint-hearted and falling ones. By spiritual discipline, we need to separate from the church those who persist in carelessness and adultery with the world.

Praise God, the cross of Jesus will be carried until time ceases! Brethren and sisters, let us stand by the cross of our children and fellow saints until our last breath.

Michael S. Martin

That which you are under, you transplant
into that which you are over...
It is the precept which you utter,
it is the throne before which you bend,
that you will see reproduced in your children.

G. Campbell Morgan, 19th Century

Tell Me, Faithful Mothers...

...there is a question I carry every day. A question I breathe when praying. A question that you, faithful mothers, found answers for long ago as you lived your story of faith. Please tell me—for my story is yet untold—how shall I bring up my children to love the way of truth?

Ruth could say, *"You cannot choose your own heritage, but you can choose your children's heritage. I chose to trust in the God of Israel and to turn from the shiny idolatrous things of Moab. You can choose to fix your heart on the pearls among God's people instead of anything "Moab" offers. You can choose to toil in a quiet corner; clear-eyed and resolved. And when you make your life a choice for God, you become a gentle force to draw your children to the truth."*

Hannah could say, *"When life seems to close its hands and withhold some good thing, pour out your plea before the Lord. When you give your children to God, plan to obey that vow, and then pour out your sacrifice. Pour out your love to your children by supplying the 'little coats' of their personal needs. Pour out a song of joy in your Rock as I did."*

Jochebed might say, *"Train your children with urgency, for swift currents and crocodiles may lie ahead. Seek out safe places for your children. Bend their wills. Hold their hearts. Verbalize your values. Work in close bond with your husband. Show your children faith, not fear. Sense the here-ness and the now-ness of life—and sow truth in their hearts!"*

And you, who have given yourself to mother God's own Son—tell me, Mary—how did you fill your place so faithfully?

Mary seems to say, *"You cannot understand all of God's purposes in your life of mothering, but you can be willing at His call. No stalling or sighs. No "why's." And when you do not understand what has come upon you, do not try to pry every perplexing thing apart, but quietly ponder. Then when you feel the hardness of the cross, the sharpness of the sword, believe that what you gain will be worth far more than it cost."*

Faithful mothers, your answers show me that I have not done what I could, until I do as you did. May my story echo yours.

V. H. K.

Our Little Ones for Thee

"Those that be planted in the house of the LORD
shall flourish in the courts of our God." Psalm 92:13

This is the promise that I claim for these
   Whom Thou hast given me, O Lord, to guide.
Strong, straight, and beautiful as living trees,
   Here in Thy house I'll set them side by side:
Down to the solid rock of Truth I'll go,
   Press close the soil of Faith with hands of Love,
Out of its depths—magnificent—shall grow
   These that shall flourish in Thy courts above.

Daily I'll water them with Thy good Word,
   And from their hearts I'll pull the weeds of sin.
This is the best that I can do, O Lord;
   But Thou wilt finish what Thou didst begin,
And I can leave them with a quiet peace:
   Man sows the seed—God giveth the increase.

Helen Frazee Bower

"Arise, cry out in the night:
in the beginning of the watches pour out
thine heart like water before the face of the Lord:
lift up thy hands toward him
for the life of thy young children."

Lamentations 2:19

Faithful women do not become
a link in the godly line haphazardly,
but by a continual choice to do right.

Quoted by Naaman R. Petre

Mothers Who Build the Church

Mother-eyes...twin beholders of things seen and unseen. They linger over her newborn, drinking in what will soon vanish into childhood. They gather golden bits of family living into memory's bank.

Mother-eyes...they glimpse the future as time wafts by and whispers, *"Today will soon be tomorrow."* And each searching mother asks, *"What do I want my children to be in that tomorrow? Will my values endure in their lives? Am I, with my husband, shaping them as living stones to build the church?"*

Mother-eyes. They long to see their children as solid blocks built into a strong church wall. That is their ideal! But mother-eyes need also to see that ideals alone are weak. Desire needs to be matched with diligence, and vision with vitality, for *build* is a doing, working verb.

Bringing ideals into reality day after brimful day makes any mother wince at her smallness, her stumblingness. But there is an Eye that sees clearer than her eyes, a strength greater than her own, a wisdom deeper than her desire...and she looks to the Lord to help her each day.

A mother who builds the church...

❖ *finds quiet quarters with God but can also commune with Him in the commotion of life. Her children do not miss seeing her Source of strength.*

❖ *wants to learn more of God's Word and His ongoing plan for the church. By little seasons, her Bible is paged, underlined, and worn into a sacred softness.*

❖ *is her husband's loyal arm, supporting his wishes for their home, reaching where he cannot reach.*

❖ *unpacks treasures of faith for her children to see. She shows them facets of truth to answer their little questions and guide their large concerns.*

❖ *covets an evenness of life.*

❖ *works out the doctrines of God in real life. She beautifies them, makes them pleasing, makes them inviting. She wants her life full of fruit, not falling leaves.*

❖ *is content to be one of many nameless mothers raising faithful followers, dutiful disciples, and behind-the-scenes builders. She teaches her children the joy of "oatmeal" work—ordinary, but fulfilling service.*

❖ *is a purposeful stranger and pilgrim. She is content within her circumstances.*

❖ *remembers that she is on a principled path, not a road of convenience. She is willing to sew a little more, pay a little more, search a little harder to supply her family with items that speak of simplicity and separation from the world.*

❖ *considers that what her children wear, displays her heart.*

❖ *loves the people she goes to church with. She is open and trusting with other sisters. She does not let misunderstandings detour her nor criticisms dismay her.*

❖ *has convictions that are not elastic.*

❖ *shows respect and appreciation for her children's schoolteachers. She sees them as fellow laborers in raising her children.*

❖ *points to the towers and bulwarks of the church and tells her children about builders of the past. Church history is not stuffy and stilted to her. It is alive with the story of faith and discipleship. She forges a link from it to her children.*

❖ *loves her children with a firm love that decidedly denies them what they do not need. There is no "yes" in her "no."*

❖ *asks when concerns are shared in church, "Is it I?"*

❖ *weaves her burden for the church and prayers for church leaders into the fabric of home life.*

❖ *raises little peacemakers. She knows that the peace of the congregation begins under her roof.*

❖ *identifies with Christ and the church in an unashamed way, even when others scoff at her stand.*

❖ *ponders the question, "Would my children die for the faith I embrace?"*

❖ *cultivates a relationship of trust and respect with her children that makes them unwilling to disappoint her.*

❖ *prepares her children daily for a land—an era of church life—that she glimpses, but cannot lead them through. Like Moses, she envisions them possessing what she possessed, building as she built.*

Mother-eyes...rewarded.

V. H. K.

Martyr's Mirror Mothers
Voices of Anabaptist Mothers from the Martyr Book

A mother writing a letter. That is not unusual; mothers often write letters. But look...this mother leans into her lines, intent, untrembling, her very heart incised on the precious paper with the stiff little straw dipped into wet-rust ink. A mother who so recently enjoyed her light, airy workroom now endures the dark, heavy odor of an ancient prison. And she, who had thought time went faster than she did, now feels as though it almost stands still. The chatter and busyness of her children is gone and the silence of unmoving stone surrounds her. *Why is this?*

She answers, *"This is no error, but the true way, and I adhere to God."* She had chosen the "true way" of discipleship, a way of unreserved obedience to the Scriptures, a way so intolerable to the authorities of her day, a way that carried a great cost: imprisonment, torture...death. But our mother understands the price. Her writing continues, furtive and single-minded in the fading light. It is her last opportunity to share her faith with her children.

❖ *Ghent, Flanders, 1560.* Soetgen van den Houte wrote her three young children these words of love and warning. Her husband had suffered and died for the faith, and she now awaited her hour of parting.

"My dear children, since it pleases the Lord to take me out of this world, I will leave you a memorial, not of silver or gold; for such jewels are perishable: but I should like to write a jewel into your heart, if it were possible, which is the word of truth.

"Suffer yourself to be instructed by those who fear the Lord. As long as you obey good admonition and instruction and fear the Lord, He will be your Father and will not leave you orphans. Keep this in your hearts, my dear lambs and guard your tongue, that it speak no evil. Always be diligent to do your work wherever you are. Be diligent in prayer and love the poor. Learn to be meek and lowly.

"Choose rather to suffer affliction with the children of God, so that you may be rewarded with them. For they are the ones to whom belong all the beautiful promises, but they must suffer much.

"O my dear lambs, see that you do not spend your youth in vanity or pride, or drinking, or gluttony, but in sobriety and humility in the fear of God. Written by...your mother in bonds, written in haste, (while trembling with cold), out of love for you all."

❖ *Rotterdam, Netherlands, 1539.* As she boarded a boat, Anneken Jans sang a hymn of faith among her fellow travelers. She was quickly arrested as an Anabaptist. Within a month of imprisonment, her death sentence came. Already a widow at age 28, she cared for her fifteen-month-old son, Isaiah, in prison. At the end, she carried him as far as she could to the place of her execution and then offered him to anyone willing to care for him. A father of six took her son with a small bag of money—and this letter.

"*My son, hear the instruction of your mother; open your ears to hear the words of my mouth. Behold, I go today the way of the prophets, apostles, and martyrs, and drink of the cup of which they all have drunk. See, my son, this way has no retreats; there are no round-about or crooked little paths. Behold, this is the way which is found by so few and walked by still far smaller number; for there are some who well perceive that this is the way to life; but it is too severe for them; it pains their flesh.*

"*My child, do not regard the great number, nor walk in their ways...where you hear of a poor, simple, cast-off little flock, which is despised and rejected by the world, join them; for where you hear of the cross, there is Christ; from there do not depart. Take the fear of the Lord to be your father, and wisdom shall be the mother of your understanding...O holy Father sanctify the son of Thy hand-maiden in Thy truth and keep him from the evil for Thy name's sake, O Lord.*"

❖ *Rotterdam, Netherlands, 1573.* A mother of four children, Maeyken Van Deventer, was imprisoned for her faith. "*She could not be turned*" from the truth and a death verdict soon followed. She wrote to her children these words about her impending execution and a personal prayer for them.

"*This I expect from day to day, that, when it pleases the Lord, I may offer up my life and body for His holy name's sake, and I trust...that the good Lord will not forget me any longer. When you hear this, sorrow not, as the world does, which has no hope; but thank the Most High, that you had a mother who was found worthy to shed her blood for the name of the Lord.*"

A PRAYER SAID BY MAEYKEN VAN DEVENTER

"*O Holy Father, sanctify the children of Thy handmaiden in Thy truth, and keep them from all evil, and from all unrighteousness, for Thy holy name's sake. O Almighty Father, I commend them unto You, since they are Thy creatures; care for them for they are Thy handiwork; so that they may walk in Thy paths. Amen.*"

V. H. K.

Her Question

An Israelite mother, Rebekah, asked it. She was concerned about her son's potential marriage to a daughter of the Canaanites. If that should happen, she asked, *"What good shall my life do me?" Genesis 27:46*

Consider her values. Rebekah was not measuring her life primarily by her living standards, her social reputation, or her own well-being. Rather, her goals lay in the future of her children and grandchildren. Should God's line of separation between Abraham's family and the Canaanites be broken down, one of the most important matters of her life would surely suffer ruin.

Where, when, and how do mothers today reveal their life values? By understanding just how direct their influence on the future is. By having a gripping conviction for separation from the world. By seeing beyond today's whims into tomorrow's appetites. By teaching their children from their earliest childhood to appreciate nonconformed attire. If simplicity—the absence of useless trimmings and features—is not practiced in our children's wardrobes, their interests will grow in directions that they will one day need to crucify. To be comfortable and cool is not the main purpose of wearing clothing. Rather, the function is to express modesty and dignity. As mothers choose, our practice becomes.

We need mothers who are not so captivated by items that are cheap or received as gifts that the principle of separation is sacrificed to economy. If the truth is going to reach the third generation, it will need to be worth its cost in the eyes of the first.

Mothers, are you, too, asking Rebekah's question? Life is too short to take a long time to discover your viewpoint. May the Lord bless each mother with a vision that calculates life in respect to the future.

Condensed from an article by Thomas D. Bender

CHAPTER 17

Mothers of Men

My Son

I hold within my arms today
A priceless bit of mortal clay;
　　Divinely fashioned and so fair,
　　The purest may a kinship share.

My soul with gratitude is filled;
My heart with mother love is thrilled;
　　My eyes brim o'er with newborn joy,
　　While gazing on my smallish boy.

Oh, precious one, through tears I see
A mighty task awaiting me.
　　My happy sky grows overcast;
　　Life's duties loom so grand, so vast.

To shield from wrong, to right incline,
This little life now linked to mine—
　　Divine the gift. Oh, may the mold
　　A heart of truth and honor hold!

Help me, kind Father, to know the way
From out the tangle of each day,
　　To guide him safe to manhood's prime,
　　And all the glory shall be Thine.

M. E. Piatt

The Little Brown Sock

I have just finished mending it—a hole in a little brown sock. I felt a mixture of emotions when I discovered it tonight as I pulled the sock off his chubby little foot. I could hardly believe that it had come so soon—the realization that the little fellow whom I had still considered a baby is no longer a baby but an active little boy, fast growing up.

There was ample reason for the hole in the sock. If it could talk, it would have an amazing tale to tell about all the things it did today, of places it went and things it heard. But a little brown sock has no way of communicating its ideas, so, begging your pardon, I would like to tell you what happened as I saw it.

The little brown sock's day began early—soon after the little boy woke with a merry call that seemed to mean, "Oh, ho! Sleepyheads!" In a moment the household was active, for there was no need to pretend that one could go on sleeping.

When the little boy was dressed, he pranced out to the kitchen while I tidied his room. Suddenly I was aware of an unhealthy silence. I have become increasingly suspicious of an unwonted quietness in a house that shelters a little boy. I investigated. I found him sitting happily on top of the kitchen table holding the empty ink bottle I had neglected to put away in one hand and with the other he gently patted the pool beside him. His hands, his clothes, and the tablecloth were as blue as the bluest ink I had ever seen.

When the last vestige of the pool on the table had been removed, we started all over in clean, dry clothes, and that is how the little brown sock was launched on its adventures.

A few moments later, unknown to me, the little boy disappeared into the bathroom. He pulled a chair to the sink and climbed up as though climbing chairs had been the diversion of his life. Then he plugged the drain and turned on the water. Perhaps his intentions were well directed, but he must have thought of something else in the meantime, for he hopped off the chair, forgetting the running water. When I discovered it, water had run over the sink to the floor, saturated the rug, and flowed under the bathtub and cupboard—and, of course, required a mop and bucket. We mopped the floor, this little boy and I; he, enjoying every moment of it.

Then there was breakfast time. Apparently, Little Boy was not hungry this morning, though that seemed incredible to me, knowing him. Hungry or no, it was soon obvious that he preferred his food in some form other than the one in which I gave it to him. When I returned after a brief absence, he was vigorously stirring his glass of milk. In it, he had carefully placed a soft-boiled egg, cereal, prunes, and a piece of toast which floated obligingly on top. I looked at it and then at him. "Can it be?" I thought. Somehow, there did not seem to be anything else to say.

At last, we started to clean the house, this little boy and I—at nine o'clock. I had planned to be half done by that time, for we were having guests tomorrow and there was much to be done. We swept, we dusted, we emptied wastepaper baskets, and while I worked, he tried on our shoes, peeped into dresser drawers, followed me about with the dustpan, occasionally putting it down at the most inopportune time and place.

Then dinnertime came. Quickly he collected his usual equipment: a pan, a lid, a spoon, a hot pad, and a chair on which to stand. He set to work to help me get dinner. Busily he stirred and measured and beat the imaginary contents of his pan. It was then that he spilled a quart of milk, and again the mop and the bucket made their untimely appearance.

I brushed my hand across my brow. Wasn't that a trace of headache that I felt there...? Is this the way to conduct a busy Saturday?

After dinner, as always, this little boy climbed up beside me to help with the dishwashing. Equipped with a pan of water, a tin cup, and a few spoons, he played contentedly until the task was finished.

At last nap time came. With many a gurgle and happy laugh, the little boy welcomed the time to rest. He went to sleep hugging his old rag doll closely to his heart, and while he slept, the brown sock also rested, lying contentedly on the floor.

So the day passed as all days do for little boys and busy mothers, and evening came, but I was not happy. At bath time, when I pulled off his brown sock, I saw this hole—the one I had just mended—and I began to think.

Yes, I had scolded and talked more loudly than I had meant to. I had been impatient. Of course, it was my fault about the ink bottle,

but I had talked as though anybody ought to know that ink bottles are not to be played with. I had expected him to know that living expenses are high and that it was extremely wasteful to spoil one's breakfast. Didn't he know that I had a headache and that I was tired and had too much to do? I expected him to understand that some other day I would take time to play peek-a-boo behind the davenport or to build blocks—but not today! There was no time to play ball or go for a walk—I was too busy.

But the hole in the little brown sock reminded me that time passes quickly; that little boys grow up too soon; that opportunities lost are lost forever! Then, as if to compensate, I held him close to my heart. We looked at the book that he likes best. We sat quietly and listened to the wind whisper outside the windows, and we looked at the stars that peeped shyly down on us. At last, as his little head began to droop on my shoulder and his arm stole around my neck—I felt forgiven.

Later when I crept into his room to lay a warm blanket on him, I stood for a moment in silence beside his bed. The subdued light from the hall shone softly upon him. On his face I saw an eloquent expression of peace and innocence and trust. I wondered why I had ever felt any annoyance or disappointment. Why, I was the most blessed person on earth! Suddenly all the weights and burdens were gone—and I knew without a doubt that no price was too great to pay—for this!

Clara Lehman Hershberger

While Singing

"Faith of our fathers! living still—"
   The noble words sound forth
   Through all God's house.
I hold you close, my son,
   Sleeping and dear.
      There is much I would say,
      But you are small
   And would not know,
   And the faith I would tell
      In glowing words
      Is oftener taught by deed.

Helen Alderfer

A Mother's Dedication

Dear Lord, I bring to Thee my son
Whose tender years have scarce begun;
    In this wee frame I know full well
    A living soul has come to dwell
Who needs me now at childhood's gate,
Ere he shall grow to man's estate;
    I covenant through hours apart
    To pray for him with fervent heart,
To teach Thy Word with winsome voice
By day and night until his choice
    Be but Thy blood for sins' deep stain,
    And my dear son is born again;
Then onward shall I pray the more
And teach Thy precepts o'er and o'er,
    That he may grow, each youthful hour
    By Thine indwelling, risen power.
Lord, some young boys with none to care
Will never hear a mother's prayer;
    Prepare my son with love aflame
    To reach them with Thy saving Name,
And make him, Lord, a polished tool,
A learner in Thy highest school.
    A mother's part seems, oh, so frail!
    But Thy strong arm can never fail.
To teach, to pray, to stand are mine;
The miracles must all be Thine.
    Expectantly, I yield to Thee
    The little boy Thou gavest me.

Louise B. Eavey

Bettering Your Boys

Into your gentle hands, God placed a pale blue bundle of boy life—raw material of the man kind. He calls for your best efforts to process and polish each of your sons from innocent babyhood into mature manhood. And you call them to do their best, not because they owe it to you...you owe it to them to raise them to be gentlemen. These questions check your progress...

1. Is the vocabulary of politeness—*"Thank you," "Please," "Excuse me"*—among your boys' early words and phrases?

2. Do your boys shake hands respectably? Not too hard or too limp? Not twisted or with exaggerated pumping?

3. Are they memorizing these hygiene facts? Water + washcloth × wiping = a fresh face and clean ears. Teeth + brush = a nice smile. Nose + hanky × discreet blowing = no sniffing.

4. Are you alerting your boys to their trails: tracks on the floor, drips of watery toothpaste over the sink, coats and boots slung inside the door?

5. Can they manage their food quietly and tidily at mealtimes? Do they take huge bites, chew with parted lips, or scatter crumbs?

6. How often do you need to tell them to use their instant refiner—a comb—on their tousled hair before meals and going away?

7. What about all those loose ends—flopping shoe laces, flapping shirttails, and belt ends? Are you showing them how to control them?

8. Tidy bedrooms do not come naturally for boys. But they can do it. Do you do it for them?

9. Can your boys (thirsty, hungry, impatient) wait in a line (long, slow, boring) without complaining or shoving?

10. Do your boys gentle down to hold a baby? Do you teach them to be kind to harmless animals? To not stomp on a caterpillar is as valuable to the boy as it is to the caterpillar.

11. Handwriting speaks. Does your son's say, *"I don't care what anyone thinks"* or *"Nothing is too small to do well"*?

12. Are your boys learning that little mouths should not make big noises in places with walls?

13. Do you teach them to not mimic others, to not snicker at unexpected noises, to not laugh uncontrollably?

14. And, lastly, do you point out bits of beauty, the finer things of life, that they miss in their boyish haste—the glorious sunset, the birdsong, the perfect spider web, or the roses at their prime? Someday they will see them for themselves—through a man's eyes.

V. H. K.

Shirts

White shirts, blue shirts,
Now-what-did-they-do shirts,
If only there were few shirts—
    I've pressed and pressed and pressed.
New shirts, torn shirts,
Fresh shirts, worn shirts,
Oh, let me never scorn shirts—
    Supposing there were less!
Piles of shirts, more shirts,
Done-fifty-times-before shirts,
But when I think of who wore shirts,
    I find that I am blessed.

Husky boys, lean boys,
Sometimes they're teasing, mean boys,
And rarely are they clean boys,
    All primly dressed for church.
Kitchen boys, chore boys,
Slamming-every-door boys,
Tracking-up-the-floor boys—
    I serve them till it hurts.
Cheerful boys, sigh boys,
Licking-up-the-pie boys,
And all of them are my boys
    In freshly ironed shirts!

Mary Beth

Dear Mother of Only Boys,

Last week, I brought a casserole and a cake to your door. It was my chance to welcome your sixth son, a perfect bundle in blue. As I held him, you must have read my thoughts, for you said, "We couldn't be happier if he was a girl. He's a precious gift."

Heartfelt words. But I also knew your family of boys might, on certain days, seem as incessant and restless as the bluest of seas. And there you are, alone on an island of femininity, surrounded by swirling building blocks and beloved toy tractors, rooster tails and cowlicks, grass stains and grease spots. I know there are times when your boys' rough edges and rambunctious ways startle you. Times when you need to deal with habits as hard to undo as a knot in wet shoelaces. And I think that from "son up to son down" your quiet times can't be many.

Then you must wonder just what it would be like to have at least one little girl's companionship.

Should I pity you? No, I know you wouldn't wish for even silent sympathy—because you have found, boy by boy, that this is God's perfect plan for your family. No little son will ever be second best to a daughter, since God's hand sends each child.

I want to encourage you, if I can...

When you are weary of making things happen—for little boys can be so oblivious to dirt, dishes, and schedules—remember you are setting patterns of order for their lives.

When you are weary of spending an hour to prepare a meal that vanishes in twenty minutes, remember the times your boys say, *"Make this again, Mama!"* You are not unrewarded, for their needs were met one more day.

When you are simply weary—your strength nearly gone—remember you are investing in lives that will outlast your own. Look ahead! You just cannot reap everything in the same season you sow.

Few people realize all your behind-the-scenes work when they see your stair-steps little men walk into church, but such things are known to God.

May He give you the serenity to welcome each man-to-be,
the courage to train them as only a mother can,
and the wisdom to know it is worth it all.

 *V. H. K.*

Your Growing Boys

Most boys go through a period when they have great need of patient love at home. They are awkward and clumsy, sometimes strangely willful and perverse; they are desperately conscious of themselves and very sensitive to the least word of censure. They are leaving childhood, but they have not yet reached the sober good sense of manhood.

Now is the mother's hour. Her boy needs her now more than when he lay in his cradle. Her fine insight and serene faith may hold him fast and prevent his drifting into dangerous courses. There is very much that only a mother can do for her son and that a son can receive only from his mother.

Above all things, mothers need faith. Genuine, hearty, loving trust in God, a life of meek, glad acquiescence in His will lived daily through years in the presence of her son, is an immense power. He never can get away from the sweet memory that Christ was his mother's friend.

Author Unknown, 1884

The Boy

Put me in touch with the heart of a boy,
Let me study his doubts and fears,
Let me show him the ways of life
And help him avoid its tears.

For the heart of a boy in buoyancy
Is one that is pure and free;
So put me in touch with the heart of a boy,
The heart of the man-to-be.

Author Unknown

 # Just a Mother?

Second Samuel, Chapter 20, tells the story of an unnamed woman who delivered a city through her courage and wisdom. She called herself a *"mother in Israel."* How this tired world needs such mothers!

Amid officers, clerks, salesmen, saleswomen, secretaries, managers, foremen, chairmen, workmen, and baby sitters, there is a scattering of folks who are "just mothers." They seem to thrive well on tiny toes, sticky saucers, prickly pins, muddy mops, sweet smiles, and every other unpoetic mixture that makes up a family.

History had them too.

—*Just a mother* who taught her little Moses to despise what most men love, and love what most men despise.

—*Just a mother* who kindled in her little Daniel the tender flame of excellence in spirit.

—*Just a mother* who hoped to see a big Timothy, and firmly trained her little one. He was a bishop in the making.

—*Just a mother* who trained her little David to become a man after God's own heart.

—*Just a mother* who lent her young Samuel to the Lord. Her toddler became a prophet.

—*Just a mother* who packed a little boy's lunch. That lunch was multiplied until it would have fed her boy for five years.

Yes, it was *just a mother* who baked bread and washed dirty shirts. She kissed little fingers and guided little feet. She washed the dishes and changed the diapers. She read Bible stories and taught little prayers. She sang babies to sleep and then prayed for them while they slept. She scrubbed the floors and made ten thousand meals.

A middle-aged man stood gazing out the window. But his thoughts were not on what his eyes were seeing. He was thinking about a group of boys out of which time had manufactured men. They were grown men. They were godly men. They were mannered men. They were grave men. They were leaders. And they were brothers. These were the words that fell from the lips of that middle-aged man, "They must have had a wonderful mother."

If God gave to church leaders the keys of the kingdom of heaven, then He didn't give much less to godly mothers. For mothers make men.

Robert L. Heatwole

Little Pictures of Good Mothers

The mother who knows three words stand between a restless preschool boy and a contented one: *Something To Do.* She takes out a defunct adding machine. In his little hand, she places a screwdriver, and now he tinkers happily.

The mother who sits in quiet awe at her son's baptism. She hears his sacred vows, sees his bowed head, the water, the welcome. Her *son* has become her *brother.* This is the *"no greater joy"* so many before her spoke of. The meaning, unsayable. The trust, unweighable. For there is no greater responsibility. See her head bow. She consecrates her life anew to guide her beloved son.

The mother who fears things creepy and crawly and her son who is a friend to things slimy and grimy. She helps him mount his collection of butterflies and beetles in a homemade cardboard display case for the kitchen wall.

The mother who helps her son wade through the heavier *abc's* of school life...*algebra.* Not that the equations excite her, or integers interest her, but she wants to offer her slight help to buoy her boy.

The mother who meets her son's girlfriend for the first time. She pushes nervousness aside and welcomes her to the family's friendship. She keeps a gracious distance and a prayerful closeness.

V. H. K.

Mother's Small Man

Two dark blue eyes, intent and wise,
This old world view with grave surprise;
   Learn from it, turn from it, all that you can!
   That is the challenge—mother's small man.

Two sensitive ears, with unknown fears,
Turn at each sound my darling hears;
   'Tis a harsh, hard world, but God has a plan,
   He'll keep from danger—mother's small man.

Each tiny pink fist, fit but to be kissed,
Waves hither and thither, wherever they list;
   Reach needs of the world with an open hand!
   Peacemaker always—mother's small man.

Two delicate feet, all dimpled and sweet,
To walk this rough earth seems strangely unmeet;
   Yet tread the pure path, it is but a span,
   Life's little crossing—mother's small man.

Author Unknown, 1896

The Praying Mother

Upstairs, in the farmhouse under the hill,
A mother kneels in the twilight still.
   She kneels and prays, as she used to pray,
   For her blue-eyed boy, who is far away.

Listen, O Father! And angels white,
Guide him and guard him, day and night!
   Keep him true to the old-time ways;
   Keep him pure while his mother prays.

James Buckham, 1907

Lord, Give Me Sons

Lord, give me sons like Daniel of old,
Who for the truth will be strong and bold.
   Sons who would dare to the Lord be true,
   Striving to please Him in all that they do.

Lord, give me sons who would dare to do right
When Father and Mother are nowhere in sight,
   Though down in Egypt they stand alone
   In the midst of a crowd to evil prone.

Lord, give me sons so yielded to Thee
That the world at a glance Thy likeness can see.
   O give sons with ambition so pure
   That naught from the path of right can allure.

Lord, of the sons Thou hast lent to me—
I gladly return them for service to Thee,
   Nor would I ever in sadness repine,
   If Thou should'st reclaim in death what is Thine.

Vera H. Miller

Felicitas with her seven sons,
Junarius, Felix, Philippus, Sylvanus,
Alexander, Vitalis, and Martialis,
put to death for the faith, at Rome, A. D. 164.

To her sons, she said: "Remain steadfast
in the faith, and the confession of Christ;
for Christ and His saints are waiting for
you...therefore fight valiantly for your souls,
and show that you are faithful in the love of
Christ wherewith He loves you, and you Him."

Read this account in Martyrs Mirror, pages 109 & 110.

"Dear Son"

When a mother wants to give her heartfelt counsel to her nearly-a-man son, when her treasury is so full she cannot keep the lid from cracking open, when the vast importance of the matter meets with the urgency of the hour, she tries to express herself: *"What advice shall I give thee...What, thou son of my prayers?...What, thou dearly beloved?"*

Then it flows. A mother warns her son of the stain of vanity, the glitterments of the world. She calls him to a pure walk. How could he know each danger? She marks any error in his life as if with earnest red ink. His circles move ever away from her, and someday he will share life with his own wife. So she imparts a lasting gift to him—a picture perfect of a true young woman of God. "She is rare, but she is real." the mother says. "Find her, my son!"

Read her words in Proverbs 31.

A Mother

A Prayer for a Son

As Thou didst walk the lanes of Galilee,
So, loving Savior, walk with him for me;
   For since the years have passed, and he is grown,
   I cannot follow; he must walk alone.

Be Thou my feet that I have had to stay,
For Thou canst comrade him in every way;
   Be Thou my voice when sinful things allure,
   Pleading with him to choose those that endure;
Be Thou my hand that would keep his in mine,
And all things else that mothers must resign.

When he was little, I could walk and guide;
But now, I pray that Thou be at his side.
   And, as Thy blessed mother guided Thee,
   So, loving Savior, guard my son for me.

Martha S. Clingan

CHAPTER 18

Mothers and Daughters

My Daughter

Into my hand, a treasure has been placed.

I, custodian of this priceless gift,
Must fashion into beauty, into grace, one
Who excels myself in things worthwhile.

I journeyed first that I might help her
Find the path I covet for her eager feet.

Each forward step
And each unfolding dream
From altar fires of life must be inspired.

For like the breeze that fans the dormant coals,
I, too, must kindle flames to glow with light,
That she may radiate the warmth and strength
Of virtues found in ideal womanhood,
Worthy to pass this glowing torch of life
Into another hand
Grown even stronger.

Ona Jane Meens

Dear Lord,
help me to lead my daughter
in Thy paths —
quietly, cheerfully;
To polish her character —
lovingly, patiently;
To be a living example before her —
meekly, openly;
To strengthen her
for the challenges of life —
serenely, courageously.

V. H. K.

Apprenticeship

When Daughter wants to help, I let her,

Though I can do it faster, better.

If I suppress my present groan,

Someday she'll do it fine alone.

Donna Evleth

"The Children Are Tender"

One day my daughter came to tell me she had swept the room as I had requested. When I went to investigate, I exclaimed, "Dear, this room isn't swept right at all!" I grabbed the broom and began vigorously sweeping as I quoted, *"Whatsoever thy hand findeth to do, do it with thy might!"*

My daughter replied in a hurt voice, "Mother, I did do the job with all my might, but I can't do it with all *your* might."

This painful memory has reminded me ever since to have more patience and regard for the not-yet-mature capabilities of our children.

"I will lead on softly,
according as...the children be able to endure."

Genesis 33:14

Author Unknown

*L*ord, give us daughters
who will be compassionate and kind,
who find contentment in the Lord,
and joy and peace of mind.
Lord, give us daughters,
strong, sincere,
who bloom through sun or wind;
and may their beauty ever be
the glow of God within.

M. W. S.

Braids
A Monosyllabic Meditation

My dear two-year-old: A tall stool is a small place for a lap-sized child to stay put, I know. Your hands want to fly. Your feet want to swing. You want to go. I clasp your head in my hands and tell you, "Now, look that way while I braid your hair." Your eyes and chin drift. I bring them back. "Hold still." As a comb and brush draw stray hair, I must train you. Pull all the parts of your will in, just as I give each swath of loose hair a neat home...We are done! You turn your head back and forth to feel the flip-flop of the wee ropes. We smile and I lift you from your seat. You will learn from my grip and my grace as we meet here each day.

My dear five-year-old: This morn you told me, "When you braid my hair, I hear a soft song. It says, '*Whisk, whisk, whisk.*'" Your ears catch the slight things that I, in my push and fret, slip over. I know I need to slow down. This is not a chore to sigh through. This is a sweet time to yield to. A time to give an ear more than a mouth, a heart as much as a hand. I need to hear of your loose tooth, your wish for a church purse, your doll's new name. I want you to feel that no thing is too small to tell me. This short space of now counts. Now is the time to braid the strands of love, trust, and joy through our lives while I can.

My dear eight-year-old: Your nose is in a book this time. Yes, you must read it for school. When did we talk of school last? I should not ask how it was, but what it was. What did you learn in math? Who did you jump rope with? Have the frog eggs hatched yet? Now I hit a snag in your hair. My care with the comb shows my care for you. Tug soft, tug firm. Is this how you will comb my grey hair some day? Once more, I work your braid in a sleek, smooth line. Can I, in the next eight years of your life, tuck in the good and make straight each muss? Make a smooth line as you grow from young child to young girl? I pray that God would guide my hand.

My dear twelve-year-old: I could let this be your task, for you are deft with your hair. But I would miss this time to be close to you. Some days we talk with ease and you show me the world as you see it. A world that swirls with all the hues of a new dawn. I find out that these things count now: to be neat, to be well thought of, to not miss the news of the hour. Some days come, too, when I need to hear what you *do not* say. I need to watch that I do not pry too long and that I do not blurt my words. I want my talk and my touch to be calm with care, for you take in my tone as if through your skin. And though you can't see how I comb your hair, you trust me. Trust me, too, when I guide your strands of thought where it is hard for you to "see."

As I back up to keep your long braid taut, I see that the space has grown since I first worked your hair. But oh, may there be no rift, no wedge 'twixt our hearts! Then when the last time slips past and the days of braids ends, I pray that you and I will be twined as one.

V. H. K.

Welcome! Enter In

Supper was over. Three girls chattered as the dishes clattered through the sink and into the cupboard. Mother sat in the next room...listening. The girl's imaginations were busy that evening and took them down numerous trails. They asked each other, *"If you could have anything at all, what three things would you wish for?"* Some wishes had a serious tone and some a not-so-serious tone.

Mother stepped to the door to listen more closely. She was quiet. Soon one of the girls turned and asked, *"Mother, what would you wish for if you had three wishes?"*

She was invited! It was her opportunity to enter their dreamland, to guide their ideas.

This is what Mother said: *"Oh, I could wish for this or wish for that, but girls, I try not to wish for anything that I could not put on my prayer list."*

These daughters shared freely. Some daughters quietly give hints. But talkative or shy, the sign over their open door is the same, "Enter here and enter now." Hear them gladly.

A Minister

Painting for Eternity

A mother sat at her sewing,
  But her brow was full of thought,
While the little girl perched beside her,
  Her own small stitches wrought.

A book of her careful choosing
  Lay open upon her knee
To the old master artists' story—
  "I Paint for Eternity."

And so I imagined her dreaming,
  As I watched her serious eye.
Then the 'broidery dropped from her fingers
  As she breathed a heart-felt sigh.

She drew her daughter nearer
  And studied her sunny face,
While sweeping the strands from her temples
  She kissed her with loving grace.

And she thought, "I, too, am an artist,
  My life-work here I see;
This sweet, dear face, my hand must trace,
  I must paint for eternity!

Hence each dark passion's shadow!
  And care's deeply graven lines!
Oh, may she reflect the beauty
  That from the pure heart shines.

But how shall I blend the colors?
  How mingle the light and shade?
Or arrange the strange surroundings
  The future has arrayed?

Alas, I am but a learner!
  So where shall I make me wise
Or obtain the rare, true colors —
  The Master's precious dyes?

I must haste to the fount of beauty,
  Must pleadingly kneel at His feet
And crave, 'mid His wiser scholars,
  The humblest pupil's seat.

Then hand and heart together
  Some grace shall add each day;
Thus, thus, shall her face grow lustrous
  With beauty that cannot decay.

My daughter! God guide my pencil
  And grant me the vision to see...
In the light of His love, without blemish or stain
  I shall paint for eternity!

Then the mother aroused from her daydream;
  But her soul the vision had caught.
It inspired her heart with courage
  That Love divine had taught.

Her fingers flew the faster
  As she sang a soft, low song;
It seemed a prayer for the child so fair,
  Her trust and her treasure lifelong.

A. C. M.

I Am My Daughter's Keeper

"Keep me!" I hear it when my house is dirt-stricken in its throughways and corners. I hear it when company is coming. And I hear it when my peaches are creeping past ripeness. The call comes softly or loudly, *"Keep me!"*

Among these voices, voices that will pass away with their season, I hear another voice, urgent and unceasing..."*Keep me! pure-hearted, open-faced, and true.*" It is my daughter. I am my daughters' keeper!

How do I keep her? Not by smothering her; not by drawing overprotective curtains around her. No, I would keep her as the bride keeps her dress from spot and wrinkle.

I would keep her modest. I would preserve her as a wrapped treasure. I would plant in her a carefulness that grows instinctive and lifelong. I would begin before her memories begin. I would train her to know that dresses stay down, that girls do not sprawl on the floor or sit carelessly. I would sew in pace with her growth. Tending a hem in time saves mine...my daughter's modesty and purity. And I would direct her big eye—the unfailing surveyor for her big "I"—the eye that catches the lacies, the puffs, the beads, buttons, and bangles. I would teach her to be unaware of herself, to be content with the plainness and sameness of her appearance, and to prize the beauty of heart and spirit.

I would keep her reserved. I would teach her shyness. Not self-conscious withdrawal. Not unsociable snobbery. But to control her eyes when a stranger (or a familiar) is too friendly and to control her ears when flattery is too close. I would teach her reserve that gives strength to step back, to turn away. I would give her words to say no in an uncomfortable situation.

I would keep her innocent. I would respect the curiosity of her growing mind. I would answer her questions as a sacred trust, so she knows her mother is the safest place to find answers about the way of life. I would pray to know the tissue-thin place between saying enough to satisfy her and not too much to stir her. I would protect her from the too-heavy burdens of the adult world: money matters, vices and violence, conflict and church issues. And should some thing pass though my shield, as a needle pierces a weakened thimble, I would know how to salve that wound.

I would keep her stable. I would be a quiet river of strength for her. Neither gusts of impatience nor tides of discouragement would I put in her way. I would keep her from extremes of emotion. Not gales of giggles (*"What is so funny?"* I ask. *"Everything!"* she says.). Nor stubborn sulkiness (*"What is wrong?"* I ask. *"Nothing!"* she says.). Neither sky high nor basement low. Just steady. I would not snatch her back from the hard path. I would urge her to step on even though her heart is faint. For her life will bring many a call to follow through. And when tears prick her eyes, I would help her to choose mellowness, not the easier path of self-pity.

I would keep her beautiful. I would allay her every-girl's-quest for acceptance. I would give her words to ring in her heart: *"I love you just as God has made you. And He has made everything beautiful. Even your freckles."* I would keep her from the vanity of too much mirror time and the pressure of peers to primp and to preen. I would point her to the virtue of *being* nice beyond *looking* nice, of giving herself rather than doting on herself. And to see true beauty's best feature: a meek and quiet spirit.

I would keep her trusting. Her dreams, her hopes, her longings... her most tender heartthrobs. I would gently catch a little thread as she unspools her thoughts to me. Then I would not let it lie on a tangled pile, but help to wind her thread around a solid core—a center of devotion. For now, that center is the simple pleasures and humble service of home life. Someday, perhaps, it will be the one man whom she will marry. I would be the keeper of her heart as she places her future in God's hands.

I am my daughter's keeper, but finally I cannot keep her. My gift, my treasure is on loan. May I give her back to God as pure as He gave her to me.

V. H. K.

Things to Teach My Daughter
Before She Leaves Home

❖ Wipe stickiness before it spreads. ❖ Serve rather than be served. ❖ Conduct yourself modestly, with poise and grace. ❖ Do not let milk heat on the stove unattended. ❖ People do not know you care until you do something for them. ❖ Fewer things equal more time. ❖ Find joy in the everyday. ❖ Make sure you have thread in your bobbin. ❖ Seldom pitch what can be patched. ❖ Keep your recipe book clean. ❖ No matter is too small to bring to God. ❖ A bargain is not always a blessing. ❖ Keeping your floors swept will make your house look tidier than it is. ❖ Your tone of voice says more than your words. ❖ Always welcome children into your life. ❖ Get ready for Sunday all through the week. ❖ When you step into friend's homes, do not take long to offer your help. ❖ Sometimes the best way to "make" money is to save it. ❖ Vanity will knock on your door. Do not answer. ❖ Be early to church. ❖ Use a spatula. ❖ Honor your father, encourage your brothers. ❖ Trust a timer rather than your memory. ❖ Try to realize your ideals, but be ready to idealize your reals. ❖ A good seamstress rips. ❖ The homey smell of fresh bread is one reward for your effort. ❖ Keep lists. ❖ Find the good and praise it. ❖ Make attractive meals with a simple set of staples. ❖ Keep a handwork project to redeem your time when resting, waiting, and traveling. ❖ Offer your guests a glass of water. ❖ Enjoy gardening inside and out. ❖ Pick up the pin or the penny out of the swept-up dirt pile. ❖ Be careful to not sacrifice the permanent on the altar of the temporary. ❖ Have an eye for what needs to be done next. ❖ Beware of piles; dirty dishes attract ants, paper clutter invites frustration. ❖ Learn strength of character by leaning on your Savior. ❖ If you do not know what to do—ask your mother.

V. H. K.

If You Are
the Mother of the Bride ...

❖ You feel as if you have plunged into a sea of details that makes you wonder when you will touch bottom.

❖ You recall how at the beginning of your daughter's courtship, she battled the butterflies and sleepless hours—thinking, thinking. And now at the end of it all, it is *you*.

❖ You may not panic, but you must keep the pressure on to reach your goals in a timely fashion.

❖ You feel so self-centered in your focus. You care about others, but cannot reach very far outside your little world of The Wedding.

❖ You struggle to let the recipes and roasters on their shelves while trying to concentrate on the message in church.

❖ You realize how important temperature management is as you thaw out, cook up, cool down, freeze through, thaw again, and heat up.

❖ You want to give her the best wedding gift that you possibly could—a perfect mother. But alas, it cannot be found.

❖ You cannot prevent the fullness of time. God wants them together. You must step back.

❖ You carry around a prayer in your heart that you would know how to mother her well during the last weeks she is in your care.

❖ You think, *After the dust settles, we'll be able to catch up with each other.* But no, she'll be g-o-n-e.

❖ You live by lists.

❖ You ask the Lord to steady your emotions.

❖ You get closer to the end of the funnel and suddenly *the sides are steeper.* You go faster, falling...trusting God's hands to bear you up until all at once you are through.

❖ You shed yet a few more happy, sad, sweet tears as you witness "what God hath joined." And you thank Him in your heart for the privilege to mother your daughter through this sacred space of time.

V. H. K.

The Three Mothers

Grandmother sits in her easy chair,
With a kindly smile and snow-white hair;
    She is gently rocking to and fro
    And thinking of days of long ago,
When children gathered around her knee,
Innocent, happy, and so carefree.
    When evening stories and prayers were said,
    She then snugly tucked each one in bed.
Her memory sweet will with us stay,
For she is the mother of yesterday.

To womanhood now her child has grown;
All girlish prattle and plays are flown.
    She now meets the sterner things in life
    And takes her place in this world of strife.
She has learned patience through many cares;
Often a smile on her face she wears;
    In her children's joys, she has a part,
    And always carries them on her heart;
She guides their little feet lest they stray,
For she is the mother of today.

Her dear little girl comes bounding in
With tearful eyes and quivering chin;
    Her mother-heart is so grieved and sad:
    The dog broke her doll—the best she had;
But as she grows up day after day,
Mother teaches her the better way.
    To trust in the Lord, whate'er betide,
    Take things as they come, though oft denied;
Be meek and true in the face of sorrow,
For she is the mother of tomorrow.

Author Unknown

CHAPTER 19

Mothers and Youth

I have

First, I held a bundle in the soft gift-wrap of innocence.

no greater joy

Then, with unskilled hands,
I pressed and polished my child to fashion his character.

than to hear

Now I behold my youth, path chosen and feet steady,
walking in a living faith.

that my children

How full my cup, as quietly I view my treasure!

walk in truth.

3 John 4

V. H. K.

To Mother Your Youth

Consider the special places your mothering fills...

1. *Be observant.* Caring mothers study their youth. The ever-so-small things, the in-between-the-lines things, the getting-to-be-a-pattern things are not missed by mothers who are unfailingly there. No one else is as close to help them as you are. Add your accents to their strengths, your counsel to their weaknesses. *Keep watch.*

2. *Be attuned.* Your youth *will* share with someone. Do not miss your moment. Your three-year-old may chatter almost incessantly—some fastens to you and some floats by. But when your youth want to talk, drop everything. *Be attentive.*

3. *Be respectful.* Those sacred confidences your youth share with you—do not leak them to your friends. Those weak spots they each have—do not complain about them to others. To do so is to add bricks to an unseen wall. *Be their trustworthy one.*

4. *Be sensitive.* Their castles may crumble, their roses may blight. The day of "rocking their hurts away" is past. Identify with them. Give them your heartfelt words, lest they cocoon themselves with their disappointments. The water of your encouragement can seep underground to heart-caverns you know not of. *Be sympathetic.*

5. *Be steady.* You want your youth to embrace your convictions as they mature. But if they question and challenge you, be one with your husband on drawing the line between safety and danger for your family. Never think you can win your youth by permitting more than their father does. Do not be intimidated, but remember that keeping boundaries brings the security of love. *Be firm.*

6. *Be calm.* "You did *what?*" (Can you hear yourself?) Reactionary mothers often curdle the situation, rather than clear the tension. Be perceptive and hold back the quickest words. If your youth fail in some way, it means they need you. Their problems are your opportunity. They often mean to do well, but need someone to quietly light the right way. *Be gentle.*

7. *Be stretchable.* The children used to swarm around you. Now they swirl away from you. So many projects, plans, and places! It can tax your mind as you calculate how many to serve from meal to meal. No longer is it your little world with its tidy schedule. But do what you have to do and do it cheerfully. Remember the cause. You are forging the link between their childhood and adulthood. *Be willing.*

8. *Be prayerful.* You used to be motheringly near when they faced a first time experience. Now there are places you cannot go with them — Bible school, courtship's path, the job away from home. But you can pray. *Ponder and pray.*

9. *Be undistracted.* Mothers are not immune to peer pressure themselves. The desire to see your youth excel others and to boost your own image through them can tug at you ever so subtly. Choose principle over popularity. *Be unswayed and predictable.*

10. *Be accepting.* If you are reluctantly resigned to see your daughter growing into singlehood, you will hinder her joy. Your wishes are more transparent than you think. For the same reason, do not compare your son's accomplishments with his brother's. God's plan for each life is like the snowflakes He created: precise, complete, unique. And often it arrives just as quietly. *Esteem His plan.*

11. *Be winning.* Bind them by many fine-spun threads to the warmth of your hearth. Be amiable and alive, not mechanical. Love and respect their father. Have a personal relationship with your heavenly Father that makes them want the same. As a mother, you may never attain the perfection of honeycomb, dripping with sweetness. But your youth know what is beautiful to you. You can attract them to love what you love. *Draw them to truth.*

12. *Be hopeful.* The full bloom takes time. Impatient mothers demand perfection and generate frustration. Suspicious mothers undermine their relationship with their maturing youth and may create that which they suspect. Patiently, lovingly continue to set your youth's feet on the path of peace and heaven. *Expect their faithfulness.*

K. & V. K.

We Cannot Choose

We cannot choose our children's path
　Or force them to the light,
But we can pray because we know
　To pray is always right.
We cannot choose but pray.

We cannot choose our children's King,
　But we can daily show
A glad submission to God's Word,
　The peace His subjects know.
We cannot choose but show.

We cannot choose our children's God;
　A million idols call,
But we can live with purpose clear—
　"We serve God, heart and soul."
We cannot choose but live.

We cannot choose our children's way,
　But we can show God's love;
That pleading, bleeding, leading love
　Shall draw their souls above.
We cannot choose but love.

And so we never cease to pray
　And in that prayer find rest,
And as we walk in holiness,
　Our labor shall be blest.
We cannot choose but pray.

Joanna F. Martin

Mothers and Their Young Men

Mary, the handmaiden of the Lord, accompanied her faithful husband on his yearly visits to the temple for the Passover. She undoubtedly rejoiced to take her oldest son along to worship when He was twelve. But this special joy turned into several agonizing days of sorrow and suspense when He proved missing. Surely her feminine constitution was at its emotional limits when finally they looked into the doctors' debate room and saw Jesus sitting there.

Did she let her emotions loose? No, in calculated motherly tones she raised a question that effectively communicated the rebuke that was on her mind. This type of rebuke, used by godly mothers of all time, seems to bring better results than the efforts of mothers who attempt to rebuke as a man.

Galen R. Weaver, Adapted

Some mothers try to aggressively dominate their older sons' behavior through whining and belittling them. This must never be done. A son will shy away from you if you lose your control. Never cut your son down and say he is a worthless person. He will then become that worthless and fruitless man and thus fulfill your words. Eliminate the scowl from your voice and face when dealing with your sons. Think of how *you* respond so much better to a kind smile and thoughtful words, rather than harsh and bitter tones. So do your sons.

Author Unknown

Christian mothers, young sons should value you and your husband's counsel higher than any other they could find. When they are tempted to go with the wrong crowd, they should see your loving face. When they are questioned concerning their position, they should mouth your gentle, thought-through answers as their own.

You, mother, must be the queen of their heart. The warmth of your hearth, surrounded by the love of God, must draw them back to your feet again and again.

John A. Baer

Zebedee to His Wife

*"Two brethren...with Zebedee their father, mending their nets;
and [Jesus] called them." Matthew 4:21*

Salome! Had you been with me in the boat,
   You would not chide and moan because our boys
Have gone with the Beloved from this our home.
   Let me, Salome, tell you how it came.
The night was still—the tide was running strong,
   Heavy our nets—the strain reached breaking point,
And while 'twas dark we docked, and as we worked
   I felt as though new strength and steady joy
Surged through my being, so I sang a psalm—
   As David sang—as one to greet the morn;
And then my heart was filled with quiet calm.

The boat was soon in order, and we turned
   To dry and mend our nets. Then Jesus came—
He called the boys, first John, then James, by name,
   And they arose and went to follow Him.

And when He climbed the hill, our sons went too—
   James was behind, and John was by His side;
And when they talked, John scarcely seemed our John—
   I felt that he had caught a marvelous light.
And all my being seemed to overflow;
   I knew that night had passed—the dawn had come,
And then I knew that we must let them go.

Author Unknown

To Mothers of Philips

"Jesus...findeth Philip, and saith unto him, Follow me." John 1:43

"Many mothers express interest in mission work, but how many are perfectly willing to have their own sons and daughters go?"

Mother-in-law of Jacob Burkhart, missionary to India, 1900

"What they do and how they live is much more important than where they live. If God wants any of my family at a certain place, that is where I want them too. I do not volunteer their service, and I do not want to hinder them either. May God's will be done."

Virgie V. Torkelson

"The call of the church has the potential to scatter our children, but if they are faithful to God, they can be closer to us than if they lived next door."

Edward R. Ker

"Seeing the Lord at work in the lives of our children and grand-children helps to fill the void of being separated from them."

Enos M. Shank

Beyond the margin of your care, but not beyond your love—
Still in the hollow of His hand who watches from above!

Alice H. Mortenson

A Paradox of Motherhood

We want to not be needed,

For they are grown and flown,

But we need to be wanted,

For they are still our own.

V. H. K.

To Let Go

To let go is not to diminish your care for your child.
It is to continue your stream of mother love,
full as ever, in new channels.

To let go is not to release your child as an autumn
leaf to tip and toss through the air. It is to guide
straight and point strong so he would *"forsake not
the law of [his] mother."*

To let go is not to shatter your golden stage of family life.
It is what you have been working for, the finished vision of
plants grown into godly young men and stones polished into
virtuous young women.

To let go is to fulfill the commitment you made to give your
little treasure back to God. It is to agree to God's greater right
to your child. It is to see the ripened fruit obtained by a tug in
the fullness of time.

To let go is not just to tolerate the changes this life-sized
adjustment brings to your mothering. It is to go beyond
the safe, tucked-in feeling of every child at home. It is
to encourage him to follow God's path for his life, secure
in your approval.

To let go of your child is to do without tangible signs
of his well-being that come through daily mother-care.
It is to move from the need to see, to the need to trust.

To let go is to let in. It is to welcome a new relationship as
adult to adult. It is to share more of life's spheres together.

To let go is to accept a second place in your child's life.
It is to realize that now he is absorbed in his new realm.
You can embrace it and grow, or resist it and struggle.

To let go is to ask yourself: "Did I pour enough good into his life?
Did I make the way clear enough? Will he see that though I stumbled, I was sincere and though I was faulty, I wanted to be faithful?"

To let go is to expect that your investment in your child's life will
not be in vain. For to let go—in God's will—truly, is to keep.

V. H. K.

It May Be

"*It may be that my sons have sinned,*" said Job.
    It may be that temptation's breeze has blown across my sons'
      paths.
    It may be that my daughters' hearts have tightened with
      stress or drained with discouragement.
    It may be that my grandchildren will stand with uncertain
      feet between white ways, gray ways, and black.
        It may be...the whispered possibilities worry me.

Job's children "*went and feasted in their houses.*"
    My children now eat at other tables, miles—even states—away.
    My children leave one by one, cleaving to their own with the
      strongest of tendrils.
    My children must decide, determine, discern life apart from me.
        My children...I glimpse their lives and wonder.

Job "*offered burnt offerings according to the number of them all.*"
    I offer trustful prayers in place of troubled cares.
    I offer kitchen sink prayers, clothesline prayers, ironing
      board prayers.
    I offer specific prayers for the constellation of interests and
      needs in each of their lives.
        I offer...this help that reaches where I cannot.

"*Thus did Job continually.*"
    Every day some blessing flows to my children through the
      channel of my prayers.
    Every day I find peace in this patient remembrance.
    Every day I pray for their growth and strength; a helpless
      mother drawing from the All-sufficient God.
        Every day...it shall be that my prayers surround their lives.

V. H. K.

The Mother and the Shepherd

The sheepfold was quiet, the flock was asleep,
But a mother watched long with a vigil to keep,
 For her lamb was not there; in the sunshiny noon
 It had frolicked away where the wild daisies bloom.

  The daisies were gay, and the springtime was fair,
  But the mother knew well of the crevices there.
   And she called to her lamb in a firm, gentle tone,
   But the lamb would not listen; it thought it was grown.

Ah, what could the mother but cry in distress,
As the lamb tumbled over the sheer mountain crest?
 And there wasn't a thing that the mother could do,
 But sorrow and bleat where the wild daisies grew.

  The sunset was red when the flock gathered home
  At the word of the Shepherd who called them to come.
   And the mother looked on as He counted the sheep,
   And she thought of her own on the precipice steep.

She watched as He bolted the door-latch, and then,
Ah, He took up His rod and His stout staff again,
 And His footsteps were firm, and his eyes were tear-bright,
 As He hastened away in the darkening night.

  The coyotes wailed wildly on yonder grim hill,
  And the lions stalked forward to ravage and kill,
   And she fancied the breeze brought her little one's cry—
   That was injured and helpless and ready to die.

The hours slipped by, and the stars turned above,
But the mother watched long in her vigil of love,
 Till the song of the shepherd was heard on the way,
 And her heart leaped with gladness to hear His lips say,

  "Rejoice, for the lamb that was lost has been found,
  And its wounds I have dressed and its legs I have bound."
   So the mother and young one made ready to sleep,
   Content in the fold, for the Shepherd would keep.

But the mother beheld as He watched by the door,
And she knew that her lamb was her own lamb no more.
  For the blood-drops dripped down from the strong hands
    pierced thro'—
  He had done for her own what she never could do.

J. F. M.

Beacon Thoughts
for Your Dark Night

❖ If your straying child knows you pray for him every day,
  your prayers have not been in vain. God alone knows the
  strength of a mother's prayer.

❖ Find peace in knowing God loves your child even more than
  you do.

❖ Your love for your child echoes God's *"great love wherewith
  he loved us, even when we were dead in sins."* Like an elastic band,
  the farther it stretches, the stronger the tension becomes. Your
  child surely knows that nobody cares for him, nobody yearns
  for him, more than his own parents do.

❖ Commit your child to God. How? Through sighs, groans,
  tears, and prayers, keep bringing him to God.

❖ When you take care of the possible, you can trust God for
  what seems impossible. Step back and let God do His work
  through your prayers.

❖ God is faithful. His Holy Spirit will keep working with your
  child where you cannot reach or see.

❖ The Lord can use your stability to work in your child's life.
  Stand firm and he will have something strong to come back to.

❖ Your pain is woven with many other pains; you feel like a
  failure, your heart is weak, you worry about your other children...but turn! There is work to do. Keep home happy for
  your loved-at-home ones.

❖ Never, never, never give up praying. Never let go of hope.

K. & V. K.

The Mother of the Prodigal Son

Where was the mother of the prodigal son
On that day so long ago?
What were her thoughts
And what were her fears
As she watched him turn to go?

How many times in the dark of night
Did the tears slide down her face?
Did she get out of bed
And fall on her knees,
Just to pray that her boy was safe?

How were the days when she did not know —
Was he alive? Was he warm? Was he well?
Who were his friends?
And where did he sleep?
Was there any way she could tell?

But, oh, on that day when she looked down the road
As she had looked since her son went away,
Did love unspeakable flood her soul?
Did she cry?
What did she say?

I think when the father had welcomed their son
And the boy had greeted his brother,
That the servants made a path
For him to enter the door
To the waiting heart of his mother.

Author Unknown

CHAPTER 20

Adoptive Mothers

To an Adopted Child

Dear, do not weep! By every act of mine
  I am your mother: by my sleepless nights
By every step in the long day's design
  That I have taken, by the sweet delights
    Of your blessed companionship; by your clear gaze
    By all my care in your beginning days.

Your warm, soft body to my heart oft pressed
  Warmed me and dried my disappointed tears.
You made a real home of our lonely nest.
  Now we look forward to the fruitful years
    With you beside us, bearing in your hands
    The love that every mother-heart demands.

I am your mother; though you may not be
  Flesh of my flesh, our love goes deeper still.
You are my heart's adopted, part of me.
  I am your mother by the power of will.
    Because we did not want to walk alone,
    From the whole world, we chose you for our own!

Anne Campbell

Doors Closed and Opened

To long for children is natural. When couples realize that children may never be born into their home, the longing becomes especially intense. Childlessness is hard to accept. But we know that childless homes are not inferior to child-filled homes. They are equally under God's blessing.

Some childless couples move forward to adopt. Others linger and struggle with nagging fears. *"What will others think of us? Are we capable of training children? What if we fail? Will we be able to bond with an adopted child as well as with a birth child?"* And almost all childless couples face envy as children are born into their friends' homes.

This turbulent time is entirely normal for those who keenly desire children in their home. But before arranging to adopt, each parent needs to bow before God and pray with utmost honesty, *"Thy will be done."* This difficult prayer requires *total surrender* to the fact that God may not choose to give children now—or ever. It calls for *absolute faith* that if He does give a child, He will have a solution for every challenge. Facing God openly on these matters builds a solid rock of confidence for the years ahead.

Remember that when God gives a child, He always has a greater investment in the child than we do. We can lay all our qualms and questions to rest with Him. Then our emotional energies are free to nurture our child. Though childlessness may seem at first like a closed door, God can open another door to the privilege of raising a homeless child for Him.

Even though we find confidence and strength in God's leading, it is a blessed support when our church family is also interested in our chosen children. Adoption is for life. In the work of child raising, all of our families, formed either by birth or by grafting, are moving together. Shoulder to shoulder, parents in the church go forward, helping each child on his personal journey to the point of decision for the Lord and beyond.

Daniel R. Lehman, Adapted

Dear Heavenly Father,

I turn to Thee at my day's end...at my strength's end.

Thou knowest how it was today...the challenges we faced...my lively-eyed children and tired-eyed me. I love each one dearly, but their doings and their undoings, their feelings and their failings concern me. I worry...Thy handmaid is small and their needs are great. How can I fill each one?

"Hast thou not known? hast thou not heard, that the everlasting God, the LORD, the Creator of the ends of the earth, fainteth not, neither is weary? there is no searching of his understanding."

Yes, I know and remember! After years of yearning, Thou hast filled our home with these precious children. And Thy strong arm is with us still! Please show me how to cherish our children without overlooking their problems. I want to love as Thou dost love.

"For whom the Lord loveth he correcteth; even as a father the son in whom he delighteth."

Oh, show me, show me how! They need so much... See how the short years of their lives are stacked so precariously, one on top of another? Such fragile security! Please grant me both gentle and firm hands to steady them.

"To give unto them beauty for ashes, the oil of joy for mourning, the garment of praise for the spirit of heaviness; that they might be called trees of righteousness, the planting of the LORD, that he might be glorified."

Please use us, my husband and me, to grow a few of Thy trees. I want to be the kind of mother my children will turn to when needy...the kind of mother that gives them courage to do right when they think of me. Oh, that these children—not born *to* us, but *for* us—and we for them—would be born into Thy family someday! I need Thy grace for every step. I thank Thee for Thy promise. It reaches me...

"Now unto him that is able to do exceeding abundantly above all that we ask or think, according to the power that worketh in us,...be glory."

In Jesus' Name, Amen.

(Isaiah 40:28; Proverbs 3:12; Isaiah 61:3; Ephesians 3:20, 21)

V. H. K.

Legacy of an Adopted Child

Once there were two women
  who never knew each other;
One you do not remember;
  the other you call mother.
One gave you a nationality;
  the other gave you a name;
One gave you the seed of talent;
  the other gave you an aim.

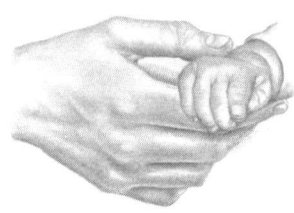

Two different lives shaped
  to make yours one.
One became your guiding star;
  the other became your sun.
One gave you emotions;
  the other calmed your fears.
One saw your first sweet smile;
  the other dried your tears.

The first gave you life
  and the second taught you how to live in it.
The first gave you a need for love,
  and the second was there to give it.
One gave you up;
  it was all she could do.
The other prayed for a child,
  and God led her straight to you.

And now you ask me through your tears
The age-old question through the years:

Heredity or Environment,
Which are you a product of?

Neither, my dear child, neither.
Just two different kinds of Love.

Author Unknown

Chosen Child

Child of that other mother, I could weep
in the sweet night watch as I bend above you,
that she could not (would not?) keep:
your baby blandishments she knows not of
nor the deep secrets of your trusting sleep
as you lie warmly circled in my love...
How can she live within such emptiness
while I have her lost mothering to bless?

Beth Duvall Russell

*When I approach a child,
he inspires in me two sentiments:
tenderness for what he is,
and respect for what he may become.*

Louis Pasteur

"*The Lord hath given me my petition*" and today I am a mother.
Where my child has come from, I really do not know.
How I deserve him, I will never understand.
And what lies in store for him, only the future will reveal;
but in him is life which will survive the ages.
And even now he is part of things eternal,
for Jesus said, "*Of such is the kingdom of heaven.*"

An Adoptive Mother

"Our Own"

"How many children do you have?"
"We have four," I replied.
She stared curiously, then asked,
"How many are your own?"
"We have four of our own,"
I quietly affirmed.
"Two by birth, two by adoption;
each one lent to us by God
for a season
to teach, to train, and love,
and then to release back to Him."

Ours by birth or by adoption,
rights and privileges all the same—
ours to provide and care for
while we live on earth.

Whether by birth or by adoption,
children may bring grief to parents.
But they need assurance
of belonging,
even at their worst.
Young hearts are, oh, so tender.
How they need to know
they belong!
Their parents have chosen them,
by birth or by adoption.
Thoughtless words so lightly spoken—
"How many are your own?"—
cause the little hearts to wonder,
"Do I belong?"
We are all adopted children,
chosen by God, for His very own.
It brings a great assurance,
to know that we belong!

Mary June Glick

Our Adopted Daughter

I gaze into her childish face,
  Brush back a tiny curl.
So sweet, so innocent she is—
  Our small adopted girl.

"Is she your own?" I have been asked.
  I firmly answer, "Yes."
Oh, how could it be otherwise?
  She's brought such happiness.

Although she was not born *to* us,
  God planned that we should meet;
I know that she was born *for* us
  To make our home complete.

When others do not understand,
  Lord, help us to forgive,
And as adopted sons of Thine,
  Oh, may we ever live.

Lord, give us grace to guide them right—
  These little ones You've giv'n—
That all of us, when life shall end,
  May dwell with Thee in heav'n.

Mary Hursh

God bless adoptive mothers, mothers who could not
have children of their own but whose tender spirits so crave
the joys of motherhood, that their restless hearts cannot be
satisfied without a child to nurture and train, mothers who
through their gentle ministrations and love teach a little
one to glory in the fact that he is a chosen child.

Author Unknown

To Baby, With Love

Many small infants are brought to my keeping,
　　Asking for nothing but motherly care;
Brown ones or white ones, there's really no difference;
　　Surely my heart has enough love to spare.
Little girls smile as they look through their lashes,
　　Fingers like rose petals brushing my cheek;
Little boys clap little hands for attention,
　　Eyes twinkle knowingly each time I speak.

Happiness now is an armful of babies;
　　Try not to think that a time comes to weep;
Try not to think, in that moment of parting,
　　Never again will I sing them to sleep.
Never again will I hush them at twilight,
　　Whispering softly a prayer for each one;
Lonely will be my tomorrow without them,
　　Empty my days when my babies are gone.

Somewhere another home waits for their presence,
　　Somewhere a new mother welcomes their charms.
They will forget that I tenderly loved them;
　　I feel the shape of them still in my arms.
Some baby feet have hard roads to travel —
　　What does life hold for them? No one can say.
Loved them and lost them, but this is my comfort,
　　Gladly I helped them one step of the way.

Martha F. Letkmen

Lullaby for a Foster Child

Sleep, my baby—
     Mine? Mine?
Sleep, my baby—
     Mine?
One mother looked at you only to name you;
Another mother will one day claim you—
     Mine?

Sleep, my babe—
     How long? How long?
Sleep, my babe—
     How long?
How long will your sweet smile answer mine?
How long will your dark eyes twinkle and shine
     Into mine?

Sleep, my babe,
     And grow—grow!
Sleep, my babe—
     And grow:
With love the climate to surround you—
With love a blanket warm around you—
     Grow!

Sleep, my baby—
     Mine. Mine.
Sleep, my baby—
     Mine.
As long as there's nobody else to claim you—
As long as there's nobody else—I name you
     Mine!

Miriam Sieber Lind

To Our Foster Children

See, my arms are open, child;
    Come, let me hold you tight,
Cuddle you close to my heart,
    And kiss your hurts aright.

No one loves you? I do, child!
    I long to mold your heart
Into God's dear plan for you
    And bid your fears depart.

You have had more than your share
    Of loneliness and grief.
May my love, as healing balm
    Bring to your heart relief.

See, my arms are open, child!
    The world's been so unkind
To you, but in our home, we pray,
    That naught but love you'll find!

Author Unknown

Foster Baby Bye

I did not cry when they came for him,
    my goodbye was suitably gay;
as if it were not a jagged-edged piece of my heart
    that was torn,
        that was torn,
            torn away.

Judy Ann Unruh

Billy!

He came into my life, a lad of fifteen months.
A baby really, and yet, he seemed so big to me,
filled such a large place in my life.
His mother, tired of little boys,
laid him upon my bed.
"He'll sleep. Don't wake him. I'll go now,"
she said, and she was gone.
I turned and viewed my charge,
and lo! The babe awoke.
He sat up straight and looked at me.
He scanned the room, his bed.
"Hello, Billy," I gently said.
Unsmiling still, he only looked and looked.
I talked to him; I gave him milk;
I stacked his blocks and knocked them down.
And then it happened!
He smiled a precious baby smile,
and slipped, so quietly, into my heart.

Months afterward, his mother came
and took my darling "son" away.

"O God, I wonder where he is tonight. I feel, again,
his tiny arms around my neck, his baby kiss upon my cheek,
his 'tanks' because I held him tight and gave him love.
Bless him tonight, O God, this child of Thine; this 'son' of mine.
He's nearly four, You know,
and little boys of four need patient mothers, God.
Father, please work a miracle again
and guard that little life,
and lead into Thy service,
the 'son' I had; the little boy I lost!"

Marie A. Yoder

The Foster Parents' Prayer

Oh, the little bits of sweetness that we hold for just awhile!
  Oh, the little souls we cherish though we call them not our own!
Oh, the little foster children, Lord, You place into our homes
  That with love's strong bond soon severed, we then find that they
    are gone.

Gone again into the world as though we never touched their lives.
  Gone again into the world of evil forces—God, You know!
You can see without our telling, how our hearts are bleeding sore
  Since we dared to give ourselves to this small child and love him so.

You have promised us reward for taking such into our care
  And we humbly thank You, Lord, for giving us this chance to share.
Yet our hearts cry out the louder—"Oh, but what about this child?
  Oh, will You, when he is older, all Your love to him declare?"

Will You, somehow, heavenly Father, just because we're praying yet,
  Give him knowledge of Your people, Your existence, and Your joy?
Will You follow him so gently all throughout his lifelong way,
  And protect him—temper evil to "our" precious little boy?

We do well to just remember that You love him more than we,
  That You notice even sparrows that may fall upon the ground;
And this precious little being that You planned to bring to earth
  Is still always in Your keeping even though we're not around.

Heal our hearts and make us conscious of Your working in our lives;
  Help us, too, be better fitted for what life may have in store.
Help us see the many blessings we received from this small child.

  We commend him to Your keeping—
  may You bless him ever more.

Paula Brubaker

CHAPTER 21

Special Mothers

Prayer for Mothers

Thy grace to every mother;
   And, oh, Thy special grace
To mothers of the children
   Whose feet do not keep pace

With the running of their playmates,
   Who do not hear or see;
Thy grace to all the mothers
   Whose wounded hearts must be

The source of reassurance,
   Encouragement, and power
To children who are different.
   Lord, give them, hour by hour,

Good cheer and faith and courage
   And steadfast self-control
To help their helpless children
   Grow strong in heart and soul.

Jane Merchant

Dear Daughter

Perhaps you'll never walk, my child.
  Your perfect feet
Will never caper, bound, or skip,
  Blithesome and fleet.
From crowds of prancing little folk,
  You sit apart...
But never mind, my dear; you've walked
Into my heart.

Perhaps you'll never write, my child.
  Your dimpled hands
Will never trace your name and date
  On sea-washed sands.
You'll never scrawl a cherished note
  Or saying wise...
But never mind, my dear; you wrote it
With your eyes.

Perhaps you'll never speak, my child.
  Your rosy tongue
Will never chant the verses that
  Through years have rung,
Or whisper, "Mother, I love you!"
  To soothe some smart...
But never mind, my dear; you spoke it
To my heart.

Perhaps you'll never sing, my child.
  Your happy voice
Will never lilt a cheery strain
  At moment's choice;
In all the mighty choirs of earth
  You'll have no part...
But never mind; my dear, you've put a song
Within my heart.

P. S. Perhaps you'll never walk; but child,
   With new-made feet
You'll walk upon the golden stretch
   Of heaven's street.
And far beyond the bonds of earth,
   With angels, ring
The holy songs unknown to man...
   There you will sing!

With love, Mother

Author Unknown

Prayer of a Mother

Help me, Lord, that others may not see
The bitter tears I cannot hide from Thee.
Help me, Lord, that I may learn to smile,
Although my heart is breaking all the while.
Let me learn to question not Thy will;
O Lord, please give me faith my fears to still!
The dreams I once held dear can never be.
But I can build new dreams with help from Thee.

Thou hast sent to me a little child
To guide, to love, to make my life worthwhile;
Give me wisdom, Lord, that I may know
The needs of this dear child who'll never grow.
Let him know he's loved and wanted here,
And let him feel Thy presence ever near.
And help me, Lord, that I may worthy be
Of this great trust that Thou hast shown to me.

Author Unknown

From Pain to Peace
Thoughts of a Mother of a Special Child

Misgivings

~Her eyes are open; looking around, but what is it about those eyes?

~Is she or isn't she? This in-between place is not a good place to be.

~It's probably just my idea. Don't all babies look a little different from each other?

The Hard News

~Solemn doctor words. It is true. There is no help. There is no cure.

~My dear little baby! Oh, Precious! Do we have enough love to cope with all that you are bringing us? A voice seems to answer, "No, mere human affection won't go very far. But the love of God is without limit."

~Does her name still fit? We didn't know we were naming a "forever child."

~A special baby. A special blessing? Dear God, please show us the blessing we cannot see though our tears!

It Just Hurts

~It's hard not to compare my friend's bright-eyed bouncy baby with my floppy, too contented baby who hardly responds to my voice.

~There is an ongoing funeral in my heart for the normal child that will never be, for the wedding that will never take place.

~Oh, my little one, you suffer so! My mother-comforts are in vain! If only I could gather my little family and fly to heaven... But I know we are here for a reason and we need to fulfill that purpose somehow.

~Only one tiny chromosome too many and we step into a new world, a massive altering of our lives. We're in an imperfect world, that is certain, but God means it for good, for the perfecting of me.

Questions Come

~How do I explain to my two-year-old that this baby needs special care when I know I can barely meet both their needs?

~Will I outlive her or will she outlive me?

~What do people at church think of the scenes we cannot always avoid? Is that pity or a frown in their eyes?

~How will I watch her closely enough to protect her from the harm she is innocent to—the hot things, the sharp things, the things she could choke on?

~Am I doing all I can for my child? When should I accept her handicaps? When should I try to help her limitations?

~What is going through the mind of my speechless child?

And Some Answers

~For today, I know a few things to do. Two years from now there will also be a few things to do, though likely not the same things. God will show us.

~A lot more is right with my child than is wrong. Her feelings show all the colors of a normal child's emotional spectrum, as familiar to me as the smell of crayons.

~I will try to train her as I do our other children whenever I can. The nonfunctioning nerves, the protruding, drooling tongue, the awkward gait are not my focus, but the small things she accomplishes. The crude little stick she gives me is as full of love as the dandelion bouquet her sister skillfully picked.

Acceptance. Again.

~If I could, I would accept God's will once and for all. But often at the bottommost part of a trial, I must do it again. God is my "very present help," and, at every point of need, I again lay down my will and take His.

~Some days I feel like giving up, but God gives me strength in those times. It comes from nowhere else but Him.

~Each mother has her load to bear...this is mine.

~Life is not fair, but God is. "Shall not the Judge of all the earth do right?"

~"Stop wondering, 'What if?'" I tell myself, "and enjoy 'What is.'" I covet my little girl's uncomplicated happiness.

~The power of my weak one to touch the strong, to mellow hearts, and to draw out kindness are miracles I am privileged to witness.

~There is pure joy knowing there is no worry for her soul. My daughter will be safe always.

~I would not wish to be handicapped as she is, but when she dies, is there anyone who would not want to be like her? Pure and at perfect harmony with God.

~We prayed for a healthy baby, but God was kind. He took the controls out of our hands and sent a blessing that surpassed our own desires.

V. H. K.

Special Mother

Blessed among mothers is she
    who has mothered a "special" child.

Those "special" little ones—
    sometimes only a slight imperfection—
        just enough to make a difference—
    the difference that brings hurts again and again.

And mothers share the pain of
    every small failure—
        every small sting.

Sometimes—so "special"
    there never is the first smile,
        the first word, the first step.

And sometimes "special" means pain
    and tears,
        crying and crying—
    unrelieved pain
        that a mother longs to endure for her child
        if only she could.

"Special" because God is
    "especially" near.

Alfreda Nightingale

*It is very good for strength,
to know that someone
needs you to be strong.*

Elizabeth Barrett Browning, 19th Century

God Chose Me?

Our children are calm, easy-going, good-natured children—except for one. That child is high-strung, hyperactive, and difficult.

Countless times, I have been brought to the end of myself—my knowledge, my patience, my strength. I have shed tears of mental exhaustion and of near despair. And I have asked myself questions that surely many mothers have also asked: *"Why was I chosen to be the mother of this child? I, who am not capable; I, who lose my patience much too often; I, who so often do not know what to do. Why was I chosen and not a mother who is wise and experienced and calm?"*

The answer comes to me: God does all things well. He makes no mistakes. Through God, I am somehow the perfect mother for my child.

Were it not for this child, we could think we have all the answers for child training. Our other children, though far from perfect, never brought us to the end of ourselves as this child has.

I never saw my own faults and weaknesses so clearly as I have in this child. I never felt my own incompetence, my own insufficiency, as I have while training up this child.

Truly, this child is training up his mother! God knew we needed this child. In His great love for our child, He puts everything we need to train him within our reach. But we must humble ourselves, we must pray, we must ask. We must be teachable as God, day by day, shows us what to do.

Yes, our little knowledge, our few loaves and fishes, will not begin to be all our child needs. But if we give it humbly in faith, then surely God will supply the basketful.

Mrs. Mark Yoder

5 Taps on a Mother's Shoulder
Some Tips for Balanced Mothering of Special Needs Children

Tap #1 Don't under-discipline your child, thinking he is too limited to behave. You only add to his handicaps. Work toward simple obedience.

Tap #2 Don't be a greater crutch for your child than he truly needs. Let him try to do something new, even if he will surely fail. Perhaps the next time he will fail better.

Tap #3 Don't place your child at the center of your family, so that too much revolves around his needs. He is a spoke, not the hub. Don't miss the silent shouts for help from the rest of your family.

Tap #4 Don't be so consumed with your child's care that you become a tired and grim mother. Your labors are intense and needful, but your refreshment is more important than covering every possible exercise and remedy for your child.

Tap #5 Don't be reluctant to admit that you need help. Your sisters in the church want to know when you are weighed down. You are not alone!

Thoughts from a Mother's Helper

A Mother Must Have Hope

They told her to plant the uncomely little stick in a simple pot. Give it a secure place to grow. Give it soil, air, water, light — all it needs to live. And above all, have patience. Long, enduring patience because, they said, it will take years until suddenly, a geyser of green shoots up...bamboo!

They told her to take her child home and love him. Teach him, nurture him, and pattern him — even if you see no improvement. Keep your faith and hope alive because, they said, if you do, a beautiful creation will develop beneath the surface. It may not be a sudden, remarkable change, but the years will tell you something that the days and weeks and months cannot. There will be fruit! A child bettered, a mother grown ever more Christlike in compassion and patience...this is why a mother must have hope.

V. H. K.

Accept and Adapt

Instead of the lively, colorful world of a normal child, Helen Keller lived in a dark, quiet world where sight barely flickered and sound scarcely whispered in her memory. It was a world that often frustrated her and from which she found no release. But with the perseverance of special teachers, little Helen broke out of her capsule and learned to relate to the world around her.

As she entered a school for the blind with her personal tutor, Annie Sullivan, Helen bumped her head on a protruding shelf. In anger, she turned to Annie and sputtered, *"Why of all places—in a school for the blind—would this corner not have been padded?"*

Annie calmly replied, *"My dear Helen, the purpose of this school is not to change the world because you are blind—it is to teach you how to exist in a world designed for those who see."*

As a parent, you cannot shield your handicapped child from all the corners of life. If you constantly cover for him, it reveals a lack of acceptance. You need to help him to *accept and adapt* to his life-long challenges. If a child does not learn to accept and, instead, allows incident after incident, stare after stare, and comment after comment to annoy him, he will probably "erupt" at the smallest corner.

The sooner you accept his handicap yourself, the sooner it turns into a blessing. A mother of a brain-injured child wrote these words: *"We would have called our daughter's handicap the greatest tragedy of our lives if it were not that through it, we came to know the Lord much better."* Although the parents were keenly disappointed when their child failed to develop normally, their child's condition helped them understand that heartaches, if properly accepted, will enrich lives in a way that may not happen otherwise.

"As for God, his way is perfect." Psalm 18:30

David A. Erb, Adapted

Heal My Child

Everywhere, everywhere, children are suffering—
    afflicted by diseases,
    broken and maimed,
    wasted and starving,
    neglected, unloved.
You have not healed them, Lord,
And I do not know why.

Nor can I yet say why
I dare to ask the strong and loving hand
that raised up Jairus' daughter from the dead
should heal my child
while others lie by companies unhealed.
    I do not know why
    and yet I cannot leave the thing unasked.

So let my prayer
Come there before Thee now, and intercede
    for children who are suffering
    for families who weep for them
    for families who do not care—
I hold them up before Thy throne.
I bring their needs before Thee, God of Love.

And Lord, my little one...
though others suffer every day
in just this way
and far, far more,
though children cry and parents groan
    and mourn,
still I cannot forbear to ask
that we be spared.

I do not understand.
I only crave Thy healing touch.
But since I darkly see Thy face
And since I dimly know Thy ways
I leave it all within Thy hand—
Thy strong and loving hand.

Janice Etter

The Vigil

Her face is so flushed, and her hand here in mine, so hot, so very hot—oven-dry and seemingly weightless. Dear Lord, she is so sick and I am so afraid. My soul whispers, *"Surrender, release her,"* and my mother heart cries in anguish "No! No, no, no..." *How can I lift her up to Thee of my own will?* My soul bends away from the possible.

Her breathing is labor, every small, beautiful muscle quiet while her body throws itself against this enemy. The waiting face of a child, even in pain, so trusting. There is no wild-eyed fear, no frantic clawing for help. Just an occasional look, a quiet, soft search for reassurance. *I am here, darling, I am here.*

My soul and heart are reaching for her, like the breath of warmth across a cool room. My will for her to live is so tangible that her small feet could walk upon it just now. All my thoughts are cables supporting this bridge for her. I hardly dare breathe for fear it will sag the short instant she may need it. My eyes burn, yet cannot leave her face. My back aches, my arm, yet even this pain is a cable for my love.

Stay close beside us, Lord, Thy love upon her and around her. I ask the knowledge of Thy presence and the assurance that Thou art here, and that I will be strong enough...

Laura Margaret Evans

*There are times,
after we have done all that we can do,
that God asks nothing of His children but
silence, patience, and tears...
And sometimes,
our helplessness is our best prayer.*

Our Rosebud

Our bud began as a lovely, small perfection...or so we thought. It unfolded as rosebuds do, slowly, quietly. A trace of color showed promise of its bloom, but then...it was too still, too much the same, perhaps it even *faded*.

Now we wait and pray and remember—remember that we cannot make the rose bloom.

We water the plant, we weed it, we dig around it. We feed it with the best nourishment we know. We work early and late, in all kinds of weather and situations, sacrificing ourselves with one goal in mind—the rose will bloom!

But in all this we must remember—we cannot *make* the rose bloom. When the garden work is too difficult and the gardener is too tired, remember—the rose will bloom. Someday, sometime, in a time and place we cannot see now—it will bloom!

No matter how tightly the bud hides within itself, seeming to resist our feeble efforts, the bud deserves a chance—a chance to bloom. And bloom it will, in its own place, in its own time.

Do not force it. Do not tug at the petals in an attempt to make the rose bloom—for you cannot. You will only ruin and damage its tender growth. You can only wait and pray and work and remember; it is not in your power to make the rose bloom.

You may be blessed to see some petals open and thrive and grow at your loving touch, and in this find some reward for your efforts; but remember—it is not *you* that makes the rose bloom. You only dig and feed and water—and wait and pray.

R. H. M.

"The desert shall rejoice, and blossom as the rose.
It shall blossom abundantly, and rejoice even with joy and singing....
Then the eyes of the blind shall be opened,
and the ears of the deaf shall be unstopped.
Then shall the lame man leap as an hart,
and the tongue of the dumb sing."

Isaiah 35:1, 2, 5, 6

CHAPTER 22

Bereaved Mothers

A Bereaved Mother Speaks

Dear God, I give Thee back Thy precious gift
    Thou gavest me so short a time ago —
In this brief space of joy of motherhood,
    Thy love, and more of faith, I've come to know.
The pain of separation sears my aching heart,
    And, while I cannot understand Thy ways divine —
While sense of loss transcends all other thoughts,
    My earnest prayer is, "Make Thy will be mine."

Be patient with me, God, a little while,
    Till empty arms and nerves, so frayed, relax.
Give richly of Thy tender store of love,
    And I will strive Thy patience not to tax.
I am so thankful in a time of loss, like this,
    There's One to whom I have been taught to go,
And easier is the pain, for rather would I give
    Him back to Thee than anyone I know.

For Thou hast gathered countless ones to Thee,
    And children ere have been Thy special care;
So I am quieted, and in my grief appeased
    To think my precious, tiny babe is there.
I would be pleased if Thou wouldst let me feel
    That, while Thou hast him, yet he's still my own,
And, when I too, am called by beckoning hands,
    I'll find my Heart's Desire near Thy throne.

George Z. Keller

Your Little Lamb

So you have been "putting away."

It was a sad business. I think I know how your heart cried, as you took the dear little garments and hid them away, out of sight.

You could not help going over the sorrowful circumstances again. You remember everything; right from the very first. There was the time when the great Hope became a certainty. Then, as day followed day, the thought became more vivid, the longing more intense. What care you took of yourself! You were careful not to overwork. You rested systematically. You took pains to cultivate your mind. You resolutely put away all doubtful thoughts. You said, "I will not think on evil things, lest I should clip my darling's wings." Often you prayed for your little child. You realized, as never before, a woman's dependence on the Life-Giver.

And thus you were brought nearer to the heart of God. You felt that He was the One with whom you, personally, had to do. Yes, the little fingers pointed you to Him.

You spent hours making dainty garments. How lovingly you planned and fashioned everything! You lined the cradle; you made the bed and tiny pillow, with many tender thoughts of the little head and the soft limbs that would soon be resting in that cozy nest.

It was all ready, and you were just waiting for the little one to come into your arms, when—all unexpectedly—the blow fell.

Your little lamb came into the world—just came—and immediately was borne away to its heavenly Home.

And so, it was all for nothing.

It had all happened to no purpose.

This was the thought that beat in upon the anguish of those first intolerable hours.

You had spent your strength for naught.

You had had your dreams in vain.

Your arms were empty, after all.

And your heart was, oh—so sore!

You lay quietly and thought about it. People were very kind; they brought flowers and books, and talked gently about all being for the best. They tried to cheer you by speaking of the future. And you listened, grateful for their kindness. But, when they had gone, you went back to your own sad thoughts.

Some said it would do you no good to dwell on the subject, and that you should be encouraged to talk of other matters. But you longed to talk about your little darling. You found comfort in going back to the morning and afternoon of that long-looked-for birthday.

I cannot think that you were wrong in doing so. When Sorrow knocks at the door, we cannot delay answering it forever. Open the door and ask Sorrow in. Sit with her for a while, and treat her as an honored guest. By and by, you will find that you have been entertaining an angel unawares.

Now you are about again. And you have been "putting away." You are supposed to have "got over" your disappointment. You are taking up life again. People tell you that you have been very strong, and that there is still much in store for you.

But I want to put into words the question I see in your eyes: "What happens to the little lost lambs?"

It seems to me absolutely true that every stillborn child lives — to God. Listen to one who lived very near to the heart of God: *"Thine eyes did see my substance, yet being unperfect; and in thy book all my members were written, which in continuance were fashioned, when as yet there was none of them." Psalm 139:16 "Thine eyes did see."* With God, to see is to take knowledge of. With Him, nothing is unimportant. There are no accidents in His writing of history. The little "substance" that was so precious to you, must be precious to Him.

Your darling never shed a tear; never knew the soil of sin; never breathed in the tainted air of earth; never turned away from the tender mercy of God.

It is true that he never wore the cozy daintiness that you made. But think, for just a moment, with what material God may array such little children. I think that He, who decks the commonest

weed with dewy wonders, may be expected to have some marvelous conception for "clothing" the little being who has been cast on Him from the very first.

It would be just like Him to take the mother's love and tenderness and longing, and to weave out of it something that shall make the small spirit so definitely and individually her own child, that she will be able to recognize her loved one when they two shall meet.

And now there is something connected with your dear Baby that you need not put away. You made clothes for him, but did he not fashion some new raiment for you? I think so.

There was the beautiful robe called Sympathy and that other garment which one wears nearer still to the heart. I mean the one called Suffering.

You will always know more than you did before, won't you? This experience has brought you into fellowship with a countless host of women. On this road you are treading today, you will see the footprints of other women who have gone this way before you.

The little one touched your eyes, and so now you see every circumstance of life more sympathetically and more lovingly than you did. The little feet made paths for themselves, and you have followed, discovering many things that once you did not care to know.

> It was not all for nothing.
> It was not a waste of time.
> Who can tell just what it was for?
> Who knows how this may link up with Eternity?
> My friend—God knows!

Fay Inchfawn

> *C*ome to My heavenly garden,
> And see there in perfect bloom,
> The flower you longed for dearly,
> But thought I plucked too soon.
> Then you will know My reason,
> Though you know it not today,
> Why in his blooming infancy
> I took your baby away.

Author Unknown

Refuge in Disappointment

When my heart is breaking—
   (Who can feel its woe?)
And my arms are aching,
   (Only mothers know!)
Lead me to Thyself, dear Lord,
   And help me *hope* in Thee.

When the strain is making
   More than I can bear,
And it seems I'm taking
   Far more than my share,
Be my Rock and Refuge, Lord,
   And help me *rest* in Thee.

Raise me from the depths, Lord;
   Let me not despair.
Teach my lips to praise Thee;
   Tune my heart to prayer!
Let me lose myself, dear Lord,
   And *find my All* in Thee.

Joy comes after sorrow;
   Peace comes after pain.
When my will's surrendered,
   I can smile again.
Thou art my salvation, Lord;
   O help me *live* for Thee!

Sharon L. Sensenig

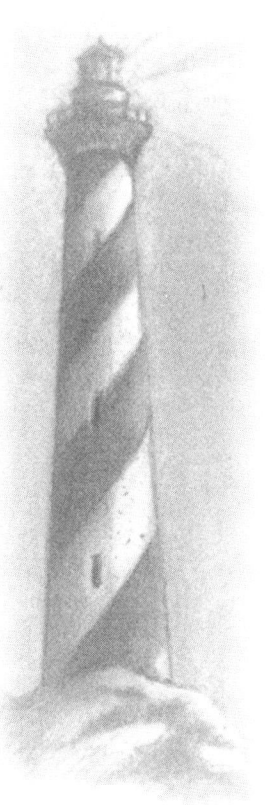

"Is it well with the child?
And she answered, It is well."

2 Kings 4:26

The Mother's First Grief

She sits beside the cradle,
    And her tears are streaming fast,
For she sees the present only,
    While she thinks of all the past;
Of the days so full of gladness,
    When her firstborn's answering kiss
Thrilled her soul with such a rapture
    That it knew no other bliss.
O those happy, happy moments!
    They but deepen her despair;
For she bends above the cradle,
    And her baby is not there!

There are words of comfort spoken,
    And the laden clouds of grief
Wear the smiling bow of promise,
    And she feels a sad relief;
But her wavering thoughts will wander,
    Till they settle on the scene
Of the dark and silent chamber
    Of all they might have been.
For a little vacant garment,
    Or a shining tress of hair,
Tells her heart in tones of anguish
    That her baby is not there!

She sits beside the cradle,
    But her tears no longer flow.
For she sees a blessed vision
    And forgets all earthly woe;
Saintly eyes look down upon her,
    And the voice that hushed the sea
Stills her spirit with the whisper,
    "Suffer them to come to Me."
And while her soul is lifted
    On the soaring wings of prayer,
Heaven's crystal gates swing inward,
    And she sees her baby there!

Robert Smyth Chilton, 19th Century

Bereaved mothers have worked for something other than the death of their child and the breaking off of their purpose. Their work shall not be in vain. Death is a great deceiver, making its power seem greater than it is. When children are taken from this world into the next, opportunities are not lost, they are only changed.

"Thus saith the LORD; Refrain thy voice from weeping, and thine eyes from tears: for thy work shall be rewarded, saith the LORD; and they shall come again from the land of the enemy. And there is hope in thine end, saith the LORD, that thy children shall come again to their own border." Jeremiah 31:16, 17

The great thing every mother should seek is such faithfulness, such wisdom, such right dealing in all ways to be a true mother to her children, however long they live. Then, whatever happens, there is the certainty, that in some way, her work will be rewarded. The work of individual obedience can never come to anything but reward in the end.

The Pulpit Commentary

Oh, when a mother meets on high,
The babe she lost in infancy,
Hath she not then for pains and fears,
The day of woe, the watchful night,
For all her sorrow, all her tears,
An overpayment of delight?

Robert Southey, 19th Century

Not Till They Are Rooted

I went into the kitchen the other day with a bit of black velvet in my hand and a whole pall of black in my heart.

All morning I had been brooding, brooding over my loneliness, shutting out the light and looking only at the darkness. A few months ago, I had lost a precious daughter, and though God had blessed me in a thousand ways, had surrounded me with love and comfort, thoughts of my loss had blighted everything.

I had tried to lift myself to such a state of trust that I could joyfully think of my daughter in far more tender care than she had with me and far safer there than in this world of temptation. There had been many hours, many of them, when I attained at least calmness; but on the morning of which I speak, the whole sky was black, with not even a star to call my look upward.

I stood at the ironing board, renewing my velvet, when one of my daughters brought in some forlorn-looking flower cuttings in clay pots.

"These need to come in whenever the sun is shining!" she said.

"Isn't the sun good for them?" asked my other daughter.

"It will be — but *not* till they get rooted!" she answered.

"*Not till they get rooted*," said I over and over to myself, as I went away. I thought, God is telling me something... He is *good* to not give me all sunshine until I am rooted. He knows I would soon wither and die. So He set me in the shadow. He wanted my roots to have the moisture of tears. And if I grow stronger through reaching after Him, little by little He will give me more sun. "Not till *she* gets rooted."

Well, I know that before my little girl died, I had given the frivolous things of life far too much of my heart. I had been swayed hither and thither by those who were not my rightful guides. I had been content with little fellowship with God. I had been far from healthy, genuine growth. The sun had withered, not strengthened me. I was not rooted.

Then let me then be rooted! Let me lift up my thoughts constantly to the Divine realm, the summer land of the soul, for help and guidance. Let me make God my own and then all that He possesses will be mine also. Let me through obedience enter into love, so shall I find all that I have lost.

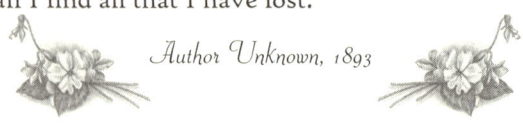

Author Unknown, 1893

Kept for You

God has taken your babes: they are safe. They did not venture out into some great void, some vague and unexplored path, where the little wanderers are left to find their own way. If there be use for angels, surely it is fitting and beautiful for them to bear in their arms and convey to the presence of the All-Loving, the tender spirits of little children.

Nor do we need to doubt that there is a place for our children in the Father's house with sweet company in perfect blessedness and gladness, innocence, and friendship, such as they could never have had on earth.

Our children are cared for. He that was grieved when the little children were kept from Him, who took them up in His arms, laid His hands upon them, and blessed them — is He any less a lover of children in heaven than He was upon earth?

But, shall *we* know them? Why not? Where does Scripture indicate this? It is not positively affirmed; but it is implied that men, dropping at death all that is of the flesh, will rise into the communion of heaven, carrying the same affection, sentiment, will, and intelligence that they had on earth. Otherwise, of what use are discipline, education, and earthly experience? It is the saint made perfect, not made out of a new pattern, that we shall meet in glory.

Let no mother be deprived of the hope of meeting her children in heaven! Let mothers comfort themselves in believing that the loves of earth will go on in heaven, and that whatever was pure, noble, and true on earth will go on with them forever. Among all other griefs, let not this unnecessary one arise — that you have lost your children forever! He who keeps you for them, will keep them for you! They will be more beautiful, sweeter, more glorious in preciousness.

Henry Ward Beecher, 19th Century

An Eastern Shepherd

An Eastern shepherd led his sheep
    Toward a river's brink,
But when they saw the stream was broad,
    Their hearts with fear did shrink;
And though the shepherd went across
    In view of all the sheep,
They did not dare to follow him
    And ford the waters deep.

And so he took a little lamb
    Right from its mother's side,
He clasped it in his shelt'ring arm,
    And with it crossed the tide.
The mother, missing what she loved,
    Was eager now to gain
The distant shore, that she might find
    Her precious lamb again.

She quickly made her way across,
    And soon the stream she passed;
And other sheep soon followed her,
    Till all had crossed at last.
She found the lamb that she had lost,
    Within the shepherd's care;
And he had used her little one,
    In leading many there.

Oh, Mother, has your little lamb
    Been carried on before?
The Shepherd wants to have you, too,
    Upon the farther shore.
And so He clasped your treasured one
    Unto His sheltering breast,
That you might come and seek it there,
    And find in Him your rest.

Author Unknown

Pass Under the Rod

I saw a young mother in tenderness bend
    O'er the couch of her slumbering boy;
And she kissed the soft lips as they murmured her name,
    While the dreamer lay smiling in joy.

Oh! sweet as the rosebud encircled with dew,
    When its fragrance is flung on the air,
So fresh and so bright to that mother he seemed
    As he lay in his innocence there.

But I saw when she gazed on the same lovely form —
    Pale as marble, and silent, and cold —
But paler and colder her beautiful boy,
    And the tale of her sorrow was told.

But the Healer was there, who had stricken her heart
    And taken her treasure away,
To allure her to heaven, He has placed him on high,
    And the mourner will sweetly obey;

There had whispered a voice —
    'Twas the voice of her God —
        "I love thee! I love thee! pass under the rod!"

Mrs. M. S. B. Dana, 19th Century

*"And I will cause you to pass under the rod, and I will
bring you into the bond of the covenant." Ezekiel 20:37*

*In Bible times, sheep passed one by one through the door
of the fold as the shepherd stood holding his rod, dipped in
vermilion dye, above them. As they came out he counted,
    "One, two, three, four, five, six, seven, eight, nine..."
And as the tenth sheep passed under, the rod descended and
marked it to be set apart for the Lord and His special purposes.*

The Cheerful Giver

"What shall I render Thee! Father Supreme,
For Thy rich gifts, and this the best of all?"
Said a young mother, as she fondly watched
Her sleeping babe. There was an answering voice
That night in dreams—
    "Thou hast a little bud
Wrapt in thy breast, and fed with dews of love;
Give Me that bud. 'Twill be a flower in heaven."

But there was a silence. Yea, a hush so deep,
Breathless, and terror stricken, that the lip
Blanched in its trance—
    "Thou hast a little harp—
How sweetly it would swell the angels' hymn;
Give Me that harp!" There burst a shuddering sob,
As if the bosom by some hidden sword
Were cleft in twain.

                Morn came. A blight had struck
The crimson velvet of the unfolding bud;
The harp strings rang a thrilling strain and broke—
And that young mother lay upon the earth
In childless agony.

           Again the voice
That stirred her vision—*"He who asketh of thee*
Loveth a cheerful giver." So she raised
Her gushing eyes, and, ere the teardrop dried
Upon its fringes, smiled—and that meek smile,
Like Abraham's faith, was counted righteousness.

Lydia H. Sigourney, 19ᵗʰ Century

CHAPTER 23

Widowed Mothers

A Young Mother's Prayer

I cannot understand, dear Lord,
 Why he was called away,
Just when I needed him so much
 To help me on my way.

He was so young, so good, so dear,
 Devoted to our sons and home;
Why must he leave me then, dear Lord,
 To carry on alone?

When the shades of night come closing in,
 And my heart breaks, Lord, I pray,
Heal my wound, and give me strength
 To face another day.

Help me rear my little sons,
 That their feet may never stray
From the path that leads to heaven,
 Where all tears are wiped away.

Author Unknown

Mothering Alone, Yet Not Alone

When our husbands are taken from this life, it falls to us as mothers to assume the role of leading out at home, whether we wish to or not.

I think for the boys to know, even when they are older teens, that they are just "the boys" in the home underscores their accountability to us as mothers. They need that.

I took the lead in family worship and in asking visitors to lead us in prayer at mealtime, even when the boys were in their upper teens and low twenties and still home. They could have been the spokesmen for me, but I wanted them to be boys while they were in our home; they would have the responsibility of being the leader later in their own home, the Lord willing. I always appreciated when other fathers led out in prayer when we were the company and my oldest boy was 14, 16, even 18, instead of asking my boy to lead out. It was so good for us to hear the father pray, so restful, so secure...

Do not lean too heavily too soon on the children's advice. It would be easy to. Know their thoughts and consider them. But lean on other mature people more.

It is most helpful to have a few trustworthy people to be your advisors—people who share your convictions and who will guide and support you in decisions that must be made. It gives the children security to know that you confer (even when they do not want you to sometimes) with Uncle Paul's or Brother John's whenever you need to—not too large a circle or you will still end up not knowing what to do.

Honor your husband's convictions and implement his ideals as much as you are able. To tell the children, "I know this is what Daddy would want us to do," gives validity to your decisions. Seeing you honor Daddy's direction will help them honor yours.

By all means possible, teach your children the joy of submission. Teach by precept, by example, by discipline. No matter what your circumstances in life, this is perhaps the most crucial lesson to be learned.

Nurture your relationship with each child. You are their only parent they can hear and see now. They *need* you. Guide their thinking—never scorn it. Be sensitive, thoughtful, and wise. Build the kind of relationship they will still want to draw from in twenty years.

We are not to be pitied because we are bereft. The same God who took, comforts the sore spots with extra special tenderness. Teach the children that the thoughtful deeds of others prove God's love to us. We are loved and cared for. Pity is weak, and weakens. True comfort strengthens. We look for comfort, but not pity.

"Keep your chin up," my uncle said. God hears our pleas for courage and wisdom. We look *up* for God's help and beyond to the comfort and joy that awaits us over there. That is what keeps us going, and we want to do all we can to bring our children with us.

Karen M. Carpenter

Mother's Easy Chair

A woman in humble circumstances, the mother of four children, was suddenly bereaved of her husband. She took up her burden with calmness and patience, toiling early and late for her children.

A friend said to her one day, "Don't you ever get tired or discouraged?"

"Oh, yes," was the reply, "quite often, but when I think I can go no further, or do nothing more, I go and rest in my easy chair."

"Easy chair?" said her friend, looking around the bare room.

"Yes," she answered, "would you like to see it? Come with me."

She took her into a small room and knelt by the bedside. The toil-worn mother prayed as if she was face to face with God.

Rising, she said, "Now I feel rested and am ready for work again. Prayer is my easy chair."

There is no home so poor and humble, no life so bare and destitute, but can have the easy chair of prayer.

Author Unknown

Ask Not Why

I know not why, I know not why
My young husband had to die,
And leave me with two children small,
Just when I need him most of all,
   I know not why.

Lord, how can I perform this task?
This question of God, you can ask.
But with my shield of faith held high
I'll trust in God and ask not why,
   I'll ask not why.

My God mistakes has never made,
And of my foes I'm not afraid,
For while I'm passing through each test—
I just remember, God knows best,
   My God knows best.

Sometime, somewhere on heaven's shore,
When all my work on earth is o'er,
When I am safe with God on high,
I then will understand just why.
   I'll then know why.

Lula Dando

Lines from a letter to a bereaved one: "It will tempt you to ask *why* this must be. *God knows why,* and that may be as good to us as though we knew a thousand reasons.

"I pray God to hold you quiet and patient and uncomplaining, and help you bear the weight of this seemingly unintelligible sorrow.

"I hope you will remember that this is the only world in which a Christian can suffer, and suffer patiently and meekly. We cannot suffer by and by. God helps us to glorify Him now, when we can."

Malthie D. Babcock, 1901

The Widow's Answer

In the quiet of her kitchen, a mother patched a pair of worn trousers and listened to the glad shouts of the children at play in the yard, two boys and one little girl. Her children! Her heart swelled with contentment. They were healthy, happy children and were growing old enough to help with many little tasks.

But, oh, how much guidance they would need in the next few years! A shadow crossed her face. Must she do it all alone? And what if she should be taken from them? Taken away, as their dear father, who had died just four years ago?

Who would feed them? Who would clothe them?

Who would mother them? The questions

blew hard on her wavering faith.

They would be so alone.

"O God," she whispered. "What can I do? Surely You would not take me from them—but what if...? Oh, show me what I can do."

As stitch after stitch fell from her busy needle, God showed her a way for widows and their children. She must give them something which would be theirs always. They must have a Friend who would go with them all the way, whether they had father or mother or not, so that when trouble came, as it surely would, they could go to Him.

"I may not be here," she thought, "while they make their way among strangers. If they do not have God to trust, whom will they have?"

She treasured her discovery as something valuable beyond price, and began to teach her children some lesson *each day* about their heavenly Father and His Son, Jesus Christ. As she saw them learning something of the One who would be their Friend as long as they followed Him, her burden became lighter. She knew that this was the dearest blessing she could possibly give her children.

Eva Metz, Adapted

The Mother's Trust

Beneath the blood-stained lintel
    I with my children stand;
A messenger of evil
    Is passing through the land!

There is no other refuge
    From the destroyer's face.
Beneath the blood-stained lintel
    Shall be our hiding place.

The Lamb of God has suffered;
    Our sins and griefs He bore;
By faith the blood is sprinkled
    Above our dwelling's door.

The foe who seeks to enter
    Doth fear that sacred sign;
Tonight the blood-stained lintel
    Shall cover me and mine.

My Savior! For my dear ones
    I claim Thy promise true,
The Lamb is for "the household" —
    The children's Savior too;

On earth the little children
    Once felt Thy touch divine,
Beneath the blood-stained lintel
    Thy blessing give to mine.

O Thou who gave them, guard them —
    Those wayward little feet,
The wilderness before them,
    The ills of life to meet;

My mother-love is helpless,
    I trust them to Thy care!
Beneath the blood-stained lintel —
    Oh, keep us ever there!

The faith I rest upon Thee,
    Thou wilt not disappoint;
With wisdom, Lord, to train them,
    My shrinking heart anoint;

Without my children, Father,
    I cannot see Thy face;
I plead Thy blood-stained lintel,
    Thy covenant of grace.

Oh! Wonderful Redeemer,
    Who suffered for our sake,
When o'er the guilty nations
    The judgment storm shall break,

With joy from that safe shelter
    May we then meet Thine eye;
Beneath the blood-stained lintel—
    My children, Lord, and I.

Author Unknown

*"The beloved of the LORD
shall dwell in safety by him;
and the LORD shall cover him all the day long."*

Deuteronomy 33:12

Alone in the Heat of the Battle

Was this a day of grief to you? A day edged in navy blue? A tunnel echoing with your lonely cry, *"How long, Lord?"* Did you feel like the bird that hit your windowpane—stunned mid-flight—as you realized anew that, *"He is gone"*? When your little girl came to your arms, wailing with a pinched finger, did you give way to tears, mixing yours with hers? Then again, did you add to the onion-tears while preparing supper? Now the meal is on the table, but no Daddy appears at the door to scoop up your children, melting away the day's frustrations. No Daddy to make everything all right.

Dear friend, draw near to the "God of all comfort"! Today's grief is not a sample of forever. Tunnels must have an end. There is a pinpoint of light ahead, but see, there are lamps along the way, too. God's mercies are right beside you! Suppertime is past and you tuck your dear ones to bed. You kneel at the staircase landing, praying for each child by name—and they hear you. Then behind your door, you pour out your strongest tears and fears to God. The balm He sends will help you be strong for your children one more day.

Was this a day of perplexities? Was it like a puzzle knocked to the floor and now five pieces are missing? Did the kitchen sink drain only gurgle and then stop? The extension table refuse to extend? The clothesline sag and the sheets drag? Did you swallow away those words of security more than once, *"Go get Daddy."* And in the background did deeper dilemmas murmur? Shall I start woodworking projects for the boys or a greenhouse for the girls? Shall my daughter accept this young man's friendship or not? How shall I step through the maze of tax work? All the while wondering, *"What would he do? What would he say?"*

Dear friend, cast all your care upon the Lord. Start by carrying one difficulty to Him at a time. Start by saying, "Come, boys, let's try to fix it as best we can." You pull together and find, that with God's help, you can do some things that it seemed you "can't." Could it be that in these troubles, God is giving your fatherless family a closeness that some fathered-families miss? Problems and burdens will keep coming, but in the midst of it, you assure your children that they are not one of them. And if the path for you and yours were a hundred times more sad and difficult, you know in your heart, that God would always be enough.

Was this a day of worry and fear? Did it seem that danger lurked like the wasp that disappeared just before you swatted it? Did it seem like pain was just waiting to happen? Did you fear for your toddler boy who loves anything connected to wheels, but has no Daddy to guard him? Was it the anxiety of not knowing how sick your little girl really is? Or the dog-barking, floor-creaking noises of night? Then there were worries that extend and eat away... How will my children know how a married couple should work together? What if I die and they become orphans? You worry; they cling. You fear; they fret.

Dear friend, trust in the Lord! He who gives the lowly sparrow its life is able to care for your little flock. God heard your plea for His peace to rule in your heart. He saw you relax your forehead and put on a real smile. Your children saw it too, for they are reading you to see if they can trust a heavenly Father. Gently lead their minds to God, who loves and cares for them more than an earthly father ever could. This day is not in your hands, but it lies securely in God's.

Was this a day of insufficiencies? Did you feel like a cup half full when the recipe calls for a whole? Did you feel torn between supervising the choring boys and guiding the kitchen girls—but really, a nap for yourself would have been most desirable? Did you see a father-hunger in your little man's eyes as he threw his ball up and down, up and down? Did you long for their Daddy to balance your extremes, be firm when you are too gentle, be calm when you are frustrated? You wonder how to be two parents when it seems you are only the remains of one.

Dear friend, let patience have her perfect work! Patiently do what you can do for your children. Try to make their lives as normal as possible. Help your fourth grader with his homework. Re-hem your twelve-year-old daughter's dress. Plant peas in the spring. Simple things that make a good mother. Trying to be more than a mother makes you less than a good mother. No one, not even you, can replace their father, but God can bless their lives with good fathering—a trusted brother, uncle, grandpa, or friend willing to stretch his arms wider than usual.

Was this a day weighted with responsibility? Was it like a greenhouse packed full of urgencies? Flat upon flat of fragile seedlings headed only one direction without your care? So many decisions and needs! Did the little ones beg to go barefoot at the first puff of warm spring air? Has your young man been drowsy in church? Did your daughter plead to wear shoes like her friend's, shoes that are not quite within your family standards? You beseech the Lord for wisdom to draw lines consistently, for strength to hold steady. You know you cannot afford to sigh and let it go.

Dear friend, continue on! God is faithful! He knows your heart's desire is for your children to make it safe home to their Daddy, to be faithful to God to the end. Explain the way of discipleship to your questioning youth. Open the door to the church house regularly. Open your door to welcome the visiting minister's family. These efforts help to tie your children to the heart-throb of the church. Your husband prayed for your children's faithfulness. Those prayers live on. He would want you to bear up and go on. You do not shoulder these desires alone.

Someday the heat will fade. Your children will have homes of their own. May you say as one widowed mother said, "My desire has been to lean heavily on my "Husband...the Holy One of Israel" so that when the children come home they can feel the comfort of the heavenly Father, who was their father's God."

And may you echo a faithful grandmother as she reflected on her years of widowhood, *"Truly, the widow's God is a great God!"*

V. H. K.

*G*limpse the rainbow after the storm.
Point your children to its sweep of color.
Clasp your youngest's head and tilt to see.
Awe in it together.

See the joy-bow after the sorrow.
Show your children the blessing of God's faithfulness.
Trace His arch over you and yours.
Smile, rejoice together.

A Mother

Close at Hand

The day is long and the day is hard,
We are tired of the march and of keeping guard,
   Tired of the sense of a fight to be won,
    Of days to live through and of work to be done,
   Tired of ourselves and of being alone.

And all the while, did we only see,
We walk in the Lord's own company;
   We fight, but 'tis He who nerves our arm,
   He turns the arrows which else might harm,
   And out of the storm He brings a calm.

The work which we count so hard to do
He makes it easy, for He works, too.
   The days that are long to live are His,
   A bit of His bright eternities,
   And close to our need His helping is.

O eyes that were holden and blinded quite,
And caught no glimpse of the guiding light!
   O deaf, deaf ears which did not hear
   The Heavenly Garment trailing near!
   O faithless heart, which dared to fear!

Susan Coolidge, 19th Century

My Hand in His

Dear God, who trims the dying day
    with gold,
I offer up my trembling hand
    to hold.
Great God! All nature small and great
    may rest
In Thee. Oh, clasp me gently to
    Thy breast.
I feel insufficient for
    my task!
Thy hand to help me, Lord, is all
    I ask.
Just fill me with Thy fullness; make
    me strong.
The burden is so great, the road
    so long.
Thus in Thy strength I journey on
    each day,
Assured that Thou art with me all
    the way.
Dear God, who trims the dying day
    with gold,
I offer up my trembling hand
    to hold.

Mrs. Nathan Zimmerman

Faint not; the miles to heaven are few and short.

Samuel Rutherford, 17th Century

CHAPTER 24

Mothers-in-law and Stepmothers

Prayer of a Mother

My little son was kneeling on the floor
Building with blocks. I stood by to adore.
   He smiled,
And blue eyes, trusting, loving, raised
"You never push things do you, Mother?"
   Praised.

My little son will build his house of life
With press of other things, a house, a wife.
   Please, Lord,
Help me to satisfy his eyes
And keep my hand from pushing,
   Mother-wise.

Author Unknown

From What I Have Heard...

Soon I will be what I have never been before—a mother-in-law. Me! Even though I am still learning how to be just a mother. I mention this to others...

"You're not really losing a son, you're gaining a daughter," a friend said after I spoke of setting one less place at the table. (*Yes, I feel like a rich woman adding to my string of pearls.*)

A mother, years ahead of me, said, "Think of her as the first flower in your bouquet! If God adds more, you'll find that each one has her own beautiful color, her own fragrance, and grace." (*And each will be my favorite, I thought.*)

"You can't imagine it now," my cousin said, "but in many ways you will become closer to your daughter-in-law who lives nearby than to your own married daughter states away. Just because you've shared so many experiences." (*One of God's sweet surprises?*)

"If she is homesick, don't think that you have failed," a young wife told me. "It's not that she doesn't like you or her new home. She's simply, and sometimes not so simply, adjusting." (*I pray for eyes to see her loneliness and make a difference.*)

"We faced a lot of things, my daughters-in-law and I," one great-grandmother reflected. "But I tried not to let anything I could help stand between us." (*If I always try to build respect, not walls, we'll both be stronger.*)

Even the minister's thought chalked across the blackboard of my heart: "When you feel small and insecure and unwise, you are in the perfect place to learn what the Lord wants to teach you." (*And I thought, we're both pupils in a new school.*)

"It will take time to be truly relaxed together," another friend shared. "But that is no wonder. You've begun a 'courtship' that your son began long before you." (*My son's choice is my choice. A friend for life.*)

V. H. K.

Dear Mother-in-law,

Please don't be afraid of me, your newest daughter! My own mother lives far away. Will you do some of the things I wish she were here to do? I know I turned down some of your first offers of help. Please don't think that you were intruding or that I am one of those "capable women." If only I were! But I am finding that I am no longer the energetic young girl I used to be. I need help at times.

Do stop by when you are on the road—just to say hello. And while you are here, I won't mind at all if you offer to clean up my morning messes of breakfast dishes and crumby floors, or help with the afternoon activities of folding the wash or reading a story or two to the little ones. They love you for doing that, Grandma.

Tell me about the child training struggles you faced when you sense that I am discouraged. Every time you say, "*I know what you mean...*" I feel less alone. Thank you for respecting my ways of keeping our home and training our children. But thank you, too, for your kind way of pointing out areas that I never thought of. I need you, my mother-in-law!

You have so kindly and willingly blessed me by your cheerful help with a job I truly abhor—butchering our chickens. I feel unworthy as I survey the packs of fresh meat in our freezer. Thank you for a gift that is better to me than a bouquet of roses!

If only I could be that kind of help to you more often. When I do manage to come and lend a hand, you don't need to tidy up before I arrive. I am glad if you treat me just like family instead of a visitor.

Today I checked the violet start you gave me. Healthy little leaves are fringing the mother leaf. It makes me think of all I wish for our relationship of quiet, steady growth. For this I know; God gave us each other.

> With Love,
> Your Daughter-in-law
>
> *Dorothy Swartzentruber*

 # Peter's Wife's Mother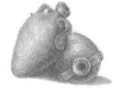

The Bible account of this ministering mother-in-law encourages and inspires us. Her record brings honor to a role that many in the world look down upon. We do not know her name, her age, or how long she lay sick. She may have been a poor woman; maybe a widow.

This mother-in-law's encounter with Christ must have been significant; for Matthew, Mark, and Luke include this story, giving similar details. She was in the household of her daughter and son-in-law, Peter. She *"lay sick of a fever."* When Jesus came, He saw her need, took her by the hand, healed her, and raised her up. Her response was immediate—*"She arose, and ministered unto them."* Matthew 8:14, 15

Observing the ministry of this mother-in-law helps us to see and understand the work and challenge of mothers-in-law today.

Her role was—

1. *A ministry in obscurity.* Jesus was the famous person in this setting. Next, there is the disciple Peter. Behind Peter is his wife. And behind her is Peter's wife's mother. A mother-in-law is not a person in life's limelight, but in the shadows.

Many consider it noble to be a mother. It is thought honorable to be a grandmother. But whoever heard of gaining renown by being a mother-in-law? But she need not despair. Jesus saw this mother-in-law behind the scenes, understood her needs, and reached out His hand to help her.

2. *A ministry in life's aging years.* Some rather youthful people can become a father or a mother, uncle or aunt, brother-in-law or sister-in-law. But God has wisely reserved the mother-in-law role for women who are middle-aged or older. It seems that God knew that filling this role would demand the experience, maturity, and wisdom that only years can bring.

A mother-in-law is called to a weighty work. Younger women are the mothers of the boys and girls. A mother-in-law serves as mother of the husbands and wives in her family. She is one of the aged women who teaches the younger women (*Titus 2:3, 4*). Though wiser, sometimes she, like Peter's wife's mother, is the weaker one in the family.

3. *A ministry to Christ.* *"She arose, and ministered unto them."*

Quite a crowd had gathered in their home that day—son-in-law Peter, his brother Andrew, and the friends James and John. Peter's family was there; maybe some of her grandchildren, too. And Christ was in the crowd she served! She was now able to minister to the One who had so graciously reached out to help her.

Life is often thankless and meaningless when one sees and serves only the crowd in the extended family. In contrast, life flows rich and full when a mother-in-law understands that ministering to her family is a ministry to Christ (*Matthew 25:40*).

4. *A ministry in service.* Faithful mothers-in-law serve, not self, but others, not in management and lordship, domineering over others, but in helpful assistance under others.

Surely, this ministry requires a special measure of grace and commitment for a mother-in-law. For many years, as a mother, she had superintended the household and family affairs. Now, as a mother-in-law, she steps down to serve as the maidservant in the home of her children.

It is the elder serving the younger; the more experienced serving the less experienced. These children whom she mothered, directed, and taught to work are now the parents whom she serves. This proves the genuine quality of a mother-in-law's life and shows the solid gold in her character. She can still practice what she, for years, has preached.

5. *A ministry in inspiration.* The sun was setting that day when Peter brought Jesus and his friends along home. Suddenly there was an immediate need—visitors to feed and care for. Was Peter's wife already weary from regular family duties and caring for the sick in her household? This mother-in-law's aid lightened more than the workload that day; it surely lifted the mother's spirit too.

A mother-in-law often brightens the day in our home. That welcome letter, call, or unexpected helping hand on a busy day does wonders to cheer the grandchildren and boost mother's morale.

6. *A ministry in impartiality.* "*She ministered unto them.*" Peter's wife's mother could have been selective in who she ministered to that day. Some of these were not close to her in the family. But no, she reached out to all who came to her house.

Often more than one in-law son or daughter is brought into a mother-in-law's family. These persons have varied personalities, talents, and gifts. Careful purpose is needed, lest a mother-in-law become partial and develop favorites in her family.

7. *A ministry in quietness.* There are no words recorded of Peter's wife's mother. Surely, she could have said much that day, talked about herself, her fever, her weakness, or her workload. She could have criticized her daughter—Why did she, the mother-in-law need to do this work? She could have scolded son-in-law Peter—Didn't he know better than to bring visitors when some were sick in the family? But *"she arose, and ministered unto them"* in quietness.

Great mothers-in-law are not known for their much speaking. They serve best in quiet, humble ways. They are careful not to be a busybody in others' home and family matters. To be on call for counsel serves far more effectively than to be in command with criticism for her in-law family.

8. *A ministry amidst commotion.* This woman was in Peter's household, possibly with children around. Her son-in-law was an impulsive individual, sometimes quite talkative. On this day, Peter's house was a hub of activity—*"all the city was gathered together at the door."* It was evening, time for quiet time, especially for one the age of a mother-in-law.

Amidst all the commotion, *"she arose, and ministered unto them."* Certainly, circumstances must have been different from what she desired, but they were beyond her control and she did her best in spite of them.

9. *A ministry in submission.* She *"lay sick of a fever."* Evidently, she had surrendered to her lot in life—failing health, physical weakness, and needing others to care for her. Sorrow may have touched her life—had her husband died?

Every mother-in-law has many opportunities to exercise this grace. In past years, God had given her responsibility; now He gradually takes it away. Children were placed into her family; now in marriage, God wills that they leave. She finds fulfillment, not in resisting these changes, but in submission.

10. *A ministry that draws on the strength of Christ.* In herself, Peter's wife's mother was weak and unable to serve. But Christ *"took her by the hand, and lifted her up."* In His help, she found the strength needed to fill this place and serve her family.

Christ is still reaching out, offering to take the hand of mothers-in-law today. He provides all the grace and wisdom that they need to be faithful and effective in this important role that they fill in the lives and homes of their in-law sons and daughters.

Simeon V. Rudolph, Adapted

In the Spirit of Naomi

Somewhere in the wilderness plain between Moab and Israel there is a three-foot patch of ground where two young women faced a life-changing decision. And there they parted ways forever.

Orpah, on one side, kissed her mother-in-law, Naomi goodbye. It was a kiss of respect; it was also a kiss of renouncement, for Orpah had no desire to live with the poor, uncolorful Hebrews. And when she took the path to Moab, she walked off the pages of the Bible altogether.

But Ruth, on the other side, *clave* to Naomi. She held fast. She was no tag-along. She was ready to identify with whatever it meant to follow Naomi's God. Read her words of commitment: *"Intreat me not to leave thee, or to return from following after thee: for whither thou goest, I will go; where thou lodgest, I will lodge: thy people shall be my people, and thy God my God" Ruth 1:16.* "They two" walked on to Israel trusting God to unfold their future.

How did Naomi inspire Ruth's unlikely devotion to God? It is a question with answers for mothers-in-law of all time.

In the spirit of Naomi...

❖ Build a relationship stronger than the "law" that binds you. Care about what concerns your daughter-in-law. Love leads to love.

❖ Focus on following God together, not on emphasizing your differing backgrounds, which you cannot change.

❖ Think not that your influence is mostly past; it is very present. Live by the fruit of the Spirit *now*. Show the marks of Christ *now*.

❖ Pay the price. A relationship worth having is never without cost. Give patience, tact, self-restraint, thoughtfulness.

❖ Be humbled by God's chastening in your life. Kneel before God when your heart aches and you do not understand.

❖ See that, if at all possible, your daughter-in-law does not leave your presence without being encouraged, appreciated, or helped.

❖ Treat her as an adult and a friend. You need each other.

❖ Talk deeper than surface subjects. Introduce issues with kindness and encourage her in a faithful walk.

❖ Desire to be where God is visiting His people, in a faithful church.

❖ Live so your daughter-in-law will say in her heart, "God has helped my mother-in-law; He will help me, too."

V. H. K.

"It'll Be All Right"

A gift one wise mother gave her daughter-in-law.

Her title of "Mrs." was as new and dent-free as the shovel she used to edge the borders of her flower beds. She loved her little home and purposed to shape it and shine it with all her young-wifely might. Memories of her mother-in-law's profuse petunias spilling over these very beds last year added to her ambition. Her compact plants needed just a bit of fertilizer to give them that overflowing look.

She poured. She mixed. And she sprayed.

Now to wait, and what a pleasure those waves of color would be to her dear, diligent mother-in-law's eyes! But — a day later, she glanced and she gasped. Her petunias were sick! They were shriveled! They were *black*! Black...the color of death for all flowers.

"Overfertilized," her husband diagnosed the trouble in the kindest possible way. But his consolations failed to quell her fear of her mother-in-law's dismay. This was not just modest mounds of petunias, it was *barren* beds.

Her mother-in-law came soon enough and the regrets tumbled from the young wilted wife. "I must have figured wrong. How could I...? I should have..."

And then the gift was given. "It'll be all right," her mother-in-law spoke so graciously, as if tucking a fretful child to bed.

Four words of understanding. Four words that released the young wife from the perfection her ideals unrealistically demanded. Four words that diffused the stress of a situation that couldn't be changed. Four words she heard again when the Sunday dinner potatoes were firm and undercooked. And when she locked herself out of the house while hanging up wash.

It was a gift the daughter-in-law would long remember. Someday she would pass it on when her own daughter-in-law was too sick to fix her new husband's meals on his birthday. And when she...

V. H. K.

A Mother-in-law Explains
Why a River
Made Her Ponder Her Words

Because a river is strong, but gentle in its lapping,
   always there, always supplying something.
It is home to flora and fauna, microbes and muskrats.
It is a long conversation
   in calming tones for those who come near.

Because a river is a path to trackless places.
It draws the newcomer around the next bend.
It introduces, invites, and shows the way most naturally.

Because a river buoys up its burden-movers.
Heavy loads find a certain weightlessness
   as they are carried on the river's imperceptible slope,
   by quiet, steady certainties that the burden-movers trust.

Because a river can hurt and destroy beyond its banks.
It swells, undiked, into a rash and roiling billow.
Or it is a gradual nosing to invade whatever it touches.
And when a river subsides, the dirty weeds and dead wood
   begrime its banks for years.

Because a river never truly ends. A river unburdens to the ocean.
The ocean whispers to a cloud. A cloud utters rain on a mountain.
A mountain chats with a creek. A creek agrees with a river.
And once again, a river unburdens to the ocean.

No water is lost, though it may seem so.
Rivers enter realms the senses cannot follow.
They, rivers and words, live on—to harm or to bless.

V. H. K.

Other Mothers

10 Things to Remember

For Mothers-in-law

1. If you are easy to borrow from, you will be easy to ask advice from.

2. "A *[foolish mother-in-law] uttereth all [her] mind: but a wise [mother-in-law] keepeth it in....*" *Proverbs 29:11*

3. Your daughter-in-law is God's gift to you. Your own girls are gone to homes of their own. Can they still sympathize with your stressful times? Not as before. Your daughter-in-law breathes the same air as you do and she cares.

4. Be relaxed—even though your thoughts fly around you like your stray gray hairs—and hers (thoughts and hair) stay together and poised.

5. Tell your married daughter what a good husband she has. Tell your married son what a good wife he has.

6. Don't make your daughter-in-law feel untalented or unskilled by saying, "Oh, in a few years, you'll learn how." She wants to do well *now*.

7. What if she reads the mail before she puts the groceries away? You wouldn't. And what if you let your wash hang out overnight? She doesn't. Keep your differences in the background and respect one another.

8. Mind your own business, but care about hers. Be on quiet standby.

9. Don't pretend. If being yourself means you tend to be a frustrated, discouraged, or bossy mother, then you have some work to do on the real you.

10. Remember the details of her life and keep in touch with her. "How did that recipe turn out? And the baby's rash...?"

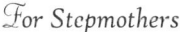

For Stepmothers

1. Sometimes it is best to be as quiet as a stitch of mending, holding things in place for everyone.

2. Sometimes you can "see the wind" as your children's unnamed emotions swirl around them. Try to not take their difficult times personally. Forget yourself and provide a safe haven.

3. It is a large step of faith to go from "me" to "we." Give yourself, your precious time and plans, to help build your new family.

4. You are a *real* mother with *real* children who have *real* needs. And their needs are much the same as any child's — to learn respect and obedience.

5. You are hoping for acceptance, but don't try to shoehorn yourself into the space your children's first mother occupied.

6. Don't continually analyze your mothering. You need that strength for all the dimensions of your charge.

7. Listen wisely and widely. Your children have a different background than you do. Be careful not to tuck the heavy blanket of your experience around all they say.

8. Be as kind as possible. It is always possible.

9. You may not be their first memory of "Mother." But you may be their last.

10. You made a commitment, a choice. As one stepmother said, "There was a need to be met. That's just the way it was." Keep a matter-of-fact faith in God as you step ahead.

For Both

1. If your children do not ask advice when you think they need it, pray, and ask God to send what they need through another source.

2. Overmothering can be smothering.

3. Be willing to be compared with mother number one. But don't contract "compar-itis" yourself.

4. When you are tempted to be the savior of the situation, a fixer, an interferer, a solution looking for a problem to solve—step back. Be calm and wait to be bidden.

5. There is no way to be a perfect "other mother." But there are many ways to be a good one.

6. Help your children through gentle, forthright conversations instead of talks that could be suffixed with "Sermon ended."

7. Count it a sweet honor and responsibility to be called "Mother." and be glad that her real mother fills a place in her life you cannot.

8. You may feel like a failure sometimes, surely. But God is faithful to bring more opportunities to overlay the past.

9. Ask yourself, "What kind of an 'other mother' would I love and respect?"

10. Yours is a calling laden with the need for wisdom. God prom- ises to hear our heart's cry for our children: *"Give therefore thy servant an understanding heart!"*

V. H. K.

They might not need me;
yet they might.
I'll let my heart be just in sight;
A smile as small as mine might be
Precisely their necessity.

Emily E. Dickinson

Happy is the mother who, by taking second place,
finds that she has earned a first place
that belongs to her alone.

George E. Sweazey

The Good Stepmother

I want to pay tribute to the good stepmother. I have no authoritative word on this, but I think she must have gotten the name stepmother because when she married, it became her job to *step* into a very difficult situation.

I admire the stepmother who understands that her new children have gone through a disturbing experience in losing their own mother. I admire the stepmother who faces honestly her own feelings, fears, and inner conflicts, admits her own failures and deals fairly and gently with those around her just as any Christian should deal with other human beings.

I admire the stepmother who understands that many of her problems with her children are just like the problems mothers have with their own "flesh and blood" children.

I once visited in a home where the mother and father had been married before and lost their companions by death. Each brought several children to the second marriage. Every one of the two sets of children had one real parent and a stepparent. But together they made up a family with as much harmony, if not more, than the average family. In fact, the mother told me that the child that gives her the most trouble is one of her own.

I admire the stepmother who carries on bravely in spite of hardships, believing that the intensity of her conflicts will be greatly reduced by the happy life that she and her husband are able to pursue together.

Ruth B. Stoltzfus

Stepmothering

Asking, Acquiring, Accepting, Adjusting, Adding, Apologizing,

Blending, Building, Balancing, Beginning, Blooming,

Considering, Comforting, Confiding, Communicating,

Deferring, Deciding, Delighting, Devoting, Diffusing, Discerning,

Easing, Echoing, Economizing, Eclipsing, Embarking, Encouraging,

Fearing, Failing, Forbearing, Forgiving, Facing, Figuring,

Grieving, Growing, Gentling, Gracing, Giving, Giving, Giving,

Hoping, Hearing, Healing, Hesitating, Honoring,

Inspiring, Interlacing, Introducing, Improvising, Identifying,

Joining, Juggling,

Kneeling, Knowing,

Loving, Living, Leaving, Letting, Learning, Listening,

Melding, Minimizing, Merging, Musing,

Noting, Needing, Nesting, Nurturing,

Overlooking, Organizing, Opening, Observing, Owning, Overlapping,

Praying, Pleasing, Purposing, Packing, Parting, Painting, Papering,

Quizzing, Querying, Questioning, Quelling,

Remembering, Regretting, Respecting, Reaching, Rejoicing,

Sympathizing, Struggling, Stretching, Stepping, Stopping, Sighing,

Talking, Transferring, Trembling, Trying, Trusting, Treasuring,

Understanding, Uniting,

Valuing, Visiting, Verbalizing,

Waiting, Welcoming, Wondering, Worrying, Working,

eXploring, eXcusing, eXchanging, eXpressing, eXtending,

Yielding, Yearning,

analyZing, stabiliZing, synchroniZing, harmoniZing.

V. H. K.

CHAPTER 25

Grandmothers

My Little Crown

"Children's children are the crown of [aged women]" Proverbs 17:6

Welcome, dear bundle, child of my child! Welcome to the arms of this mother of a new mother! Welcome, little unearned treasure! My little crown!

A *crown* to show a special position... Suddenly I qualify. Small as I feel as a mother, you have made my life grand—grand with a love that is quietly tucking in around my heart.

A *crown* to show a lofty honor... I bow to think how God gives a perfect parcel of innocence to mere men and says, "Raise this child to be My heritage."

A *crown* wrought with jewels and golden detail... I am a small part of a beautiful plan. As my duty-worn hands cradle your dewy-soft form, I pray that my past may supply something for your future.

A *crown* to polish and to protect... I tremble knowing the uneven, darkening terrain your feet will tread. Oh, that I could keep you from danger! I will pray and point and believe that God makes a way for every generation to be faithful.

A *crown* to complete my work in the world... You are the prize I would gain. For there is no greater joy than to know my grandchildren walk in truth.

V. H. K.

God's Plan

O mothers, lonely in your house today,
  From whence the voice of glad, young life has flown,
Where joy once reigned, sits silence cold and gray;
  The children now have dear homes of their own.

That this might come to us one day we knew,
  For always, ere the frost had kissed the flowers,
The full-fledged birdlings from the home-nest flew;
  But, ah, the autumn seemed so far from ours!

And not for us, the hope the fond birds share,
  That brings them hastening over hill and plain
To build and rear anew with tend'rest care;
  For never may we build and rear again.

But would we keep our dear ones, tho' we might?
  Nay, mother hearts, not self-love, do we know;
When once they prove their strong young wings in flight,
  We hide our tears and, smiling, bid them go.

Someday, perhaps, when little fingers twine
  In clinging trustfulness about our own,
And eyes so strangely like to yours and mine
  Look up with loving glances we have known,

With joy we'll clasp the precious thing and say,
  "This is reward for all our loss and pain;
This is God's plan, that haply thus we may,
  Through children's children, build and rear again."

Helen Marquis

A Wish for My Old Age

Let it be said that while she was living
Her body's truest beauty was giving;
    That never her hand or her heart was turning
    From hands in need, or hearts in yearning;
That never her mate sat by her side,
Hungry and cheerless and oft-denied;
    That never her child reached out to find
    His mother sterile in soul and mind.

May it be said, to the end of her knowing,
Her mind was a kingdom forever growing,
    Forever eager, forever willing,
    Forever wide to the Truth's infilling;
That its smallest gift was not abused;
That the lamp God lit there was ever used.

And may it be said, through gladness and grieving,
Through ebb and through flood, she was always believing;
    Though the flesh mocked the will, and the will leaned to fall,
    The voice from within was still urgent, though small;
And the faults of her youth wore finally thin,
And the graces of God shone pleasantly in.

Miriam Sieber Lind

*The greatest contribution
[grandmothers] can make
is not in the gifts they give,
but in the lives they live.*

Eby W. Burkholder

Godly Grandmothers I Have Known

I have not forgotten it. A Sunday evening visit with Grandmother Verna, our firstborn sprawled on the floor in a sudden
pouty tantrum, and my embarrassed excuse, "Oh, she's just tired."
"No..." Grandmother Verna turned to me with kind, instructional
eyes, "*that* is her *will!*" And then, one time after a quilting, she
fingered a child's jacket. "You know, these frills and embroideries
don't look so innocent to me anymore." Her regret was quiet but
clear. I knew that through the years, her walk had grown closer
to the Lord and the church, but her children... My friend found a
Bible at a used bookstore. Inside it said, "*TO: Merle FROM: Father
& Mother.*" It was her son's, discarded. But Grandmother Verna
did not waver. She was not discouraged. She warned younger
mothers to not let any link of faith or practice grow weak. And
she helped to strengthen the church in her corner.

I think she had an elastic heart. As a mother of many, Grandmother Alta must have held her last baby and thought, *surely this is
not the end.* And it wasn't. As a grandmother, she welcomed each
grandchild, and then stretched beyond her ample family to mother
many motherless ones—unconditionally and non-provincially.
It seemed she had a little tablet in her heart where she wrote the
names of needy ones so she could recall them with great warmth
upon meeting again. They surely felt like strangers taken in.
Perhaps her grandchildren thought they had much less of their
grandmother-to-all than if she had focused exclusively on them,
but they gained far more by her example of generous mothering.

"*I*'ll be there, but you won't see me." Grandmother Leah spoke
to her grandson of his wedding that she could not attend. Surely she felt the same about others in her far-spread family—her
granddaughter's baptism, her son's ordination. She was a praying grandmother. Every morning she took the Bible-sized piece
of cardboard covered with fine-point-penned names of her children, grandchildren, and great-grandchildren. Every morning
she propped it on the back of her chair, and knelt there. Every

morning she took each name to her heavenly Father and asked Him to keep them faithful and to meet their needs. Even though she followed their experiences closely, Grandmother Leah knew that better than her being there, is for the Lord's presence to go with them.

When you stepped into Grandmother Mary's kitchen, you could not miss her blackboard. Just a plain, chalky rectangle of slate, but it seemed to frame her outlook of grandmothering. You might have seen a trail of uneven 8's drawn by a first-grade hand, a lollypoppish flower garden along the bottom, a number puzzle, or a rough-sketched layout of someone's new house with the address in the top corner. "Whatever you are doing, I am interested; whatever you need, I will try to supply" was the unspoken message from Grandmother Mary's heart. Her back room was piled with goods from hither and thither, but she just might have shoes to fit her little grandson or a sweater for his big sister. And was some little person not well? She could tell a fever with the back of her hand, and her keen interest took her to their bedside. She kept giving till she was gone.

Though tiny and untiring, Grandmother Hannah was not fussy. Like the tick-tock of the little chime clock in her house, she was uncomplicatedly happy, serenely precise. Her dishes and cups nested in a lone cupboard; her tattered cookbooks and buffed silverware lay in their drawer. A little square of a mirror was all she needed to comb and veil herself. Less is more, she and Grandfather Abram believed. The less time and energy for themselves, the more they had to share with others. And so, when he and she drove in their children's lanes, it was a welcome sight. Perhaps Grandmother Hannah would bring a few tomatoes or extra onion bulbs. Then she would take up her quiet presence, mending, peeling, scrubbing, while the family noise surged all around her. "Such little things," she would discount her day's work in her bright and busy way. She deeply underestimated. Her labors of love went beyond her to influence those whose voice of thanks she would never live to hear.

V. H. K.

Full Circle

She began to run. The limp bouquet of violets clutched in her eager hands was clenched tighter.

"Wait! Please wait for me!" The childish plea went unheeded. Short, five-year-old legs could not keep up.

"Are the bigger children going too fast for you?" Grandma's voice was like music, like birds singing and water splashing and something more. "You may walk with me. I think we walk the same fast."

The little girl smiled happily, as she slipped her hand into Grandma's. She skipped a few steps. "Grandma, here are some violets for you," she said shyly, lifting the bedraggled bunch.

Down the lane the young girl dashed, raising a cloud of butterflies from the clover as she passed. If she went any faster, she would be skimming with the swallows themselves. Into the green shadows of the woods she flew and leapt onto a log with youthful exuberance.

A pleased grin spread across her face as she stood there waiting for her brother. He was a few paces slower. She had won!

The young man and the young woman walked up the aisle between the rows of family and friends. At the end of this walk, at the front of the room, they would be joined together for life. Their steps were confident.

"Come to Mama. Yes, you can!" she coaxed. And Baby's squeals of delight mingled with mother's joyous laugh as he toddled precariously across the vast three feet of space into her arms.

Briskly she marched. The strong wind tore at her skirts and frolicked with a stray wisp of hair, helping her forget her weariness.

"Hurry, children!" she ordered. "Try to keep up. We want to get home in time for supper."

Her smallest child whimpered and dragged his feet. "I'm tired." She felt a flash of sympathy amid the other duties crowding her mind, and scooped him up.

"I'll carry you then."

She strolled slowly, reveling in the warmth of the sun on her back and breathing deeply of the April air. Up ahead the grand-children scampered, shouting gleefully, kicking stones down the path, plucking wild flowers. They were lambs let out on a spring meadow, she reflected.

And she noticed the littlest one was falling behind. "Wait, wait!" she would cry, but no one paid any heed.

"Are the bigger ones going too fast for you? You may walk with me. I think we walk just the same fast."

The dark-eyed girl turned shyly, happily, and held up a trusting hand for Grandma's. With the other, she lifted a squeezed bunch of treasured violets. "Here, Grandma, these are for you."

The years walked swiftly... She eased one trembling foot be-fore the other. Her knees shook and she clung to her cane and to the arm of her young friend. The young woman smiled under-standingly. "What do you think? Would you like to sit out on the porch? I will help you."

It was such a long way to walk, but, yes, she wanted to—just to be outside and breathe the clean air and give thanks for the years.

She was so grateful for the young hands and young feet to as-sist her. Grateful, too, that always, always God had walked with her. And grateful as well for the privilege she had been granted to see life come full circle.

Rachel M. Stauffer

Good Grandmothers

...are tellers of stories. They open the faucet of the past to quench their grandchildren's story thirst, and are careful not to flood them with too many, "I remembers..."

...are askers of questions. "Is math any easier by now?" "What did you name your puppies?" "Is your new dress finished yet?"

...are wielders of peelers. Their swift hands make the pear pile smaller, the kitchen less steamy, and the hours shorter on canning day.

...are noticers of everyday things. School art on the wall, birds at the birdfeeder, sandbox setups of farms and roads are noteworthy because they are part of their grandchildren's lives.

...are bringers of bags. "What's in your bag, Grandma?" More often, it is books and animal crackers rather than toys and candies.

...are sermons in sweaters and shawls. They are the real-life picture of what many a minister has preached about godly older women: meekness, sobriety, and kindheartedness personified.

...are accepting of each and all. Their family spectrum started with the primary colors of blue, yellow, red, but each of their children blended with another into shades of violet, turquoise, goldenrod. Every color in their growing family is well-loved.

...are inviters of children. Their homes are child-friendly nests, not showcases of fragile knickknacks.

...are bridgers of miles. They are close to faraway grandchildren in ways that surpass geography.

...are menders of rends. They keep a thimble in their apron pocket. They remember how it is when both house and hands are full, and they offer their help.

...are wipers of tears. They rock away little hurts and wipe little noses as if they had never missed a beat between these new little ones and their own.

...are watchers of behavior. They quietly guide the little hand that pulls away. They wisely settle the silly laughing and sibling spats. And they share what they see with the parents.

...are tenders of home fires. Even though there are not as many cords to bind them to home, they are still faithful keepers. They take good care of Grandfather.

...are mothers of a thousand hearts. They are careful where the invisible finger of their influence points. They know that their opportunity is short, but their motherhood is long.

...are absorbers of noise. They are willing to have their stillness broken by the happy commotion of many families packing into their little home.

...are readers of books. They have time to read the same story over and over to little ears and eyes—and they don't skip pages.

...are guardians of innocence. Parents need not fear what their children may discover on Grandmother's bookshelf or in her toy box.

...are keepers of vigils. The sick ones, the erring one, the facing-a-crossroads ones are in their day and night prayers. Their loved ones can say with surety, "Grandmother prays for me."

...are listeners to little ones. There are no unimportant words from their grandchildren.

...are promoters of conviction. They take care that the clothes they make or buy for their grandchildren are not for pride's sake.

...are supporters of discipline. "What your parents say is how it will be." They are not soft or spoiling. They are fellow-sharpeners to make an arrow that will fly true.

...are encouragers of every one. Little words commending the good they see, little notes at special times, written by their hand, their shaky hand, all say, "I care!"

...are accumulators of good things. Their true treasures are not in the clutter of the years, but in the thoughts and truths that have strengthened them through their years. From this, they will share.

...are passers on of the faith. Their vital interest is that the span from their foremothers to the mothers-to-come would not have one fragile link. They know the faith will never be outdated if it is firm on the Rock and lived out with joy.

V. H. K.

For grandmothers who lie awake at night, thinking of their loved ones.

Be Still

Tonight, my soul, be still and sleep;
The storms are raging on God's deep—
God's deep, not thine;
 Be still and sleep.

Tonight, my soul, be still and sleep;
God's hands shall still the tempter's sweep—
God's hands, not thine;
 Be still and sleep.

Tonight, my soul, be still and sleep;
God's love is strong, while night hours creep—
God's love, not thine;
 Be still and sleep.

Tonight, my soul, be still and sleep;
God's heav'n will comfort those who weep—
God's heav'n, not thine;
 Be still and sleep.

Tonight, my soul, be still and sleep;
God's eyes will watch thy dearest sheep—
God's eyes, not thine;
 Be still and sleep.

Author Unknown, Adapted

From Life Songs, Number Two
 Song #65

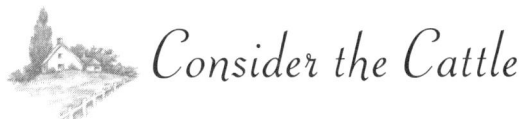 # Consider the Cattle

The mother read the verses again in Titus, *"The aged women like-wise...that they may teach the young women..."* She pondered, *"There are many young mothers in our church and though I am definitely not the oldest, I do have grown children. How shall I practice these verses?"*

It was not the first time she wondered so. *"My friends would think it strange indeed if I would visit them one day and begin telling them what I have learned."* She gasped at the absurd idea. *"I know it doesn't mean that! But Lord,"* she prayed, *"please show me what I should do. I do want to obey Your Word."*

A few days later, as the mother swept her back porch, she noticed the herd of cows lumbering toward a cluster of shade trees. Each calf bobbed along, trying to match its mother's pace.

The lead cow bustled ahead, but her calf was not so well coordinated and soon fell behind. Back came Bossy to nudge her calf along. Then she marched ahead once more, not even waiting for her baby to follow. The calf took a couple steps and finding itself motherless, gave up. Back again came Bossy, bellowing with frustration.

Meanwhile the rest of the herd, cows and calves, gradually found their way to the shade. The quiet cows gently licked their babies and softly mooed to them, even though their progress was slow.

Her sweeping forgotten, the mother watched as Bossy finally hustled her calf to the shade trees, but not before the quiet cows arrived. In spite of her big ado, Bossy had not gained time at all.

To the mother, it was as if God had tapped her shoulder right there with the answer to her days-ago prayer. She seemed to hear, *"You must teach the younger women by your quiet example of love and patience to your children and husband. Nurture your children gently as you turn their attention to Me and My Word. Other mothers will observe and learn from your life."*

It was too easy for her to scold and nag, she knew. She breathed an answer back, *"Help me, Lord, to overcome and to be a true mother for You."*

She continued her sweeping. "Mother," her little son spoke from the porch swing, "why do you watch the cows so much? Do you really like them?" "Yes, I like to watch the cows with their calves." she answered smiling. "Sometimes I learn things from them."

Susan Schwartz

All That She Could Do

Great-grandmother sat in her little, low swan-neck rocker turned just enough toward the window to glimpse the home folks as they hustled to and fro. Into the empty box of her day, she gathered those glimpses as if they were gems to treasure. Dear ones, each of them. Of late, her world had narrowed to the confines of her little house tucked next to theirs. Time drifted as slowly as the laying of dust. But what a joy when they would come to visit and place the great-grandbabies on her lap. Oh, they melted into her arms as her thoughts melted back to her own babies. She held them more firmly than her frail arms generally held herself. *She did what she could do.*

Great-grandmother knew which chair was hers in each of their homes. She wanted to help; she always helped. And they wanted her there. They might need to take out her widely crooked hand-stitching after she left, but she would try. Her shelled peas seemed a pittance next to their bowlfuls, and the nuts she had sorted would need sorting again. *But she did what she could do.*

Great-grandmother sat by the soft light of her reading lamp, surrounded by a deep, inky silence. She held her Bible open with a sense of waitingness. The things of earth sank into the encircling darkness. The Lord was so near that she wished He would come now to take her home. But she knew her work would not be ended till He called her. She would pray and be faithful to the end. *What more could she could do?*

It was the obony hours of early morning. The next-door family was leaving for a long trip; a trip that would be far longer to Great-grandmother than to them. She had begun to miss them even before they were gone, but she would never want to stand in the way of their need to go. A spark of light shone from Great-grandmother's usually dark porch. They crept past. They did not want to disturb her. But there...there, steadied by the porch railing was Great-grandmother, waving. *She did what she could do.*

V. H. K.

CHAPTER 26

Mothers at Heart

Alabaster

Not every sister becomes a mother, but that need not hinder any woman from accepting the Lord's will for her life or from finding ways to pour out her love.

God has given many women, who are not mothers, mother hearts. They can offer a touch of kindness to other mothers' children. By breaking their alabaster boxes on others' lives, they *make* opportunities wherever they go.

The gift or touch of kindness that truly costs something, speaks. God takes notice. Sisters with a mother heart have found the blessedness of doing the will of God, even though they will never cradle their own child. Motherhood, though noble, is *not* the highest calling in the kingdom of God. But doing the will of God is.

*"Yea rather, blessed are they that hear
the word of God, and keep it."*
Luke 11:28

Harry M. Erb

"Mother" Is a Verb
A Creative Definition

mother vt. moth·ered; moth·er·ing \ˈməth·(ə-) riŋ\ **1:** to give life to, to inspire, to instill, to infuse new life, to exercise a capacity given to all women transcending biological relationships. [By *mothering* many little children, she turned her loneliness into lovingkindness.] *also* the function of a childless mother. **2 :** to look after, to watch, to care for and protect [As a little girl, she *mothered* her dolls so devotedly, that it was no wonder to see her heart lean out to *mother* other peoples' children when she was grown.] **3 :** to cultivate, to teach so as to treasure each child, to cherish purposefully [Was there a child in her classroom that was clueless, friendless, tuneless? She *mothered* him through his difficulty.] **4 :** to influence as far as possible. [Through her *mothering* ways, she gave her nieces' and nephews' a living, faithful example of truth.] **5 :** to pour in, to fill the cup [She saw the emotional gaps in the little girl's heart and *mothered* in all the love she could during the time she had.] **6 :** to soothe, to comfort [She went on to *mother* many unmothered and undermothered children and thereby lightened the heaviest load she had to carry—empty arms.] **7 :** to sacrifice unselfconsciously, to care deeply at a great cost [Her practical nature said "No time for it!" But her giving heart spoke louder, saying, "Drop what you are doing and go *mother* her, now!"] See NURTURE

V. H. K.

Bestowing Your Treasure

You thought once to bestow all your heart's wealth on dear little ones of your own, and little by little you found that treasure denied by God. By God, not man. But that desire to mother is still a treasure. Believe now that the Giver of all good would have you spend your treasury in a way far better than you intended. He would have you spread it among many more little ones than what you imagined with your own small circle.

Therefore, let each child you meet have a share in the treasure. Show interest in their interests, be an example of contentment and modesty in a world of temptation. Enrich their lives with good reading, smile at them, and greet them by name. Give love, though it may be with an aching heart; give it tenderly on all sides, and God, who sees, will accept the sacrifice.

Author Unknown, 1859

Second Witness

Single sisters can have a strong positive influence on nieces and nephews (and others too) by their example and words of encouragement. When a close friend promotes the same ideals and a strong faith in God, the word of parents is strengthened. Sisters working in the home or teaching school have the opportunity of being a second witness to truth.

Marvin B. Good

When Children Are Treasured

Even those with no children to claim as their own can invest in this precious resource. Anyone can take the time to listen to the chatter of a child, with an ear open for opportunities to encourage them in the right. Anyone can spend time in prayer for youth who are facing the challenges of adolescence. The outgoing single may count more children than the mother of a full house.

Stephen J. Champ, Adapted

A Single's Prayer

My Father in heaven, I wonder sometimes
Just why You've said no to this longing of mine;
  It only is natural to wish for a home,
  A place to abide in—no longer to roam...

  Complete with a husband who's godly and strong,
  A place where we both would be shielded from wrong;
    A place where there's peace and contentment and rest.
    Yes, this is my longing. I would be so blessed.

And then there'd be little ones...innocent, fair,
Bright jewels from heaven; how sweet and how rare;
  Eternal and precious, entrusted with love
  To mold and to shape for that mansion above.

  This great, awesome charge we together would share,
  Our hearts, lives, and work would be bathed in much prayer.
    With always the burden of pleasing the Lord,
    Yes, living and following His blessed Word.

But, Lord, this has not been Your plan for my life.
You've called me to singlehood...I'm not a wife.
  And though I cannot understand Your great plan,
  I'll humbly submit just the best that I can.

  I know there are still many blessings in store,
  And ways I can enter the "motherhood door."
    Each niece and each nephew should have a dear aunt
    Who shows from experience the "singlehood slant"!

And then many teachers are needed in schools.
When yielded to God they are valuable tools.
  They lead boys and girls into God's holy way,
  And find great fulfillment there day after day.

  Sometimes little folk need a friend after church;
  How special if one on my lap finds a perch!
    To tell them a story or sing them a song
    Will help fill the void, and I'll think I belong.

Then how many times is a mother made glad,
Because I am willing to lend her my hands.
    She's usually quite happy to share girls and boys;
    Again I can revel in motherhood joys.

So, Lord, I accept and will follow Your choice;
It's not what I wished for, but I'll still rejoice.
    So many dear children are following me,
    And, Lord, by Your grace a true pattern I'll be.
Amen.

A Sister

A humble teacher in a school, or a missionary, can often live a rather quiet life. Showy talents, entertaining ways — before these the world yields its homage — while the lowly teachers and friends of the poor and ignorant are forgotten. Only remember that in the sight of the everlasting Eye, the one is creating sounds which perish with the hour that gave them birth, the other is doing a work which is forever.

To teach a few Sunday school children week after week commonplace, simple truths — persevering in spite of dullness and weak capacities — is a more glorious occupation than the highest meditation or creations of genius which edify or instruct only our own solitary soul.

This is the lesson for all; for teachers who lay their heads down at night, desponding over their thankless tasks. Remember the power of *indirect* influences, those which distil from a life, not from a sudden, brilliant effort. The former never fails, the latter often. Not in the flushing of a pupil's cheek or the glistening of an attentive eye, not in the shining result of an examination, does your real success lie. It lies in that invisible influence on character, which God alone can read.

Frederick William Robertson, 19th Century

The Mothering Impulse

The city behind her was loud with weeping as the Hebrew mother picked her furtive way across the muddy river flats. For three months, she had hidden her baby in the house—three months with her hand hovering close to stifle the beginning of each cry, three months of cringing terror at the sound of every unexpected footstep. Now, with the danger grown too great to be endured, she had brought the baby to the Nile, in literal obedience to the pitiless decree—*"Every son that is born ye shall cast into the river."* But with her wits sharpened by the weeks of fearful hiding, the mother had determined a desperate plan. As she went back from the river, a tiny boatman was still safe upon its waters.

On that day, another woman took the same path down to the river and walked along its bank. She was Pharaoh's daughter. The historian Josephus says that her name was Thermutis and that she was childless. In a flurry of excitement, her maidens found the floating cradle and brought it to her. Then came that tense, dramatic moment—in that moment the destiny of the Hebrew people, and through them, the destiny of the world hung in the balance. The baby there had been condemned to death by this woman's own father. There was every reason to expect her to obey his decree.

But God was there too, and it was His purpose to preserve a leader for a nation. It was His intention to have the future law-giver receive his training in the palace of a king. Through him, the riches of the highest culture that was known were to be transmitted to a people out of bondage. And how were these purposes achieved? See how God was working, not by might, not by power, but by His Spirit in the mysterious depth of a human soul. God put a mothering impulse into the childless woman's heart and let that do His work. The princess bent over the little ark. *"And when she had opened it, she saw the child: and, behold, the babe wept. And she had compassion on him."*

How different were those two women who came down to the riverbank that day! The trembling daughter of bondage had come there upon a desperate errand; the self-assured daughter of the king had come for pleasure. One had at least three children; the other was childless. But in one important point, these two were just alike, and that was in the mothering impulse which God had given them.

Into the hearts of unselfish women, God puts His impulses of love. He gives to them a mothering sympathy and patience. He equips them for their high task, as He equips mothers, with vision and faith and spiritual beauty. Then into their hand, God entrusts many of the great issues of human destiny.

Think of those whose mothering has been added to that of a mother's; teachers who have, with a mother's faith and patience guided children through difficult periods of their lives; devoted women at church who have illuminated youth by the light of their radiant ideals; and those who have stood beside mothers and shared their tasks. Much is owed to those who have shared in this wider motherhood. God has given them a great place.

Mothering qualities are not blocked when turned toward children other than one's own. For God never lets "fate" put any kind of padlock on our hearts. We may have assumed that our gifts should be used in one way, while all the while God intends to use them in another. We may sit down baffled and puzzled when some door that we have been walking toward turns out to be tight shut. But when we look around, we find that God has never closed all the doors.

The title *"mother in Israel"* belongs to those who have no children of their own as well as to those who do. It is the title of those by whom a religious organization is made into a church home. It is the radiant spirits of such women that keep the light shining there. Their energetic zeal keeps its hearth fires glowing. It is their mothering gentleness that makes the church a home for the young and a shelter for the weak and heavy-laden.

George E. Sweazey

"Sing, O barren, thou that didst not bear;
break forth into singing, and cry aloud...
for more are the children of the desolate
than the children of the married wife,
saith the LORD."
Isaiah 54:1

The Teacher of Children

"How are you so cheerful, gentle Edith Lane?
Be it bright or cloudy, fall of dew or rain?
    In that lonely schoolhouse, patiently you stay,
    Teaching simple children all the livelong day."

"Teaching simple children? I am simple, too;
So we learn together lessons plain and true,
    From this thumb-worn Bible, full of truth's best store;
    Or, to read another, just unlatch the door."

"Can I but be cheerful while I bid them look
Through the sunny pages of each opening book;
    Showing tracks of angels, on the foot-worn sod;
    Listening to the music nature makes to God?"

"Have you then no sorrow, smiling Edith Lane?
Where the barberry's coral rattles on the pane,
    Where in endless yellow, autumn flowers I see.
    Working for a living were a woe to me."

"Sorrow! I—a woman, and in years, not young?
Of the common chalice, drips are on my tongue.
    What of that? No whisper to my heart is lost,
    From the barberry clusters sweetened by the frost,

"From the rooted sunshine—goldenrod in bloom,
Lighting up the hillsides, for November's gloom.
    Shall I blot with weeping Nature's joy and grace?
    Rather be her gladness mirrored in my face.

"'Working for a living? May no worse befall!
Love is always busy; God works over all.
    Life is worth the earning, for its daily cheer,
    Shared with those who love me, in yon cottage dear.

"If you can, young lady, see my little throne.
Leave me with the children, dear as if my own.
Leave me to the humming of my little hive,
Glad to earn a living, glad to be alive!"

Lucy Larcom, 1868

Song of the Teacher

Dear Master, Thou who taught, pardon my shortcomings as a teacher.

Dear Master, Thou who alone dost worthily bear the name of Teacher, Thou who didst teach while Thou wert on this earth, give me an unparalleled love for my school.

Master, grant me continual fervor, and that any disenchantment may be fleeting. Tear from my heart that impure desire for punishment that disturbs me, the petty insinuating protest which rises in my breast when the children irritate me.

May their lack of understanding not distress me and may their forgetfulness of what I taught them not sadden me.

Make me more a mother than mothers are, that I may be able to love and protect as they do, that which is not flesh of my flesh.

Grant that I may make one of my children my perfect verse and that I may leave entwined in her soul my most enduring melody against the day when my lips shall sing no more.

Show me the might of Thy Gospel in my time that I may not give up the daily and hourly battle to spread the good message.

My true Friend, accompany me and sustain, for I cannot go forward without Thee at my side.

Grant me simplicity and at the same time grant me profundity.

Free my daily teaching from being too complicated or too trivial.

Keep me from bringing my little worries to the school.

Let me put spirit into the very bricks of the building.

Gabriela Mistral

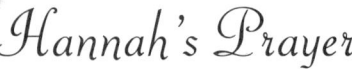

Hannah's Prayer

When lamplight glows on silent wall
And dark, mysterious shadows fall,
Deep in my heart a strange throb swells
With ache of arms that cruelly tells

> My arms are empty! Could I but press
> Close to my heart in warm caress
> A silken head and velvet cheek—
> I dare not dream, or I shall weep!

For dreams are nothing: prayer is real.
Thou knowest, Lord, just how I feel!
This ache—too deep for words to touch,
This dream—too real; soul-pain—too much!

> Like old-time Hannah, on my knee
> I stretch my hands and plead to Thee.
> With silent lips but heartfelt cry,
> I ask a thousand times, "Lord, why?

My arms are empty—Father, fill
Not with my wants, but Thine own will!"
These sobs of soul swell into tears
But not with anguished dream of years.

> My alabaster box is broken—
> "Teach me Thy prayer—Gethsemane's token;
> A precious gift I've offered Thee—
> I want Thy will, whate'er it be!

O Father, bless me with Thy keeping;
I ask Thy comfort while I'm weeping.
Twine with each thorn a rose of rest;
Teach me to say, "Thou knowest best!"

Author Unknown

"Great is our Lord, and of great power:
his understanding is infinite."

Psalm 147:5

Childlessness

Dear Lord, You brought me to a halt
  By placing this upon my way,
And though I wish to pass it by,
  You calmly bid me wait and pray.
To do Your will is my desire,
  But still I do not wish to stay—
  I must go on; the others may!

I do not understand Your plan.
  I do not know the reason why,
And all I want to do, O Lord,
  Is beat against the barrier high—
To beat it down, to see it fall,
  Or just to sit, despair, and cry...
  The self within me sobs a sigh.

The barrier stays; I have a choice:
  To beat against it injures me
Nor ever changes anything
  To what I wish my life would be.
So rather, Lord, I'll sit and wait:
  I'll sing and pray, and thus I'll see
  A wondrous way unfold for me.

It may not be the way I choose,
  But I will rest within Thy care
Much more than if I stubbornly
  Insist You move the barrier there.
So be my Guide; make me content;
  And while I wait, my life I'll share
  With other worn ones waiting there.

Sylvia Shirk

*"For he performeth the thing that is appointed for me:
and many such things are with him."*

Job 23:14

The Little Child That Never Was

The Little Child That Never Was is a very beautiful child. He is absolutely without faults or flaws or disfigurements of any kind. He is all, all, all that his father, his mother, would have him to be.

And he has a great work to do in the world—that Little Child That Never Was. He will either sweeten the life of his poor lonely father or mother or else make it as bitter as wormwood. He will wonderfully soften or cruelly harden them. The Little Child That Never Was calls his solitary father and lonely mother to the service of the world's childhood.

It is a great thing for the world that there are men and women with no children of their own. For there are little children without fathers and without mothers, and there are little children with fathers and mothers who would be better off if they had none.

And the lonely men and women are called by the Little Child That Never Was to devote their lives to the service of the lonely little children. And in ministering to the world's childhood they will lose their loneliness and their longing, for the Little Child That Never Was will become incarnate in the little children around them, and they will hear his laughter and wipe away his tears after all.

Frederick W. Boreham

Nobody who has Christ in his heart
is excused from making a mark on
the children around him.

Author Unknown

CHAPTER 27

A Mother's Hope

The Long View

Some day of days! Some dawning yet to be
I shall be clothed with immortality!

And, in that day, I shall not greatly care
That Jane spilt candle grease upon the stair.

It will not grieve me then, as once it did,
That careless hands have chipped my teapot lid.

I groan, being burdened. But, in that glad day,
I shall forget vexations of the way.

That needs were often great, when means were small,
Will not perplex me any more at all.

A few short years at most (it may be less),
I shall have done with earthly storm and stress.

So, for this day, I lay me at Thy feet.
O, keep me sweet, my Master! Keep me sweet!

Fay Inchfawn

Surrendered Love

In my boy's loud laughter ringing,
In the sigh more soft than singing
Of my baby girl that nestles up,
Content with me to rest,
And in every voice most dear
Comes a whisper—*"Rest not here."*
"And the rest Thou art preparing, is it best,
Lord, is it best?"

"Lord, a little, little longer!"
Sobs the earth-love, growing stronger:
He will miss me, and go mourning
Through his solitary days.
Could my prayers still reach from heaven
If these lambs which Thou hast given
Were to slip out of our keeping
And be lost in worldly ways?

"Lord, it is not fear of dying,
Nor an impious denying
Of Thy will, which evermore
On earth, in heaven, be done:
But the love that desperate clings
Unto these my precious things
In the beauty of the daylight,
And the glory of the sun.

"Ah, Thou still art calling, calling,
With a soft voice unappalling;
And it vibrates in far circles
Through the everlasting years;
When Thou knockest, even so!
I will rise and go."

Dinah Maria Muloch Craik, 19th Century

Dying Mother

Lord Jesus, Comforter Divine,
When rests this weary soul of mine,
   Hear Thou the wounded cry;
Cause childish heart and grieving man
To understand Thy wondrous plan.
   Quell Thou each sorrowing sigh;
The sobbing little bosoms plead
A mother's love; Lord, Thou wilt heed.

Earth's anguished tribulations cease;
I fold my toil-worn hands in peace;
   To friends the burdens fall;
"Break ye not faith nor fail to keep
This sacred trust, that I may sleep."
   I gave my earthly all;
Lord Jesus, Comforter Divine,
Be Thou e'er near these babes of mine.

N. M. Bearinger

The Perfect Time

If Time should close my world's last door tonight,
   Let no one say, "Too soon she left this earth,
Her work unfinished..." though a hoe may lie
   In garden midst...a half-laid fire on hearth...
     If partly-written letter, or a line
Half-filled with clothes bespeaks too quick a death,
   Or threaded needle piercing stitching-frame,
Should cause a dear one tears or sighing breath...
     Fear not—God beckons at precision-time!
And though some "work" may stand like unreaped wheat,
   If I've not failed what He's required of me—
When His voice calls, my work will be complete!

Ila R. Monday

A Little Parable for Mothers

The young Mother set her foot on the path of life.

"Is the way long?" she asked.

And her Guide said, "Yes. And the way is hard. But the end will be better than the beginning."

But the young Mother was happy, and she would not believe that anything could be better than these years. So she played with her children, and gathered flowers for them along the way; and the sun shone on them, and life was good. And the young Mother cried, "Nothing will ever be lovelier than this."

Then night came, and storm, and the path was dark, and the children shook with fear and cold, and the Mother drew them close and covered them with her mantle, and the children said, "Mother, we are not afraid, for you are near, and no harm can come." And the Mother said, "This is better than the brightness of day, for I have taught my children courage."

And the morning came, and there was a hill ahead, and the children climbed and grew weary, and the Mother grew weary. But at all times she said to the children, "A little patience, and we are there." So the children climbed and when they had reached the top, they said, "We could not have done it without you, Mother." And the Mother, when she lay down that night, looked up at the stars, and said, "This is a better day than the last, for my children have learned fortitude in the face of hardness."

And the next day came strange clouds which darkened the earth; clouds of war and hate and evil, and the children tripped and stumbled. And the Mother said, "Look up! Lift your eyes to the Light." And the children looked and saw above the clouds an Everlasting Glory, and it guided them and brought them beyond the darkness. And that night the Mother said, "This is the best day of all, for I have shown my children God."

And the days went on, and the weeks and the months and the years, and the Mother grew old, and she was tired and weary. But her children were tall and strong, and walked with courage. And when the way was hard, they helped their Mother; and when the way was rough, they lifted her and carried her; and at last they came to a hill, and beyond the hill they could see a shining road and golden gates flung wide.

And the Mother said, "I have reached the end of my journey. And now I know that the end is better than the beginning, for my children can walk alone, and their children after them."

And the children said, "You will always walk with us, Mother, even when you have gone through the gates."

And they stood and watched her as she went on alone, and the gates closed after her. And they said, "We cannot see her, but she is with us still. A Mother like ours is more than a memory. She is a living presence."

Temple Bailey

Their Works Follow Them

Blessed are the dead who die in the Lord. They rest from their labors — all their struggles, failures, are past and over forever. But their works follow them. The good which they did on earth — that is not past and over. It cannot die. It lives and grows forever, following on in their path long after they are dead, and bearing fruit unto everlasting life, not only in them, but in men whom they never saw, and in generations yet unborn.

Charles Kingsley, 19th Century

Children Are a Heritage

What shall the swift hands do
When the night pulls down like a shade
And the garment is but half made?
What shall the swift hands do?

They shall rest — the swift with the slow —
The task dies not with the dead.
Another shall take up the thread
Where the swift hand let it go.

And what of the golden note
When a soft hand covers the lips
And the urgent summons grips
As the first song spills from the throat?

It shall rest — with the voice of the low —
The song dies not with death...
Another shall take up the breath
Where the high voice let it go.

Yea, the song that thy lips had meant,
Thy daughter's daughters shall sing;
Yea, sons' sons hands shall bring
To fruition, thy heart's intent.

For naught that's begun shall cease
While sons and daughters arise;
While daughters and sons arise
We may go to the grave in peace.

Miriam Sieber Lind

*D*oes it seem that the dazzling
  Of noonday glare and heat
Is a fiery veil between thy heart
  And visions high and sweet?
What though a "lull in life"
  May never be made for thee?
Soon shall a "better thing" be
  Thine—the lull of Eternity.

Frances Ridley Havergal, 19th Century

Death Is Not Death

Death is not death, if it takes away from a mother forever all a mother's anxieties, a mother's fears, and lets her see, in the gracious countenance of her Savior, a sure and certain pledge that those she has left behind are safely trusted to Christ, through all the changes and dangers of this mortal life.

Death is not death, if it rids her of doubt and fear, of chance and change, of space and time, and all that space and time bring forth, and then destroy.

Death is not death; for Christ has conquered death for Himself and for those who follow in Him.

Charles Kingsley, 19th Century

I sometimes feel the thread of life is slender
And soon with me the labor will be wrought:
Then grows my heart to other hearts more tender.
  The time is short.

Dinah Maria Muloch Craik, 19th Century

The Voice in the Twilight

I was sitting alone in the twilight,
  With spirit troubled and vexed,
With thoughts that were forlorn and gloomy,
  And faith that was sadly perplexed...
    Some well-known work I was doing
      For the child of my love and care.
    Some patches a-wearily stitching,
      In the endless need of repair.
But my thoughts were about the "building,"
  The work someday to be tried;
And that only the gold and the silver
  And the precious stones should abide;
    And remembering my own poor efforts,
      The feeble work I had done,
    And, even when trying most truly,
      The meager success I had won.
"It is nothing but 'wood, hay, and stubble,'"
  I said; "it will all be burned—
This useless fruit of the talents
  One day to be returned.
    And I have so longed to serve Him,
      And often I know I have tried;
    But I'm sure when He sees such building,
      He never will let it abide."
Just then, as I turned the garment,
  That no rent should be left behind,
My eye caught an odd little bungle
  Of mending and patchwork combined.
    My heart grew suddenly tender,
      And something blinded my eyes
    With one of those sweet intuitions
      That sometimes makes us so wise.
Dear child! She wanted to help me.
  I know 'twas the best she could do.
But, oh! what a botch she had made it—
  The gray mismatching the blue!
    And yet—can you understand it?—
      With a tender smile and a tear,
    And a half compassionate yearning,
      I felt she had grown more dear.

Then a sweet voice broke the silence;
And the dear Lord said to me,
"Art thou more tender for the little child
Than I am tender for thee?"

And straightway I knew His meaning,
So full of compassion and love,
And my faith came back to its Refuge
Like the glad, returning dove.

For I thought, when the Master Builder
Comes down His temple to view,
To see what rents must be mended,
And what must be builded anew,

Perhaps as He looks o'er the building,
He will bring my work to the light,
And seeing the marring and bungling,
And how far it all is from right,

He will feel as I felt for my darling,
And will say, as I said for her,
"Dear child! She wanted to help me,
And love for Me was the spur.

And for the true love that is in it,
The work shall seem perfect as Mine,
And because it was willing service,
I will crown it with plaudit divine."

And there in the deepening twilight,
I seemed to be clasping a Hand,
And to feel a great love constrain me,
Stronger than any command.

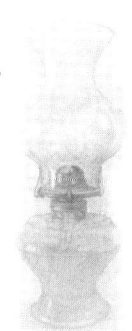

Then I knew, by the thrill of sweetness,
'Twas the Hand of the Blessed One,
That will tenderly guide and hold me
Till all my labor is done.

So my thoughts are nevermore gloomy,
My faith no longer is dim,
But my heart is strong and restful,
And my eyes are looking to Him.

Mrs. Herrick Johnson, 19th Century

*Live every day with your children so that if
it were your last, all would be well...
and someday it will be.*

When He Comes

Thus may it be (I thought) at some day's close,
Some lilac-haunted eve, when every rose
   Breathes forth its incense. May He find me there,
   In holy leisure, lifting hands of prayer,
In some sweet garden place,
To catch the first dear wonder of His Face!

Or, in my room above,
In silent meditation of His love,
   My soul illumined with a rapture rare.
It would be sweet, if even then, these eyes
Might glimpse Him coming in the Eastern skies,
   And be caught up to meet Him in the air.

But now! Ah, now, the days
Rush by their hurrying ways!
   No longer know I vague imaginings,
   For every hour has wings.
Yet my heart watches...as I work I say,
All simply, to Him: "Come! And if today,
   Then wilt Thou find me thus: Just as I am—
   Tending my household; stirring gooseberry jam;
Or swiftly rinsing tiny vests and hose;
With puzzled forehead patching someone's clothes;
   Guiding small footsteps, swift to hear and run,
   From early dawn till setting of the sun."

And whensoe'er He comes, I'll rise and go,
Yes, all the gladlier that He found me so.

Fay Inchfawn

The Children With Me

In the hope that I have of His coming,
    With its splendor and brilliant display,
When heaven will be filled with His glory
    On the saints' resurrection day,
There's one sweet moment of gladness
    I long for most eagerly —
To stand with all of my children
    Before Him who gave them to me.

The burdens that came with their training,
    The long hours of teaching, will be
All just a glorious privilege
    In the light of eternity.

The heavens will blaze with His brightness
    When I say, "I have waited for Thee.
I want to present now the children
    Thou graciously gave unto me."

Oh, often I let my mind picture
    His coming to earth once again —
To stand with the ransomed before Him
    And shout the Amen and Amen;
The myriads of angels, and Jesus
    In all of His beauty to see —
And the prayer of my heart is always
    For the children given to me.

Helen Cooper

Space Soliloquy

A journey into outer space
Is one I do not care to face:
To give Orion merry chase,
The orbit of the moon to trace,
To view three sunsets in one day,
While floating weightlessly away,
    I do not yearn.

But let me see the happy stars that rise,
In healthy, happy children's eyes;
And this the weightlessness I prize—
A conscience pure, where no guilt lies.
One day, transfigured, I shall climb,
Beyond all bounds of space or time,
    And not return.

Ada L. Wine

A mother's last longing in life—

"*Therefore, my [children]dearly beloved
and longed for, my joy and crown,
so stand fast in the Lord,
my dearly beloved.*"

Philippians 4:1

ACKNOWLEDGMENTS

Our thanks to each author and copyright holder for their contribution. Effort has been made to trace and to ask permission for all copyrighted material in this book. If any acknowledgments have been missed, the publishers welcome information to give full credit in any future editions.

CHAPTER 1   *The New Mother*

p. 1   "Motherhood" by Ida Mae Leatherman. From *Gospel Herald*, June 11, 1946.
         Used by permission of MennoMedia.

p. 3   "First Born" by Edith S. Witmer. From *Family Life*, January 1995, p. 34.
         Used by permission of Pathway Publishers and the author.

p. 7   "New Mother" by Jane Merchant. From *In Green Pastures* by Jane Merchant,
         © 1959 by Abingdon Press. Used by permission. All rights reserved.

p. 13   "Why Baby Cries" by B. Zimmerman. *From Family Life*, February 1995, p. 40.
         Used by permission of Pathway Publishers and the author.

p. 14   "Peace in the Storm" by Naomi Yutzy. *From Family Life*, December 2005, p. 9.
         Used by permission of Pathway Publishers and the author.

p. 15   "Hand in Hand" Author Unknown. From *Gospel Herald*, July 15, 1952.
         Used by permission of MennoMedia.

p. 16   "Precious in His Sight" by Rachel E. Myer. Used by permission.

CHAPTER 2   *A Mother's Trust*

p. 18   "A Young Mother's Prayer" by Audre Pitts. From *The Mennonite*, August 5, 1952.
         Used by permission of *The Mennonite*, 718 N. Main St., Newton, KS 67114

p. 19   "Mother's God" by Carolyn Eberly. Used by permission.

p. 21   "A Most Sacred Call" by A. S. From *Family Life*, March 2001, p. 37.
         Used by permission of Pathway Publishers and the author.

p. 22   "Things a Mother Cannot Do" by Harry M. Erb. Used by permission.

p. 27   "Worthy Motherhood" by Lois Gingerich. From *Gospel Herald*, July 5, 1934.
         Used by permission of MennoMedia.

CHAPTER 3   *A Mother's Influence*

p. 31   "Each Day" Author Unknown. From *Mother's Golden Now Magazine*, © 1931 by
         David C. Cook Publishers. All rights reserved. Used by permission.

p. 32   "The Twig Bender" by H. Charles Gallap. Our sincere thanks to the author whom
         we were unable to locate.

p. 33   "You Are a Mother" by Geneva Showerman. Our sincere thanks to the author
         whom we were unable to locate.

p. 34   "The Rose Garden." From *Family Life*, May 1989, p. 17. Used by permission of
         Pathway Publishers.

p. 35   "Little Coats" Author Unknown. From *Gospel Herald*, July 28, 1953.
         Used by permission of MennoMedia.

p. 36   "A Mother's Far-reaching Influence" by Mast P. Stoltzfus. Used by permission.

p. 38   "The Margin of Life" by Jessie Whitney Mayshark. From *Mother's Golden Now Magazine*,
         © 1930 by David C. Cook Publishers. All rights reserved. Used by permission.

p. 39   "More Is Caught" by Cynthia Ruchti. Adapted from a *Heartbeat of the Home* script
         by Cynthia Ruchti. Used by permission.

p. 40   "Our Children" by Polly Petersheim. Our sincere thanks to the author whom we
         were unable to locate.

p. 41   "Never feel that because ideal conditions..." Author Unknown. From *Mother's
         Golden Now Magazine*, © 1930 by David C. Cook Publishers. All rights reserved.
         Used by permission.

p. 143   "A Mother's Reflections" by Virginia Gibbons. From *Pictures in Verse* by Virginia Gibbons, © 1954. Our sincere thanks to the author whom we were unable to locate.

p. 145   "Thorns and Roses" by Marcia K. Leaser. Used by permission.

CHAPTER 13   *The Singing Mother*

p. 148   "Mothers..." by C. C. C. From *The Christian Example*, February 19, 1971. Used by permission of Rod and Staff Publishers.

p. 152   "Knowing the Joyful Sound" by Stanley C. Wine. From *The Eastern Mennonite Testimony*, June 1996, article: "Singing in Everyday Life." Used by permission of Eastern Mennonite Publications.

p. 153   "The Remedy of Song" by Mrs. Curtis Yoder. From *The Christian Example*, March 12, 1976. Used by permission of Rod and Staff Publishers.

CHAPTER 14   *The Mother Who Reads*

p. 158   "Read, Mother, Read" Author Unknown. From *Christian Monitor*, July 1924. Used by permission of MennoMedia.

p. 160   "To a Good Mother" Author Unknown. From *Mother's Golden Now Magazine*, © 1930 by David C. Cook Publishers. All rights reserved. Used by permission.

p. 161   "Please, Mother, Read to Us" From *The Christian Example*, April 21, 1967. Used by permission of Rod and Staff Publishers.

p. 162   "Effective training to respect and love..." by Lloy A. Kniss. *From Practical Pointers for Training Your Child* by Lloy A. Kniss, © 1975 by Christan Light Publications, Inc., PO Box 1212, Harrisonburg, VA 22803, p. 800-776-0478. All rights reserved. Used by permission.

p. 162   Quotations from *The Book of Life* by an unknown author, © 1923.

p. 163   "Mothers, read Bible stories..." by Jesse Neuenschwander. From *The Christian Contender*, November 1996, article: "Christian Reading Practices." Used by permission of Rod and Staff Publishers.

p. 163   "The Good Shepherd's final words..." by Bruce A. Good. From *The Eastern Mennonite Testimony*, July 1998, article: "Reading Bible Stories." Used by permission of Eastern Mennonite Publications.

p. 163   "Consider that when we read..." by Peter Baer. From *The Christian Contender*, March 2008, article: "Keeping Innocent Children Innocent." Used by permission of Rod and Staff Publishers.

p. 166   "Reading, however slow and plodding..." by David L. Martin. From *The Literature Lamplighter*, September/October 2008, Pen Pointers article, "He Got It Out of a Book" by David L. Martin. Used by permission of Lamp and Light Publishers, Inc., 26 Road 5577, Farmington, NM 87401.

CHAPTER 15   *The Mother's Devotional Life*

p. 167   "She who sits and waits..." by Ella May Miller. From *Heart to Heart*. Used by permission of MennoMedia.

p. 169   "Finding Time with God" by Ruby L. Mack. From *Home Horizons*, January 2008. Used by permission of Eastern Mennonite Publications.

p. 170   "The Quiet Hour" by Mary S. Stover. From *Mother's Golden Now Magazine*, © 1929 by David C. Cook Publishers. All rights reserved. Used by permission.

p. 171   "Mother's Morning Prayer Time" by Romayne Allen. From *Gospel Herald*, June 27, 1961. Used by permission of MennoMedia.

p. 171   "On the Wing" Author Unknown. From *Sourcebook for Mothers* by Eleanor Doan, © 1969 by Zondervan Publishing House. Used by permission of Zondervan, 5300 Patterson S E., Grand Rapids, MI 49530.

INDEX OF AUTHORS

INDEX OF FIRST LINES AND TITLES

Z

Encouraging Words
for MOTHERS

1-4 books . . . . $14.95 each
5-10 books . . . . $13.95 each
11 or more books . . . . . $12.95 each

❧ *Please contact us for wholesale pricing or for shipping to Canada.*

❧ *Georgia residents add 8% sales tax.*

SHIPPING & HANDLING
One book $4.00
Each additional book, add 80¢

Quantity	Title	Price Per Book	Amount
	Encouraging Words for Mothers		
	Shipping & Handling		
	Tax		
❧ ORDER BY FAX, MAIL, OR PHONE.	Total		

Payment: ☐Check ☐Money Order ☐Visa ☐Mastercard ☐Discover

☐☐☐☐ ☐☐☐☐ ☐☐☐☐ ☐☐☐☐

Exp. Date ☐☐/☐☐   3-Digit Code ☐☐☐

Signature _____

Name _____

Address _____

City/State/Zip _____

Phone _____

Make checks payable to:

ENCOURAGING WORDS BOOKS
1231 Twin Pine Road, Metter, GA 30439
phone: 912-685-3936 ❖ *fax:* 912-685-7463

Thank you for your order!